An Exposition
of the Ten Commandments

Other Titles from SGCB

In addition to *An Exposition of the Ten Commandments*, Solid Ground Christian Books is delighted and honored to offer the following outstanding titles:

The Afflicted Man's Companion by John Willison
The Life & Letters of James Renwick by W.H. Carslaw
The Sufferings of the Church of Scotland by Robert Wodrow
The Scottish Pulpit by William Taylor
Precious Seed: Discourses of Scots Worthies
The Doctrine of Justification by James Buchanan
Paul the Preacher by John Eadie
Greek Text Commentary on Galatians by John Eadie
Greek Text Commentary on Ephesians by John Eadie
Greek Text Commentary on Philippians by John Eadie
Greek Text Commentary on Colossians by John Eadie
Greek Text Commentary on Thessalonians by John Eadie
Divine Love: A Series of Discourses by John Eadie
Lectures on the Bible for the Young by John Eadie
Opening Scripture: Hermeneutical Manual by Patrick Fairbairn
Martyrland: A Tale of Persecution by Robert Simpson
The Preacher and His Models by James Stalker
Imago Christi: The Example of Jesus Christ by James Stalker
Sabbath Scripture Readings from the OT by Thomas Chalmers
Sabbath Scripture Readings from the NT by Thomas Chalmers
Lectures on the Book of Esther by Thomas M'Crie
The Psalms in History and Biography by John Ker
A Pathway into the Psalter by William Binnie
Heroes of Israel: Abraham – Moses by William G. Blaikie
Expository Lectures on Joshua by William G. Blaikie
Expository Lectures on 1 Samuel by William G. Blaikie
Expository Lectures on 2 Samuel by William G. Blaikie
Luther's Scottish Connection by James McGoldrick

AN

EXPOSITION

OF THE

TEN COMMANDMENTS

EZEKIEL HOPKINS

SOLID GROUND CHRISTIAN BOOKS
BIRMINGHAM, ALABAMA USA

Solid Ground Christian Books
PO Box 660132
Vestavia Hills AL 35266
205-443-0311
sgcb@charter.net
solid-ground-books.com

An Exposition of the Ten Commandments
by Ezekiel Hopkins (1633 – 1690)

First Solid Ground Edition July 2009

Taken from the 19th century edition published by the American Tract Society, New York, NY

Cover design by Borgo Design, Tuscaloosa, AL

ISBN: 978-159925-215-5

NOTICE OF BISHOP HOPKINS

~~~~~~~~~~~~~~

Ezekiel Hopkins was born at Sanford, county of Devon, England, about the year 1633, where his father was many years a laborious minister. He was educated at Oxford, where he was some time chaplain of Magdalen College. From Oxford he went to London, where he was assistant to Dr. William Spurstow till the act of uniformity. After this he was preacher at St. Edmunds, Lombard Street, and subsequently was chosen minister of St. Mary Arches, in Exeter, where he was much admired. From Exeter he was transferred to the deanery of Raphoe, Ireland, and from the deanery was promoted to the bishopric, which he occupied about ten years, when he was transferred to the bishopric of Derry. Here he continued about seven years, till the papists got the sword into their hands, when he fled for his life to England, and became minister of St. Mary, Aldermanbury, in London, 1689, where he died, about seven months only after his establishment there.

As a *preacher*, Bishop Hopkins was esteemed one of the first of the age in which he lived, being much admired and followed after in all places where he preached.

As a *writer*, he was eminent above most authors for the combination of clear statements of *doctrinal* and *practical* truth, with an eloquent application of it to the heart and conscience. Scarcely any other writer has, within an equal compass, so ably discussed, and applied with such energy the whole range of Christian truth. His works are published in four volumes, edited by the late Rev. Josiah Pratt, of London, who in his dedication of the volumes to William Wilberforce, Esq. says, "That author is of special value whose works supply, within a moderate compass, the most complete refutation of whatever can be urged against true religion, by exhibiting her in her most beautiful proportions. Such an author is Bishop Hopkins." His works embrace the following subjects:

Vanity of the World
Exposition of the Lord's Prayer
Exposition of the Ten Commandments
Discourses on the Law
Discourses concerning Sin
The Doctrine of the Two Covenants
Doctrine of the Two Sacraments
The All-Sufficiency of Christ to Save Sinners
Excellency of Heavenly Treasures
Practical Christianity
Assurance of Heaven and Salvation
On Glorifying God in His Attributes
Almost Christian
Conscience
Great Duty of Mortification
Death Disarmed
Miscellaneous Sermons

As a *divine,* Bishop Hopkins was one of the sound theologians to which the Reformation gave birth, and he unequivocally and openly held and inculcated the pure doctrines of the Reformers, opposed as they are to the pride and passions of unsanctified men. On the difficult questions concerning the grace of God and the obligation of man, he adopted those views which most naturally reconcile with one another the *declarations* and *exhortations* of Scripture. Few writers have entered so unequivocally into the extent of man's responsibility, and at the same time so strongly insisted on the sovereignty, and so graphically described the operations of the grace of God.

Contents

Introduction   7

    The time of the delivery of the Ten Commandments   9
    The Reason   10
    The Manner   11
    Are they abrogated?   19
    General Rules for rightly understanding them   29
    Their order   48

Preface to the Commandments   50

FIRST TABLE

The First Commandment   58

    Requires the love, fear, and praise of God   61
    Forbids Atheism—proof of the being of God   68
        Ignorance of the true God   92
        Profaning his name, attribute, time, ordinances   101
        Idolatry   120

The Second Commandment   126

    The Prohibition, As to the worship of God,
        external and internal   127
    As to the sins here forbidden—Superstition   139
    The Threatening, Visiting the iniquities of the
        fathers upon the children   148

The Third Commandment   165

    Profaning the name of God—Oaths   166
    The folly of this sin—Directions   186

The Fourth Commandment   192

    Primitive Institution of the Sabbath   195
    Its morality and perpetual obligation   196
    Change to the first day of the week   201
    The manner in which it is to be kept   204

SECOND TABLE

Introduction to the Second Table	225
The Fifth Commandment	228
Duties of parents and children	233
Magistrates and those subject to them	251
Husbands and wives	261
Masters and servants	279
Ministers and their people	301
Superiors and inferiors, or those who differ in the gifts of God's grace, or his common bounty	316
The promise, "That thy days may be long..."	328
The Sixth Commandment	332
The sin of murder	333
Causes and occasions leading to	345
Rules for restraining and governing anger	352
The Seventh Commandment	359
The sin forbidden	359
Its heinousness	365
Cautions and directions	370
The Eighth Commandment	373
Of theft in general	376
Many kinds of theft	379
The duties here required	389
The Ninth Commandment	395
The value of a good name	397
The sin of lying	399
Aggravations of this sin	406
The sin of slander—rules and directions	409
The Tenth Commandment	430
The sin of concupiscence	431
The whole practically applied	437

EXPOSITION

OF

THE COMMANDMENTS.

THE INTRODUCTION.

Two things in general are required to perfect a christian; the one a clear and distinct knowledge of his duty, the other, a conscientious practice of it, correspondent to his knowledge; and both are equally necessary. For, as we can have no solid or well-grounded hope of eternal salvation, without obedience; so we can have no sure established rule for our obedience, without knowledge. Therefore, our work and office is, not only to exhort, but to instruct; not only to excite the affections, but to inform the judgment: we must as well illuminate as warm.

Knowledge, indeed, may be found without practice; and our age abounds with speculative christians, whose religion is but like the rickets, that makes them grow large in the head, but narrow in the breast; whose brains are replenished with notions, but their hearts straitened towards God, and their lives black and deformed. I confess, indeed, their knowledge may be beneficial to others; yet, where it is thus overborne by unruly lusts, and contradicted by a licentious conversation, to themselves it is most fatal: like a light shut up in a lantern, which may serve to guide others, but only soots, and at last burns that which contained it.

But, although knowledge may be without practice, yet

the practice of godliness cannot be without knowledge. For, if we know not the limits of sin and duty, what is required and what is forbidden, it cannot be supposed but that, in this corrupted state of our natures, we shall unavoidably run into many heinous miscarriages.

Therefore, that we might be informed what we ought to do and what to avoid, it hath pleased God, the great Governor and righteous Judge of all, to prescribe laws for the regulating of our actions; and, that we might not be ignorant what they are, he hath openly promulgated them in his word. For when we had miserably defaced the law of nature originally written in our hearts, so that many of its commands were no longer legible, it seemed good to his infinite wisdom and mercy to transcribe and copy out that law in the sacred tables of the Scriptures; and to superadd many positive precepts and injunctions not before imposed. Hence the Bible is the statute-book of God's kingdom, wherein is comprised the whole body of the heavenly law, the perfect rules of a holy life, and the sure promises of a glorious one.

And the Decalogue, or Ten Commandments, is a summary, or brief epitome of the law, written by the immediate finger of God, and contracted into an abridgment not only to ease our memories but to gain our veneration; for sententious commands best befit majesty. And, indeed, if we consider the paucity of the expressions, and yet the copiousness and variety of the matter contained in them, we must needs acknowledge not only their authority to be divine, but likewise the skill and art in reducing the *whole duty of man* to so brief a compendium. The words are but few, called therefore *the Words of the Covenant,* or *the Ten Words* Ex

34 : 28; but the sense and matter contained in them is vast and infinite : the rest of Scripture is but a commentary upon them, either exhorting us to obedience by arguments, or alluring us to it by promises; warning us against transgression by threatenings, or exciting us to the one, and restraining us from the other, by examples recorded in the historical part of it.

But before I speak of the Commandments themselves, it will be necessary to premise something concerning, 1. the *time*, 2. the *reason*, and 3. the *manner* of their delivery; 4. how far the laws given by Moses are *abrogated;* 5. some rules for *rightly understanding* the Ten Commandments; and 6. a few words respecting their *order*

I. The TIME. According to the best chronology it was about 2,460 years after the creation, 220 after Israel's descent into Egypt, and the third month after their departure out of Egypt, Exod. 19 : 1; before the birth of Christ almost 1,500 years, and therefore above 3,000 before our days. God now first selected to himself a national church; and therefore it seemed expedient to his wisdom to prescribe them laws and rules, how to order both their demeanor and his worship. Before this the law of nature was the rule; but because it was blotted and razed by the first transgression, it was supplied in many particulars by traditions delivered down from one to another. And those of the patriarchs who, according to the precepts of this law, endeavored to please God, were accepted of him, and frequently obtained especial revelations, either by dreams or visions, or heavenly voices, concerning those things wherein they were more particularly to obey his will. Then, too, God made no distinction of people or nations; but, as it is since the wall of partition is broken down, and the Jewish economy abrogated by the death of Christ, so was it before, that, in every nation, he that feared God and wrought righteousness was accepted of him. Acts, 10 : 35.

II. The REASON. This was because the world was now so totally degenerated into vile superstitions and idolatries, that the knowledge and fear of the true God was scarcely to be found but only in the family and posterity of Abraham; and even among them we have reason to suspect a great decay and corruption, especially in their long abode among the idolatrous Egyptians; yea, the Scripture expressly charges them with it, Josh. 24 : 14; Ezek. 20 : 7, 8; and probably they took the pattern of their golden calf from the Egyptian Apis. God, therefore, justly rejects all the rest of the world; but, being mindful of his promise to their father, *the father of the faithful*, he appropriates this people to himself as his peculiar inheritance. And *because* it was manifest by experience that neither the law of nature nor oral tradition was sufficient to preserve alive the knowledge and worship of the true God, but the whole earth was become wicked and idolatrous; therefore that this people whom God had now taken to himself might have all possible advantages to continue in his fear and service, and that they might not degenerate as the rest of the world had done, he himself proclaims to them *that law* by which he would govern them, writes it on tables of stone, commits these into the hands of Moses, whom he had constituted his lieutenant, and commands them to be laid up in the ark as a perpetual monument of his authority and their duty. How wretchedly depraved are our natures, when even that which is the very light and law of them is so obliterated and defaced that God would rather entrust its preservation to stones than to us, and thought it more secure when engraven on senseless tables, than when written on our hearts!

III. The MANNER in which this law was delivered is described to have been very terrible and astonishing. God designed it so, on purpose to possess the people with the greater reverence of it, and to awaken in their souls a due respect to those old despised dictates of their nature, when they should see the same laws revived and invigorated with so much circumstance and terror; for, indeed, the Decalogue is not so much the enacting of any new law, as a reviving of the old by a more solemn proclamation. And mark the circumstances of majesty and solemnity in the action:

1. *The people were commanded to prepare themselves two days together, by a typical cleansing of themselves from all external and bodily pollutions before they were to stand in the presence of God.* So we find it enjoined: they were to be sanctified, and to wash their clothes, and *be ready against the third day,* when *the Lord* would *come down in the sight of all the people, upon Mount Sinai.* Exod. 19 : 10, 11. This teaches us,—

That we ought to be seriously prepared when we come to wait before God in his ordinances, and to receive a law at his mouth.

The dispensation of the Gospel is not indeed such a ministry of terror as that of the Law was. God doth not now speak to us immediately by his own voice—which they that heard it were not able to endure: he doth not pronounce his law in thunder, nor wrap it up in flame and smoke; but he speaks to us in a still voice, by men like ourselves; and conveys the rich treasure of his will to us in earthen vessels of the same mould and frailty with ourselves. He treats with us by his messengers and ambassadors; whose errand, though it be delivered with less terror, yet ought not to be received with less reverence: for it is God himself who speaks to us in them and by them; and every word of truth which they deliver in his name and by his authority, ought to be received with as much prostrate veneration and affection as though God did himself speak it immediately from heaven.

Think, then, how solicitous the Israelites were in fitting themselves for that great and dreadful day of hearing the law; a day more great and dreadful than ever any shall be except that of judging men according to the law. Think how their hearts throbbed and thrilled when they heard the clang of the heavenly trumpets blended with loud and terrible thunder, both giving a signal of the near approach of God. Think, if you can, what thoughts they had, when they saw the mountain burning with fire and enveloped with clouds and smoke, out of which on every side shot fearful lightnings. Think how they trembled when they saw the mountain tremble and totter under the weight and greatness of God descending upon it. And bring with you the same affections—if not so terrified, yet as much overawed—whensoever you come to wait upon his holy ordinances; for it is the same God that speaks to you; and he speaks the same things as then he did: not indeed with such amazing circumstances, yet with the very same authority and majesty.

Were God now to come down among you in his terrible majesty, or should a thick cloud fill this place and lightnings flash out of it; should you hear the thunder of his voice, *I am the Lord: thou shalt have no other gods before me;* certainly such a dreadful glory would make your hearts tremble within you and the very earth tremble under you. And could you then give way to sloth and drowsiness? Could your hearts run gadding after vanities and trifles? Or could any earthly object divert your thoughts and affections from so terrible a glory? Believe it then; God is as really present here as when he thus manifested himself to the Israelites; and present upon the very same occasion too. He is now delivering his law *to us;* pronouncing his high and sovereign commands: and if he so far consults our weakness as not to do it in such an astonishing manner; yet far be that disingenuousness from us, that we should be either the less careful to prepare for or the less reverent in attending on the declarations of his high will and pleasure, though he makes them known to us by men of the same temper with ourselves.

And if the Israelites were to sanctify and prepare themselves to appear before God at Mount Sinai, how much more ought we to sanctify ourselves that we may be meet to appear before God in heaven! That glory which God manifested when he delivered the law is not comparable to the infinite glory which he always reveals to the saints in heaven: and yet if the people of the Jews were not allowed to see God, though veiled with a cloud and thick darkness, without being first carefully prepared for such a glorious discovery; how much more carefully ought we to prepare ourselves, to wash our filthy garments, and to cleanse our souls from all defilements both of flesh and spirit, that we may be prepared to stand before God, and see him there where he darts forth the full rays of his brightness, and causeth his glory for ever to appear without any check or restraint, without any cloud or veil.

2. *The mount on which God appeared was to be fenced and railed in!* This was with a strict prohibition that none should presume to pass the bounds there set, nor approach to touch the holy mount, under the penalty of death. So we have it Exod. 19 : 12, which intimates the due distance we ought to keep from God; and teaches us to observe all that reverence and respect which belong to him as being infinitely our superior. Certainly the very places where God manifests himself, at least while he doth so, are venerable and awful: therefore, when God revealed himself to Jacob in a dream, and gave him the representation of a ladder reaching from earth to heaven—angels on every round of it, and God on the top—we find with what awe he reflects upon it, in his waking thoughts: "Surely the Lord is in this place, and I knew it not. And he was afraid, and said, How dreadful is this place! this is none other but the house of God, and this is the gate of heaven." Gen. 28 : 16, 17.

This setting bounds and limits to the mount, signified also, as in a type, the strictness and exactness of the law of God. His law is our boundary, a boundary set on purpose to keep us from rushing in upon his neck, and upon the thick bosses of his buckler: and that soul that shall presume so to break these bounds and commit a trespass on the Almighty, shall surely die the death; even that eternal death which he hath threatened against all violaters of his law.

3. *God appeared to pronounce his law in thunders, and lightnings, and earthquakes, and fire, and darkness:* these were the introduction to it; and so dreadful were they that they caused not only the people to remove and stand afar off, as not able to endure such terrible majesty, Exod. 20 : 18, but even affrighted Moses himself, who was to be *Internuncius Dei,* "the messenger and herald of God." This we find intimated, Exod. 19 : 19, "When the voice of the trumpet sounded long, and waxed louder and louder, Moses spake." What he said is not mentioned; but probably he then spake those words recorded by the Apostle, "So terrible was the sight, that Moses said, I exceedingly fear and quake." Heb. 12 : 21.

This dreadful appearance of God in the delivering of the law served to affect them with *a reverent esteem* of those commands which he should impose upon them; for, certainly, unless they were most grossly stupid, they must think those things to be of vast concern which were attended with such a train of amazing circumstances; and it is natural for men to be awed by pomp and solemnity, the majesty of the commander adding a kind of authority to the command.

Again, it served to put them in mind, as it should us also, that if God were so terrible only in delivering the law, how much more terrible he will be when he shall come to *judge* us for transgressing the law.

Indeed the whole apparatus of this day seems to be typical of the Last Day : only (as is true of all types) it shall be far outdone by its antitype. Here were voices, and fire, and smoke, and the noise of a trumpet; and these struck terror into the hearts of the people, who came only to receive the law: but, oh, think what con sternation will seize the hearts of sinners, when "the Lord shall descend from heaven," at the last day, "with a shout, with the voice of the archangel, and with the trump of God," as the apostle describes it, 1 Thess. 4 : 16 ; when, not a mountain only, but the whole world shall be burning; heaven and earth all on a light flame about them; when they shall hear the terrible voice of the Majesty on high calling to them, "Awake, ye dead, and come to judgment :" when the earth shall be universally shaken, and the dead shaken out of their graves : when whole crowds of naked nations shall throng and cluster about the Great Tribunal, not to receive a law but a sentence, a sentence that shall determine their final and eternal estate! Certainly if the giving of the law were so full of terror, much more terrible shall be our being judged according to that law.

4. When God himself had, with his dread voice, spoken to them these ten words, their affright and astonishment was so great that they *entreated Moses to be a mediator, or interpreter between God and them :* they said to Moses, "Speak thou with us, and we will hear; but let not God speak with us, lest we die." Exod. 20 : 19.

This may intimate how the law, as dispensed to us only from God, is in itself the ministration of death and condemnation; but, as delivered by a Mediator, our Lord Jesus Christ, of whom Moses here was a type, it may be the means of our obtaining eternal life, not *for*, but *through* our obedience to it.

Therefore the law is said to be "ordained by angels, in the hand of a mediator;" Gal. 3 : 19; that is, it was solemnly dispensed by the ministry of angels, and then delivered into the hand of Moses, to be by him communicated to the people; which intimates how the severity and terrors of the law were intended to drive us to Christ, as here they drove the Israelites to Moses, the type of Christ; from whose mouth the law spake not so dreadfully as it did from God's.

5. Upon this intercession and request of the people, *Moses is called up into the mount, and the law deposited in his hands*, engraven in two tables of stone, by the finger and impression of God himself: the most sacred relic the world ever enjoyed; but at length lost, together with the ark that contained it, in the frequent removes and captivities of that people.

This, too, may intimate how our hearts are naturally so hard and stony, that it is only the finger of God that can make any impression of his laws upon them. The ark was a famous type of Christ: and the keeping of the tables of the law in the ark, what doth it mean, but to prefigure to us how the law was to be kept and observed in him who fulfilled all righteousness? And when God again writes his laws on our hearts, we also keep them in Christ our ark, whose complete obedience supplies all our imperfections and defects.

6. Whereas this law of the Ten Commandments was *twice written by God himself*, once before and again after the tables were in a holy zeal broken by Moses: this also may intimate the twice writing of the law on the hearts of men; first, by the creating finger of God, when he made us perfectly like himself; and then again, by his regenerating power, when he creates us anew in Christ Jesus, giving us a new impression, and as it were setting us forth in a new edition, but yet containing the same for substance as when we came forth at first out of the crea-

ting hand of God: for regeneration and the new birth is but a restoring us to the image of God, which we defaced by our fall in Adam; and, as it were, a new stamping of those characters of himself in righteousness and knowledge, which were obliterated.

7. When Moses came down from the mount after his long converse with God, *his face shone with such a divine and heavenly lustre that the Israelites were dazzled with the brightness, and could not steadfastly look upon him:* therefore he was forced to put a veil over his face, to allay and temper those beams which the reflection of God's face and presence had cast upon him; but this veil he laid aside when he turned into the tabernacle to speak with God. Exod. 34 : 29, &c.

The significancy of this the Apostle expressly gives us, 2 Cor. 3 : 13-15, that there was a veil on the heart of the Jews, so that they could not see to the end of the law, which is Christ Jesus, who was the end of the ceremonial law, in that he put an end to it in its abrogation; and who is the end of the moral law, because in him it attains its end, which is by convincing us of our own weakness and inability to perform it, to lead us to Christ, by whose righteousness alone, and not by the works of the law, we are to expect justification before God. Yet there was so thick a veil cast over the law, that the Jews could not look through it upon the glory that shone in Christ, of whom Moses was still the type: but, when they shall turn to the Lord this veil shall be taken away; and then shall they discern the significancy of all those ritual observances, and perceive spiritual things after a more sublime and spiritual manner.

Thus I have shown the time, the reason and the man

ner of the delivery of this epitome of the law in the Ten Commandments; wherein are delineated and shadowed out many excellent gospel truths.

IV. And now if any one ask, "What need all this long discourse about the law? Is it not fully ABROGATED by the coming of Christ? Shall we be again brought under that heavy yoke of bondage, which neither we nor our fathers were able to bear? Doth not the Scripture frequently testify that we are not now under the law, but under grace? that Christ was made under the law, to free those who were under the law? and, therefore, to terrify and overawe men's consciences by the authority of the law; what is it but to make the Gospel a legal dispensation, unworthy of that christian liberty into which our Savior hath vindicated us, who has by his obedience fulfilled the law, and by his death abolished it?"

To this I answer: Far be it from every christian to indulge himself in any licentiousness, from such a corrupt and rotten notion of the law's abrogation; for, so far is it from being abolished by the coming of Christ, that he himself expressly tells us, he came not *to destroy the law, but to fulfil* it, Mat. 5:17; that is, either to perform or else to perfect and fill up the law; and, v. 18, he avers that "*till heaven and earth pass, one jot or one tittle shall in no wise pass from the law till all be fulfilled,*" that is, till the consummation and fulfilling of all things; and then the law which was our rule on earth shall become our nature in heaven.

When therefore St. Paul speaks, as he frequently does, of the abrogation and disannulling of the law, we must carefully discern and distinguish both what is taught us respecting *the law*, and what is taught us respecting *the abrogation* of the law, or any part of it.

The law, which God delivered by Moses, was of three kinds: Ceremonial, Judicial, and Moral.

The *Ceremonial* Law was wholly taken up in enjoining those observances of sacrifices and offerings, and various methods of purification and cleansing, which were typical of Christ, and that sacrifice of his, which alone was able to take away sin.

The *Judicial* Law consisted of those constitutions which God prescribed the Jews for their civil government, and was the standing law of their nation. For their state was a theocracy; and, as in other commonwealths the chief magistrates give laws to the people, so in this, the laws for their religion and for their civil government were both immediately from God. By this law were to be tried and determined all actions and suits between party and party: as in all other nations, there are particular laws and statutes for the decision of controversies that may arise among them.

But the *Moral* Law is a body of precepts, which carry a universal and natural equity in them; being so conformable to the light of reason and the dictates of every man's conscience, that as soon as ever they are declared and understood, they must needs be subscribed to as just and right.

These are the three sorts of laws which commonly go under the name of the Law of Moses: all of which had respect, either to those things which prefigured the Messias to come, or to those which concerned their political and civil government as a distinct nation from others, or to such natural virtues and duties of piety towards God and righteousness towards men, as were common to them with all the rest of mankind.

And now as to the abrogation or continued obligation of these several laws, I desire you heedfully to attend to the following propositions.

1. The CEREMONIAL LAW is, *as to the Jews, properly abrogated, and its obligation and authority utterly taken away and repealed;* for so the apostle is to be understood, when, in his epistles, he so often speaks of the abrogation and disannulling of the law: he speaks, I say, of the ceremonial law and Aaronical observances; which, indeed, were so fulfilled by Christ as to be abolished. For this law was given to be only an adumbration or faint representation of Christ. As in the night, while the sun is in the other hemisphere, yet we see its light in the planets and moons which shine with a borrowed and derived brightness; but when the sun is risen and displays its beams abroad, it drowns and extinguishes all those petty lights; so, while Christ the Sun of Righteousness was yet in the other hemisphere of time, before he was risen with healing under his wings, the Jews saw some glimmering of his light in their ceremonies and observances; but, now that the day of the Gospel is fully sprung, and that light which before was but blooming is fully spread, those dimmer lights are quite drowned and extinguished in his clear rays, and an utter end is put to all those rites and ceremonies which both intimated, and in a kind supplied the absence of the substance. So that, to maintain now a necessity of legal sacrifices, and purifyings, and sprinklings, is no less than to evacuate the death of Christ; and to deny the shedding of that blood that alone can purify us from all pollutions: which is but to catch at the shadow and lose the substance.

And as to us, who are the posterity and descendants of the Gentiles, it is more proper to affirm that *the ceremonial law was never in force,* than that it is truly abrogated; for the ceremonial law was national to the Jews, and, in a sort, peculiar to them only; neither did God intend that the observance of it should be imposed upon any other people, as a thing necessary for their future happiness, even though they should be proselyted.

And this appears, both because God expressly commands all those who were to be subject to the ceremonial law, that they should appear at Jerusalem, thrice in the year, before the Lord, Exod. 34 : 23, 24, which would have been impossible for those in countries far remote from Jerusalem; and because all their sacrifices and oblations, in which consisted the chiefest part of the ceremonial worship, were to be offered up only at Jerusalem; which would have been alike impossible, if this command of sacrificing had been intended by God to be obligatory on all the world. Therefore, doubtless, that command, even whilst it was in force, obliged none but the Jewish nation.

We find also that, even before Christ's coming, the Jews themselves did not impose the observance of the ceremonial law alike upon all proselytes; but their proselytes were of two sorts. Some, indeed, as the *Proselyti Legis,* became perfect Jews in religion, lived among them, and engaged themselves to the full observance of the whole law; yet some, called *Proselyti Portæ,* were only so far converted as to acknowledge and worship the only true God, but obliged not themselves to the performance of what the Levitical law required. These the Jews admitted into participation of the same common hope and salvation with themselves, when they professed their faith in God the Creator, and their obedience to the law of nature, together with the seven traditional precepts of Noah.*

For the farther clearing of this matter, moreover, we must know, that, in the very beginning of the church, there arose great dissension between the believing Jews and the believing Gentiles, concerning the necessity of observing the Levitical law. For we find, Acts, 15 : 5, that certain of the sect of the Pharisees which believed, affirmed that it was needful to circumcise the Gentiles, and to command them to keep the law of Moses : which yet was greater rigor than was formerly used to the proselyte party.

To determine this question, the apostles and elders meeting in a council at Jerusalem, decided in brief: That the believing Jews might still, without offence, observe the rites and ceremonies of the law : though the necessity of them were now abrogated, the use of them might, for a season, be lawfully continued: "dead" they were; but, hitherto, not "deadly:" they were expired; yet some time was thought expedient for their decent burial. Hence we find St. Paul himself, who so earnestly in all his epistles opposes the observance of the ceremonial law, yet submits to the use of those rites, Acts, 21 : 26, and 16 : 3, by which he evidently declares that those believers who were of that nation, though they were freed from the

---

* These precepts were: 1. The administration of justice upon offenders. 2. Renouncing of idolatry. 3. Worshipping the true God, and keeping the Sabbath. 4. Abstaining from murder. 5. From fornication. 6. From robbery. 7. From eating of blood, or any member of a beast taken from it alive.

necessity, yet they might lawfully, as yet, observe the Aaronical constitutions; especially, when, to avoid giving offence, it might be expedient so to do. So tender a thing is the peace of the church!

But then, concerning the Gentiles; although, before the coming of Christ, they might become perfect proselytes to the whole law of Moses, and receive the seal of circumcision, as many of them did: yet, after the evangelical doctrine was consummate, and the Apostles sent into all the world to preach it to every creature, they, by the Holy Ghost, determine, in that first council of the church, that the Gentiles should by no means be burdened with any of those impositions, that they should not subject themselves to the dogmatizing commands of false teachers, who required them to be circumcised and to keep the ceremonial law; but that they be required only to abstain "from meat offered to idols, and from blood, and from things strangled, and from fornication," that is, as judicious Mr. Hooker very probably interprets it, from incestuous marriages within prohibited degrees. And all those commands, laid upon them by the apostles, are the very precepts of Noah. But circumcision and other observances of the ceremonial law they were not obliged to: yea, they were obliged not to observe them, as being subversions of their souls. Acts, 15 : 24. And therefore we find that the same holy apostle, who himself circumcised Timothy because he was the son of a Jewess, when he writes to the Gentiles, tells them expressly, that if they be circumcised Christ shall profit them nothing. Gal. 5 : 2.

Thus we see how far and in what sense the ceremonial law is abrogated.

2. As to the JUDICIAL LAW, and those precepts which were given to the Jews for the government of their civil state, that law is not at all abrogated.

Not to us, for it was never intended to oblige us. Neither, indeed, is it at all necessary that the laws of every nation should be conformed to the laws which the Jews lived under; for, doubtless, each state has its liberty to frame such constitutions as may best serve to obtain the ends of government.

Neither is the judicial law abrogated to the Jews: for though now, in their scattered state, the laws cease to be of force, because the Jews cease to be a body politic; yet, were their dispersion again collected into one republic, most probably the same national laws would bind them now, as did in former times, when they were a happy and flourishing kingdom.

3. Concerning the MORAL LAW, of which I am now to treat more especially, that is partly abrogated and partly not: abrogated, as to some of its circumstances; but not as to any thing of its substance, authority and obligation.

(1.) *The Moral Law is abrogated to believers, as it was a Covenant of Works.*

For God, in man's first creation, wrote this law in his heart; and added this sanction to it, *If thou doest this, thou shalt live; if not, thou shalt die the death.* Now, all mankind sinning in Adam, and thereby contracting an utter impotency of obeying that law, that we might not all perish according to the rigorous sentence of it, God was graciously pleased to enter into another covenant with us; promising a Savior to repair our lost condition, and eternal life upon the easier terms of faith and evangelical obedience. Indeed, all those, who either never heard of Jesus

Christ, or who reject him, are still under the law as a covenant, and therefore their estate is most wretched and deplorable; for, being transgressors of the law, there remaineth nothing for them but a certain fearful looking-for of wrath and fiery indignation to devour them as the adversaries of God. But those who are true believers are under a better covenant, even the Covenant of Grace; wherein God hath promised to them eternal life, upon condition of their faith; and they may, with full assurance of hope, to their unspeakable joy and comfort, expect the performance of it. Therefore,

(2.) *To believers the Moral Law is also abrogated as to its condemning power.*

Though it sentenceth every sinner to death, and curseth every one who continueth not in all things written therein to do them; yet, through the intervention of Christ's satisfaction and obedience, the sins of a believer are graciously pardoned, and the curse abolished, it being discharged wholly upon Christ, and received all into his body on the cross. Gal. 3 : 13. "Christ hath redeemed us from the curse of the law, being made a curse for us;" so that we may therefore triumphantly exult with the apostle, Rom. 8 : 1, "There is now no condemnation to them that are in Christ Jesus."

In these two respects believers are indeed freed from the moral law; as it hath the obligation of a covenant, and as it hath a power of condemnation.

(3.) But, *as it hath a power of obliging the conscience as a standing rule for our obedience, it remains still in its full vigor and authority.*

It still directs us what we ought to do; binds the conscience to the performance of it; brings guilt upon the soul, if we transgress it; and reduces us to the necessity either of bitter repentance, or of eternal condemnation. for, in this sense, heaven and earth shall sooner pass away than one jot or tittle shall pass from the law.

Therefore Antinomianism is to be abominated, which derogates from the value and validity of the law, and contends that it is to all purposes extinct to believers, even as to its preceptive and regulating power; and that no other obligation to duty lies upon them who are in Christ Jesus, but only from the law of gratitude : that God requires not obedience from them upon so low and sordid an account as the fear of his wrath and dread severity; but all is to flow only from the principle of love and the sweet temper of a grateful and ingenuous spirit.

This is a most pestilent doctrine, which plucks down the fence of the law, and opens a gap for all manner of licentiousness and libertinism to rush in upon the christian world; for, seeing that the Moral Law is no other than the Law of Nature written upon man's heart at the first, some positives only being superadded; upon the same account as we are men, upon the same we owe obedience to the dictates of it.

And, indeed, we may find every part of this law enforced in the Gospel; charged upon us with the same threatenings, and recommended to us by the same promises; and all interpreted to us by our Savior himself, to the greatest advantage of strictness and severity. We find the same rules for our actions, the same duties required, the same sins forbidden in the Gospel as in the law.

Only, in the Gospel we have these mitigations, which were not in the Covenant of Works:

That God accepts of our obedience, if it be sincere, in earnest desires and endeavors. Although we cannot attain that perfect exactness and spotless purity which the law requires, yet we are accepted through Christ, according to what we have, and not according to what we have not, if so be we indulge not ourselves in a wilful sloth and contempt of the law.

That the Gospel admits of repentance after our falls, and restores us again to the favor of God, upon our true humiliation: while the law, as a Covenant of Works, left no room for repentance, but required perfect obedience without the least failure; and, in case of non-performance, nothing was to be expected but the execution of that death which it threatened.

Yet, withal, a higher degree of obedience is now required from us under the dispensation of the Gospel than was expected under the more obscure and shadowy exhibitions of gospel-grace by legal types and figures. We confess that the Israelites, before the coming of Christ, were no more under a Covenant of Works than we are now; but yet the Covenant of Grace was more darkly administered to them: and therefore, we having now received both a clearer light to discover what is our duty, and a more plentiful effusion of the Holy Ghost to enable us to perform it, and better promises, more express and significant testimonies of God's acceptance, and more full assurance of our own reward, it lies upon us, and we are under obligation, having all these helps and advantages above them, to endeavor that our holiness and obedience should be much superior to theirs; and that we should serve God with more readiness and alacrity, since now by Jesus Christ our yoke is made easy and our burden light

So that you see we are far from being released from our obligation to obedience; but rather, that obligation is made the stricter by Christ's coming into the world: and every transgression against the Moral Law is enhanced to an excess of sin and guilt, not only by the authority of God's injunction, which still continues inviolable; but likewise from the sanction of our Mediator and Redeemer who hath invigorated the precepts of the law by his express command, and promised us the assistance of his Spirit to observe and perform them.

V. But before I come particularly to treat of the words of the Decalogue, I think it requisite to propound some GENERAL RULES FOR THE RIGHT UNDERSTANDING AND EXPOUNDING OF THE COMMANDMENTS, which will be of great use to us for our right apprehending the full latitude and extent of them.

The Psalmist tells us, the commandments of God are *exceeding broad*, Psalm 119 : 96. And so indeed they are in the comprehensiveness of their injunctions, extending their authority over all the actions of our lives; but they are also exceeding strait, as to any toleration or indulgence given to the unruly lusts and appetites of men.

Now that we may conceive somewhat of this breadth and reach of the law of God, observe these following rules:

1. *All those precepts which are dispersed in the holy Scriptures, and which concern the regulating of our lives and actions, although not found expressly mentioned in the Decalogue, may yet very aptly be reduced under one of these ten commands.*

There is no duty required nor sin forbidden by God but it falls under one, at least, of these Ten Words, and sometimes under more than one; and therefore, to the right and genuine interpretation of this law we must take in whatsoever the prophets, apostles, or our Lord himself hath taught, as comments and expositions upon it; for the Decalogue is a compendium of all they have taught concerning moral worship and justice.

Yea, our Savior epitomizes this very epitome itself, and reduces these ten words to two: *love to God*, which comprehendeth all the duties of the first table; and *love to our neighbor*, which comprehendeth all the duties of the second table: and he tells us, that " upon these two hang all the law and the prophets," Mat. 22 : 37–40. And certainly, a due love of God and of our neighbor will make us careful to perform all the duties of religion to the one, and of justice to the other; and keep us from attempting any violation to his honor, or violence to their right: therefore the Apostle tells us that " love is the fulfilling of the law," Rom. 13 : 10; and, 1 Tim. 1 : 5, that "the end of the commandment is charity," or love : the end, that is the completion or the consummation of the commandment, is love, both to God and to one another. But concerning this I shall have occasion to speak more largely hereafter.

2. Since most of the commandments are delivered in negative or prohibiting terms, and only the fourth and fifth in affirmative or enjoining, we may observe this rule : that *the affirmative commands include the prohibition of the contrary sin ; and the negative commands include the injunction of the contrary duty.*

That the contrary to what is forbidden must be commanded, and the contrary to what is commanded be forbidden, is manifest. As, for instance, God in the third commandment forbids the taking of his name in vain: therefore, by consequence, the hallowing and sanctifying his name is therein commanded. The fourth requires the sanctifying of the Sabbath-day: therefore it surely follows that the profanation of it is thereby forbidden. The fifth commands us to honor our parents: therefore it forbids us to be disobedient or injurious to them. And so of the rest.

3. Observe, also, that *every negative command binds always, and to every moment of time; but the affirmative precepts, though they bind always, yet they do not bind to every moment;* that is, as to the habit of obedience, they do; but not as to the acts.

To make this plain by instance.

The first commandment, "Thou shalt have no other gods before me," bindeth always, and to every moment of time; so that he is guilty of idolatry whosoever shall at any time set up any other god to worship besides the Lord Jehovah. But the affirmative precept, which is included in this negative, namely, to worship, to love, to invoke, to depend on God, though it obligeth us always, (for we must never act contrary hereunto,) and likewise obligeth us to every moment of time, in respect to the *habits* of divine love, and faith, and worship; yet it doth not oblige us to every moment in respect of the *acts* of these habits; for it is impossible to be always actually praying, praising, and worshipping God, neither is it required, for this would make one duty shock and interfere with another.

So, likewise, the fourth commandment, which is affirmative, "Remember that thou keep holy the Sabbath-day," obligeth always; and whosoever at any time profanes the Sabbath, is guilty of the violation of this law but it doth not, it cannot oblige to every moment of time, since this day only makes its weekly returns, and every parcel of time is not a Sabbath-day.

So, likewise, the fifth commandment is positive, "Honor thy father and thy mother," and binds always; so that we sin if at any time we are refractory and disobedient unto their lawful commands: but it doth not oblige to the acts of honor and reverence in every moment of time, for that is impossible; or were it not, it would be but mimical and ridiculous.

But now the negative precepts oblige us to every moment of time; and whosoever ceaseth the observance of them for any one moment, is thereby involved in sin, and becomes guilty, and a transgressor before God: such are, "Thou shalt not take the name of the Lord thy God in vain: Thou shalt not kill: Thou shalt not steal: Thou shalt not commit adultery," &c. Now there is no moment of time whatsoever that can render the non-observance of these commands allowable, nor are there any circumstances that can excuse it from guilt. Whosoever profanes the name of God by rash swearing or trivial or impertinent uttering of it, whosoever sheds innocent blood, whosoever purloins from another what is rightly his, whosoever is guilty of any uncleanness; let it be at what time, in what place, after what manner soever, let it be done passionately or deliberately, whether he be tempted to it or not; yet he is a transgressor of the law, and liable to that curse and death which God hath threatened to inflict upon every soul of man that doeth evil. Whereas, in the affirmative precepts, there are some times and seasons to which we are not bound, so as actually to perform the duties enjoined us. This I suppose is clear, and without exception.

4. Observe this rule also: that *the same precept which*

forbids the external and outward acts of sin, forbids likewise the inward desires and motions of sin in the heart: and the same precept which requires the external acts of duty, requires likewise those holy affections of the soul that are suitable thereunto.

As, for instance, the same command that requires me to worship God, exacts from me not only the outward service of the lip or of the knee, but much more the inward reverence and affection of my soul: that I should prostrate, not my body only, but my very heart at his feet; fearing him as the great God, and loving him as the greatest good, and with all the tenderness and dearness of a ravished soul cleaving to him and clasping about him as my only joy and happiness. Therefore, those are highly guilty of the violation of this command who worship God only with their bodies, when their hearts are far estranged from him; offering up only the shell and husk of a duty, when the pith and substance which should fill it is given either to the world or to their lusts: such as these are guilty of idolatry even in serving and worshipping the true God; for they set up their idols in their hearts when they come to inquire of him, as the prophet complains, Ezek. 14 : 7. So, likewise, that positive command, "Honor thy father and thy mother," not only requires from us the external acts of obedience to all the lawful commands of our parents and magistrates, and those whom God hath set in authority over us; but requires farther, an inward love, veneration and esteem for them in our hearts. For, though men can take no farther cognizance of us than by our overt-acts; and if those be regular, they are likewise satisfactory to all human laws: yet this is not sufficient satisfaction to the law of God, for God is the discerner and judge of the heart and soul; and *his* law hath this special prerogative above all others, that it can with authority prescribe to our very thoughts, desires and affections.

And then, as for *negative* commands, they forbid not only the external acts of sin but the inward motions of lust, sinful desires, and evil concupiscence. Thus we find it at large, Mat. 5, where our Savior makes it a great part of his object in his sermon on the mount, to clear and vindicate the moral law from the corrupt glosses and interpretations of the Scribes and Pharisees; and to show that the authority of the law reached to prohibit, not only sinful *actions*, as that corrupt generation thought, but sinful *affections* too: v. 21, "Ye have heard that it was said by them of old time, Thou shalt not kill; and whosoever shall kill shall be in danger of the judgment." Here they stopped in the very bark and rind of the command, and thought it no offence, though they suffered their hearts to burn with wrath, and malice, and revenge, so long as they pent it up there, and did not suffer it to break forth into bloody murder. But what saith our Savior, v. 22? "But I say unto you, that whosoever is angry with his brother without a cause, shall be in danger of the judgment; and whosoever shall say to his brother, Raca, shall be in danger of the council; but whosoever shall say, Thou fool, shall be in danger of hell fire." You see here, that not only the horrid sin of murder is forbidden by the law, but all the incentives to it and degrees of it; as anger conceived inwardly in the heart, or expressed outwardly in words.

I cannot pass this place without giving you some light for the right understanding of it.

Here are three degrees of sin short of murder; yet all forbidden by the same precept which forbids that. *Causeless anger* against thy brother; calling him *Raca;* and calling him, *Thou fool:* whereof the one still exceeds the other in guilt. *Raca* signifies a simple witless fellow, commonly used to upbraid such as were weak and ignorant. *Thou fool,* signifies one that is not only ignorant, but wicked and ungodly, as the Scripture frequently useth the word in that sense, which is a far greater reproach than merely to call him weak or silly. Now, according to these three degrees of sins our Savior proportions three degress of punishment to be inflicted on those that are guilty of them, each severer than the other. *Causeless anger* shall bring them in danger of the judgment; *Raca,* in danger of the council; and *Thou Fool,* in danger of hell fire: that is, they shall make them liable to the punishments inflicted by these.

But, to understand the full scope and meaning of our Savior in these allusions, we must have recourse to the history of the Jewish commonwealth; and there we find that they had two courts of judicature, the lesser and the greater sanhedrim.

The lesser consisted of twenty-three persons; and was erected, not only in Jerusalem, but in every considerable city among the Jews where there were six score householders. These had authority to inflict capital punishments on malefactors; but yet, as the highest crimes fell not under their cognizance, so neither were the severest punishments under their award. And this consistory our Savior calls here the Judgment; and tells us, that whosoever is angry with his brother without a cause, shall be liable to a punishment correspondent to that which this sanhedrim was empowered to inflict; still applying temporals to spirituals, that is, he shall be liable to eternal death, though not so severely executed as it would be for crimes of a more heinous nature.

Their greater sanhedrim was their supreme court of judicature, and consisted of seventy elders, besides their chief speaker or moderator. You will find their first institution to have been by divine authority, Num. 11 : 16. They sat only in Jerusalem. Their sentence was decisive and determining, from which there lay no appeal. They were to judge of all harder matters which could not be determined by other courts: as causes concerning a whole tribe or the whole nation; causes of war and peace ; causes concerning the high-priest, and the mission and authority of prophets that spake unto them in the name of the Lord: and this may be the occasion of that speech of our Savior, "It cannot be that a prophet perish out of Jerusalem," Luke, 13 : 33, because in Jerusalem alone was this sanhedrim constituted which was to judge of the prophets whether they were true or false. This sanhedrim our Savior here calls the Council. And they had power, not only of life and death, as the other had; but likewise of inflicting death in a more severe and tormenting manner than the other: and therefore our Savior saith, Whosoever shall call his brother *Raca*, a vain witless fellow, shall be in danger of the council. Wherein he still brings the degrees of punishment among the Jews to allude to the punishment of sins in hell: and so the meaning is, that as he who shall causelessly be angry with his brother exposeth himself to the danger of eternal death; so he that shall suffer his anger to break forth into any reproachful or reviling language, although his taunts be not very bitter nor biting, only to call him a weak silly person, yet hereby he incurs the danger of a severer sentence, and execution of it upon him for ever.

But the severest sentence which this sanhedrim could pronounce against the greatest malefactors was that they should be burnt alive with fire. This execution was always performed in the Valley of Hinnom, joining to Jerusalem: which being a place wherein were frequent fires made, both in idolatrous times for the sacrificing of their children to Moloch, and in their purer times for consuming the filth of their city, and that which was as bad, their malefactors; it is not unfrequent in the Scripture to denote hell by this Tophet, this valley of Hinnom; which, for its continual fires, was a lively type and representation of it: yea, the very scripture name for hell, *Gehenna*, seems to be derived from the valley of Hinnom. Now, as burning of malefactors in Gehenna, or the valley of Hinnom, was among the Jews one of their highest and severest punishments, and never inflicted but where the crime was very gross and flagitious; so, saith our Savior, he that saith to his brother, *Thou fool*, shall be in danger of Gehenna, of hell-fire; that is, of a severer punishment in the true hell than those who were either causelessly angry or expressed their anger in more tolerable reproaches; although even they also shall, without repentance, be eternally punished.

So that the sense of our Savior in all this allusion seems to be this: that whereas the Scribes and Pharisees had restrained that command, *Thou shalt not kill*, only to actual murder, as if nothing else were forbidden besides open violence and blood; our Savior, contrariwise, teacheth, that not only that furious and barbarous sin of murder, but also rash and causeless anger, though it only boil in the heart, much more if it cast forth its foam at the mouth in reviling speeches, falls under that prohibition, "Thou shalt not kill." All these degrees deserve to be punished with eternal death; but, as among the Jews, some were punished with lighter, others with more grievous penalties, so shall it be at the Great Judgment: anger in our hearts shall be condemned with eternal punishment; but, if it break forth into reviling expressions the condemnation shall be more intolerable, and by so much more, by how much the reproaches are more bitter and sarcastical.

This, in brief, I take to be the true meaning of this difficult speech of our Savior: the whole scope whereof shows, that not only the gross acts of sin, but also the inward dispositions and corrupt affections unto sin, and every degree and tendency towards it, are forbidden and threatened by the holy law of God.

So, likewise, verse 27 of this 5th chapter: "Ye have heard that it was said by them of old time, Thou shalt not commit adultery; but I say unto you, that whosoever looketh on a woman to lust after her, hath committed adultery with her already in his heart." Here our Savior brings inward concupiscence to the bar; and makes the heart and eye plead guilty, although shame or fear might restrain grosser acts.

Thus it appears that the same precept which forbids the outward acts of sin, forbids likewise the inward desires and motions of sin in the heart.

And, indeed, there is a great deal of reason for it. For God, who is our lawgiver, is a spirit. He seeth and converseth with our spirits. There is not the least thought that flits in thy soul, not the least shadow of an imagination cast upon thy fancy, not the stillest breathing of a desire in thy heart but God is privy to it: he sees to the very bottom of that deep spring and source of thoughts that is in thy heart: he beholds them in their causes and occasions; and *knows our thoughts,* as the Psalmist speaks, *afar off:* he beholds our souls more clearly and distinctly than we can behold one another's faces; and therefore it is but fit and rational that his laws should reach as far as his knowledge; and that he should prescribe rules to that, the irregularity of which he can observe and punish.

Hence it is that the apostle, considering what an energy the law has upon that part of man which seems most free and uncontrolled, his mind and spirit, calls it a *spiritual* law: " We know," saith he, "that the law is spiritual," Rom. 7:14; and that, because the searching and convincing power of it enters into our spirits, cites our thoughts, accuses our desires, condemns our affections: which no other law in the world besides this can do. For how justly ridiculous would men be, who should command us not to think dishonorably of them, not to desire any thing to their detriment and prejudice; and should threaten us with punishment in case of disobedience : but the law of God comes into our consciences with authority; and, in the name of the great God, requires his peace to be kept among our tumultuous and seditious affections, beats down their carnal weapons, and gives conscience a power either to suppress all rebellious insurrections against the majesty of heaven, or else to indite, accuse, and torment men for them. And therefore "the Word of God is" by the apostle said to be "quick and powerful, and sharper than any two-edged sword, piercing even to the dividing asunder of soul and spirit, and of the joints and marrow, and is a discerner of the thoughts and intents of the heart." Heb. 4 : 12.

It is therefore a fourth rule for the right understanding of the extent and latitude of the commands, that the same precept which forbids the outward acts of sin, forbids also the inward desires and motions of sin in the heart.

5. Another general rule is this: that *the command not only forbids the sin that is expressly mentioned, but all occasions and inducements leading to that sin.*

And therefore we may observe that there are many sins that are not expressly forbidden in any one commandment, but yet are reductively forbidden in every one towards the violation of which they may prove occasions. And as some one sin may be an occasion to all others, so it may be well said to be forbidden in every precept of the Decalogue.

I shall instance only two of this kind: and they are—familiarity with evil persons, or keeping evil company; and the sin of drunkenness.

As for *evil company*, it is evident that though it be not expressly forbidden in any one commandment, yet, as it is a strong temptation and inducement to the violation of all of them, so it is a sin against them all. There are no such sure factors for the devil as wicked company, who will strive to rub their vices upon as many as they can infect. And therefore, thou, who delightest in the company either of atheists, or idolaters, or swearers, or sabbath-breakers, or disobedient rebels, or murderers, or whoremongers, or thieves, or perjured persons, or covetous muck-worms, thou art guilty of the breach of each of these commandments; for thou runnest thyself into the very snare of the devil, and takest the same course to make thyself so which made them such. And therefore we are all forbidden to keep company with such profane and profligate wretches by the very same commandment which forbids their impieties, whatsoever they be.

And as for *drunkenness*, whereas in the apostle's days, even among the heathen themselves, shame so far prevailed upon vice and debauchery, that it left sobriety the day, and took only the night to itself, 1 Thess. 5 : 7 ; yet now among us christians wickedness is grown so profligate that we meet the drunkard reeling and staggering even at noon-day, ready to discharge his vomit in our faces or our bosoms.

Possibly, some who are besotted with this loathsome vice may think it no great wickedness, because it is not expressly forbidden in the summary of the law; and so they cry Peace, peace, to themselves, although they go on to add drunkenness to thirst.

But of this sin I say that it is not against any one particular commandment of the law, but against all ; for since the moral law is the law and rule of right reason, the whole of it must needs be broken when reason itself is perverted by riot and intemperance, the man turned out of doors, and the beast taken in. So that, indeed, drunkenness is not so much any one sin, as it is all. The drunkard hath put off the man and hath put on the swine; and into such swine it is that the devil enters, as surely as ever he entered into the herd of the Gadarenes, and drives them furiously down the precipices of all manner of sins and vices, till at length he plungeth and drowneth them in the lake of fire and brimstone.

Therefore, whatsoever is commanded, or whatsoever is forbidden, drunkenness is forbidden, as being the greatest advantage the devil hath to prompt men to those abominations, that, were they in their right senses, they would abhor and detest. Is he, think you, fit to worship God, and to take him for his own God, who is not himself his own man? Is not he guilty of idolatry who makes Bacchus his deity, giving him the libations of his vomits, and falling prostrate before him? Can he forbear taking the name of God in vain who hath taken the creatures of God to his bane? whose tongue is set afloat with his excessive cups, and whose mouth the devil taps to let his blasphemies, and oaths, and curses, and fearful execrations run out the more fluently? Can he keep holy the Sabbath-day whose last night's drunkenness and excess rocks him asleep either in his own house or in the house of God? Is he fit to honor his parents who dishonoreth his own body? Can he abstain from murder who first takes the ready way to destroy his own body and damn his own soul; and then, through the rage of wine, is ready upon every slight provocation to mingle his vomit with the blood of others? Can he keep himself from uncleanness whose riotous table doth but prepare him for a polluted bed? Shall not he assever that which is false whose reason is so blinded by the fumes of his intemperance that he knows no longer the difference between truth and falsehood? And, finally, what bounds can be set to his concupiscence, who by thus blinding the eyes of his reason hath only left him fancy and appetite, both which the devil rules and governs?

Thus you see there are some sins which though not ex

pressly forbidden in the Decalogue, yet are virtually and reductively forbidden, as being the fomenters and occasions of others; and among these, drunkenness especially, which strikes at every law that God hath enjoined us, the guilt whereof is universal as well as the sin epidemical.

6. Another rule for the understanding of the Decalogue is, that *the commands of the first table are not to be kept for the sake of the second; but the commands of the second are to be kept for the sake of the first.*

The first table commands those duties which immediately respect the service and worship of God; the second, those which respect our demeanor towards men. Now the worship and service of God is not to be performed out of respect to men; but our duty towards men is to be observed out of respect to God. For he that worships God that he might thereby recommend himself to men, is but a hypocrite and formalist; and he that performs his duty towards men without respecting God in it, is but a mere civil moralist. The first table commands us not to worship idols, not to swear, not to profane the Sabbath. The laws of the magistrate command the very same; and those who are guilty of the breach of them are liable to human punishments. But if we abstain from these sins solely because they will expose us to shame or suffering among men; if we worship God merely that men may respect and venerate us, all the pomp and ostentation of our religion is but hypocrisy, and as such shall have its reward; for God requireth to be served not for man's sake, but for his own.

The second table prescribes the right ordering of our conversation towards men; that we should be dutiful and obedient to our superiors, loving and kind to our equals, charitable and beneficial to our inferiors, and just and righteous towards all. These duties are not to be done only for man's sake, but for God's; and those who perform them without respecting him in them, lose both their acceptance and reward. And therefore our Savior condemns that love and beneficence which proceeds merely upon human and prudential accounts. Matt. 5 : 46. "If ye love them which love you, what reward have ye? do not even the publicans the same?" And Luke, 6 : 33, 34, "If ye do good to them which do good to you, what thank have ye? for sinners also do even the same. And if ye lend to them of whom ye hope to receive, what thank have ye? for sinners also lend to sinners, to receive as much again."

We ought not therefore to serve God for man's sake; but we ought to love man for God's sake, and to perform the duties of the second table out of conscience and respect to God. We ought to do this in obedience to his authority; for what we do for men is an acceptable work and service when we do it out of a sincere principle of obeying the will and command of God. We ought to do it in conformity to his example; and this our Savior urgeth, Matt. 5 : 45, "That ye may be the children of your Father which is in heaven: for he maketh his sun to rise on the evil and on the good, and sendeth rain on the just and on the unjust." We ought to do it, in view of a comfortable hope and expectation of his eternal reward. Luke, 6 : 35. "Love your enemies, and do good, and your reward shall be great." And this is the way to exalt morality to be truly divine; and to make whatsoever we do towards men, to be an acceptable service to God. By this means we interest him in all the acts of our charity, justice and temperance; and we may be assured that what we thus do for his sake, shall in the end be graciously rewarded by his bounty.

7. Another rule is, that *the commands of the first table, so far forth as they are purely moral, supersede our obedience to the commands of the second table, when they are not both consistent.*

As, for instance: we are in the second table required to obey our parents, and to maintain and preserve our own lives; yet, if we are brought into such circumstances as that we must necessarily disobey either God or them— either prostitute our souls to guilt, or our lives to execution—in such a case our Savior hath instructed us, Luke, 14 : 26, "If any man come to me, and hate not his father, and mother, and wife, and children, yea, and his own life also, he cannot be my disciple." Indeed, a positive hatred of these is unnatural and impious; but the hatred which our Savior here intends is *comparative;* that is, a *loving them less* than Christ, less than religion and piety. And if the commands of the one or the concerns of the other are at any time to be violated or neglected, it must only be when we are sure that they are incompatible with a good conscience and true godliness.

8. Again, whereas, in the first table, there is one command partly moral and natural, partly positive and instituted, and that is our observation of the Sabbath, we may observe that *our obligation to the duties of the second table often supersedes our obedience to that command of the first table.*

It frequently happens that works of necessity and mercy will not permit us to be employed in works of piety, nor to sanctify the Sabbath after such a manner as else we ought; for the Lord requireth mercy rather than sacrifice. Hosea, 6 : 6. And this our Savior allegeth, Matt. 9 : 13. In which sense it holds true, that "The Sabbath was made for man, and not man for the Sabbath." Mark, 2 : 27. Whatsoever therefore is a work of necessity, or a work of charity and mercy, and that not only towards man, but even towards brute beasts themselves, may lawfully be done on the Sabbath-day, without bringing upon us the guilt of profanation; for that which is purely moral in the second table doth in a sort derogate from what is but positive and instituted in the first.

9. Another rule is, *whatsoever is forbidden in any command, both all the signs and symptoms of it, and likewise all the effects and consequents of it, are forbidden in the same.*

Thus, under the prohibition of idolatry, falls the prohibition of feasting in the idol-temples, and eating meats sacrificed to them, as being too evident a sign of our communion with them.

So, in the commands in which pride is forbidden, (which are chiefly the first and second, for a proud man sets up himself for his god, is his own idol, and is his own idolater,) in the same are forbidden all the signs and effects of pride; as a lofty look and a mincing gait, an affected behavior and vain fantastic apparel, against which the prophet largely declaims, Isa. 3 : 16-26; because, although pride doth not formally consist in these things, yet they are signs and effects of pride, and contrary to that modesty and decency which God requires.

10. The last rule is this: *The connection between the commands is so close and intimate, and they are so linked together, that whosoever breaketh one of them is guilty of all.*

Now that bond which runs through them and knits them thus together, is the authority and sovereignty of God enjoining their observance: so that whosoever fails in his due obedience to any one, doth virtually and interpretatively transgress them all.

Thus we find it expressly affirmed, James, 2 : 10, "Whosoever shall keep the whole law, and yet offend in one point, he is guilty of all." Not as though the violation of one precept were actually the violation of another; for many may steal, and yet not actually murder; many again may murder, and yet not actually commit adultery: but this place of the apostle must be understood of violating that authority which passeth through them all, and by which all the commandments have their sanction. For since the authority of the great God is one and the same in all these laws, he that shall so far disrespect this authority as wilfully to break one of them, evidently declares that he owns it not in any. And although other considerations may restrain such a one from those crimes which are forbidden by some commandments, yet his observance of them is no part of obedience, nor can it be interpreted to be performed out of conscience and respect towards God; for were it so, the same authority which withheld him from murder, or theft, or adultery, would likewise restrain him from lying, or taking the name of God in vain; and he that is guilty of these offences, is likewise guilty of all, because the same authority is stamped upon them all alike, and is alike violated in the transgression of each. And this very reason the apostle subjoins to his assertion, verse 11, "He that said, Do not commit adultery, said also, Do not kill. Now, if thou commit no adultery, yet if thou kill, thou art become a transgressor of the law: yea, of the whole law, as breaking that fence which God had set about his law, even his sovereign and absolute authority.

These are the rules which may direct your understandings to a right knowledge of the latitude and comprehensiveness of the law. The application of them to particular cases I must leave to the judgment of christian prudence, except as various illustrative examples may be given in the ensuing treatise.

VI. Before entering upon the consideration of the commandments in particular, it only remains to speak briefly —and that chiefly because others have spoken so much— concerning the ORDER of these commands.

The number of them is no way questioned; for God himself hath determined them to be *ten*, Exod. 34 : 28; but the method and disposition of them is much controverted, and I think with more heat and contention than the cause deserves; for if all that God hath spoken be entirely delivered to us, what great concern is it whether this or that command be reckoned the second, third, or fourth? This certainly tends but little to piety; and we had need rather to employ our care how to keep them, than how to reckon them.

Therefore, waiving all other differences, (as that of Hesychius, making the first command to be this, "I am the Lord thy God," which we, with good reason, affirm to be only a part of the preface;—and the leaving out of the fourth, concerning the sanctification of the Sabbath;— and the placing of "Thou shalt not kill" after "Thou shalt not commit adultery, Thou shalt not steal," whereas we, according to the Hebrew verity, place it before;) all that I shall remark is, the difference between the Papists and us in the enumeration of the Ten Commandments.

They generally hold that there are but *three* commands in the first table, and therefore make *seven* in the *second:* and so, to complete this number, they join the *first* and *second* into one, and divide the *tenth* into *two.*

Concerning this division or union we would not be much contentious with them, were there not a sacrilegious and idolatrous design couched under it, as manifestly there is: for finding the second commandment to strike so directly at their image worship, they think it expedient to deny it to be any distinct precept of itself; and reckon it but only an appendix or exposition of the former, " Thou shalt have no other gods before me;" that so they might with the better color omit it; as generally they have done in all their books of devotion and of instruction for the people. So that of those few among them that can rehearse the Decalogue, you shall find none that will repeat, " Thou shalt not make unto thee any graven image: thou shalt not bow down thyself unto them, nor serve them;" they not knowing that any such thing is forbidden them by God. And yet, that they may make up the full number of the commandments, they divide the tenth into two: one, forbidding the coveting of our neighbor's wife; and the other, the coveting of any other of his possessions.

The only authority they produce from antiquity for this order of the Decalogue, is that of St. Austin: and it is true, he doth in many places of his works so conjoin and divide them; yet not from any design of promoting idolatry, or keeping the people in ignorance, that the worshipping of images was forbidden. But in this particular he went contrary to the current of all former antiquity; yea, contrary to the very order of the Scripture: for whereas they say that the ninth commandment is, Thou shalt not covet thy neighbor's *wife;* and the tenth, Thou shalt not covet thy neighbor's *house, nor his servant, &c.* if we consult Exod. 20 : 17, we shall find that the command runs thus : *Thou shalt not covet thy neighbor's house, thou shalt not covet thy neighbor's wife, &c.* from which it certainly follows that they cannot make two precepts, but appertain to one.—But enough of this: which I had not mentioned, had it not been conceived out of such an impious design.

We now proceed to the commandments themselves, in which we have the *preface* and the *precepts.*

PREFACE TO THE COMMANDMENTS.

I AM THE LORD THY GOD, WHICH HAVE BROUGHT THEE OUT OF THE LAND OF EGYPT, OUT OF THE HOUSE OF BONDAGE.

This preface carries an equal respect and reverence to all the commandments; and contains a strong argument to enforce obedience to them. As kings and princes usually prefix their names and titles to the laws and edicts they set forth, to gain the more attention and the greater veneration to what they publish; so here the great God, the King of kings, being about to proclaim a law to his people Israel, that he might affect them with the deeper reverence of his authority, and make them the more afraid to transgress, displays and blazons his name and his style before them—*I am the Lord thy God, which have brought thee out of the land of Egypt, and out of the house of bondage*—that they might learn to fear his *glorious and fearful name*, THE LORD THY GOD. So we find it, Deut. 28 : 58.

And here, as all the arguments which are most prevalent and cogent are adapted to work upon one of these two passions by which we are swayed in all the actions of our lives, either our fear or our love, so God accommodates himself to our temper and proclaims, *first, his authority*, to beget *fear :* "I am the Lord thy God;" and then, *secondly, his benefits* and *mercies*, to engage *love:* "The Lord thy God, that brought thee out of the land of Egypt, out of the house of bondage." And both these he proclaims, that, having so strong an obligation on our very natures as the motives of love and fear, he might the more readily work us to obedience. For what motives can be urged more enforcing than these, which are drawn both from power and goodness ; the one obliging us to subjection, the other to gratitude?

1. *He is the Lord God, the great creator, the only proprietor, the absolute governor and disposer of all things;* therefore on this account we owe *an awful observance to all his laws and injunctions.* It is but fit and just that we should be subject to him that created us, and who hath infinite power, for our contumacies and rebellions, eternally to destroy us.

He is the Lord God, the great and glorious One, whose kingdom is from everlasting to everlasting, and whose dominion hath no bounds, either of time or place. "Behold," saith the prophet, "the nations are as a drop of a bucket, and are counted but as the small dust of the balance: behold, he taketh up the isles as a very little thing. All nations before him are as nothing; and they are counted to him less than nothing and vanity." Isa. 40 : 15, 17. His voice shakes the heavens, and removes the earth out of its place. His way is in the whirlwind. Storms and tempests are his harbingers; and the clouds are the dust of his feet. The mountains quake at his presence; at his displeasure the hills melt away; the world and all the inhabitants of it are dissolved. His fury is poured out like fire, and the rocks are thrown down by him. His hand spans the heavens, and he holds all the waters of the sea in the hollow of it. Heaven is the throne of his glory, and the earth his footstool: his pavilion round about him, dark waters and thick clouds of the sky. Ten thousand times ten thousand glorious spirits stand alway ministering before him: they fly on his errands, and are ready to execute his sovereign will and pleasure. "Who is like unto thee, O Lord, glorious in holiness, fearful in praises, doing wonders?" and therefore, who would not fear thee, O King of nations; and tremble and be astonished, when once thou art angry?

Wilt thou then, O vile and wretched sinner, despise the authority and majesty of the great God, before whom all the powers of heaven and earth lie prostrate? Darest thou infringe his laws and violate his commands, who is so great and terrible a God that he can destroy thee by the very breath of his nostrils? "By the breath of his nostrils are they consumed." Job, 4 : 9. Yea, he can look thee to death. "They perish at the rebuke of thy countenance." Psalm 80 : 16. Art thou able to contend with this God? Art thou a fit match for the Almighty? Can thy heart endure, or thy hands be strong in the day when the Lord shall deal with thee, and come to recompense vengeance upon thee for all thy transgressions? Who among you can dwell with the devouring fire? who among you can dwell with everlasting burnings?

Certainly, did we but frequently thus overawe our hearts with the serious consideration of the dread majesty and supreme authority of the great God, we should not dare so presumptuously to provoke him as we do. Fear is a most excellent preservative from sin, and a strong fence that God hath set about his law to keep us from breaking those bounds which he hath prescribed us. Therefore the wise man gives us this advice, Eccl. 12 : 13, "Fear God and keep his commandments;" and the Psalmist, Ps. 4 : 4, "Stand in awe and sin not."

2. As the authority of God is set forth to move us to obedience by working on our fear, so *his benefits and mercies are declared to win us to it from a principle of love and gratitude:* "The Lord thy God, who hath brought thee out of the land of Egypt, out of the house of bondage." And indeed this, though a soft, is yet a most powerful and effectual argument.

Hath God surrounded thee with blessings, and loaded thee every day with his benefits? Hast thou received thy life, thy being from him; and so many comforts in which thou takest delight, and he allows thee so to do? Hast thou been delivered by his watchful providence from many deaths and dangers; restored from sickness, or preserved in health? Doth he feed thee at his table, and clothe thee out of his wardrobe? Nay, what is infinitely more, hath he given thee his only Son, and his Son given thee his life and most precious blood? Hath he sent thee his Gospel; and in it the exceeding great and precious promises of eternal glory, a glory which hope durst not be bold enough to expect, nor is imagination large enough to conceive? Hath he sent thee his Spirit to seal and ratify all these promises to thee? Hath he crowned thy head with many rich blessings here, and will he crown it with joy and blessedness hereafter? And canst thou, O soul, be so unkind and disingenuous as to deny any thing to that God who hath denied nothing to thee? Canst thou refuse him the only thing he requires of thee, the only testimony which thou canst give that thou hast any sense of his favor? and especially considering he requires it only that he may reward it with farther blessings?

Canst thou wrong that God who hath been so kind and gracious unto thee, and is continually doing thee good? Canst thou despise his precepts, who hath regarded thy prayers? Wilt not thou hear him speaking unto thee, who hath often heard thee when thou hast cried unto him, and hath helped and saved thee? Certainly, the ingenuousness of human nature forbids it: the love of God constraineth otherwise; especially since he hath required obedience from us as the evidence and expression of our love to him: John, 14:21, "He that hath my commandments, and keepeth them, he it is that loveth me; and in 2 John, 5:6, "This is love, that we walk after his commandments." And that, which is a most cogent motive, thine own interest and eternal concernments engage thee to it; for, "what doth the Lord thy God require of thee, but to fear the Lord thy God—and to love him—and to keep his commandments—which I command thee this day for thy good?" Deut. 10 : 12, 13.

God might have required from us the very same obedience which now he doth, without promising us any reward for it; for we owe him all that we can possibly do, as he is the author of our beings, and every power and faculty of our souls ought to be employed for him who gave them unto us. But when the great God hath been so far pleased to condescend from his prerogative as to command us nothing but what hath already brought us very great advantages, and will for the future bring us far greater, when his hands shall be as full of blessings as his mouth is of commands; when he enjoins us a work that in itself is wages, and yet promiseth us wages for doing that work; when the mercies he hath already given us do oblige us, and the mercies he hath promised yet to give do allure us, certainly we must needs be the most disingenuous of all creatures, and the greatest enemies to our own happiness, if these considerations do not win us to yield him that obedience which redounds not at all to his profit and advantage, but to our own.

Thus you see how God hath enforced the observance of his law upon us, both by his authority and by his mercy: the one to work upon our fear, the other upon our love; and both to engage us to obedience.

Here it is observable, that, in the rehearsal of those mercies which should oblige to duty, mention is made only of those which seem to concern the Israelites, and no other people : *I am the Lord thy God, which brought thee out of the land of Egypt, out of the house of bondage.* From which some would infer that the Decalogue only respects them; and that the commands then given do not at all appertain to us any more than the benefits commemorated.

But the answer is easy. For this mercy here mentioned, of deliverance from Egypt and the house of bondage, is to be understood as well *typically* as *literally.* If we understand it literally, it indeed refers only to the people of Israel, whom God brought out of Egypt with a mighty hand and a stretched-out arm, and by such a series of miracles that they were almost as ordinary as the common effects of his providence. But if we understand it typically and mystically, it is true that God hath brought *us* also out of Egypt, and out of the house of bondage; and therefore the enforcement of the commandments on this account belongs to us christians as much as it did belong to the church of the Jews; for, if we run up the allegory to the spiritual sense of it, we shall find a wonderful agreement betwixt them and a near representation of our state in the state of the Israelites. Let it suffice to compare them together only in a few remarkable instances.

Thus as they were kept in bondage under the rigorous tyranny of Pharaoh, who sought both by policy and power to destroy them; so were we kept in bondage under the tyranny of the devil, of whom Pharaoh was a black type and shadow. And as God delivered them from his hand by a temporal salvation, so hath he delivered us from the power of the devil by a spiritual salvation; redeeming us from the slavish bondage of sin through the blood of his Son, by whom all our spiritual enemies are destroyed;

and conducting us through the wilderness of this world unto the promised Canaan, that land that floweth with milk and honey, the seat of rest and eternal joy and felicity, even heaven itself: and, therefore, if the consideration of a temporal deliverance were so powerful a motive to engage the Israelites unto obedience, how much more effectually should we be obliged unto it whose deliverance is far greater than theirs was; for God "hath delivered us from the power of darkness, and hath translated us into the kingdom of his dear Son," Col. 1:13; he hath "delivered us from the wrath to come," 1 Thes. 1:10; he "hath abolished death, and hath brought life and immortality to light through the Gospel," 2 Tim. 1:10. And therefore as our deliverance is spiritual, so ought our obedience to be; that being delivered from the justice of God, the condemning power of the law, the reigning power of sin, the sting of an accusing conscience, the rage and malice of the devil, and the intolerable torments of hell, we might, with all love and thankfulness, cheerfully serve that God whose mercy hath been extended towards us in those things which are of highest and most precious concernment.

Thus you see the reason of this preface, "I am the Lord thy God, which brought thee out of the land of Egypt;" and how it is both applicable and obligatory to *us Christians* as well as to the *Jews;* containing a declaration of God's authority to enforce and of his mercy to oblige us to the obedience of those laws which he delivers.

But I come now to the *precepts* themselves.

THE FIRST COMMANDMENT.

Thou shalt have no other gods before me.

This first and chiefest of the ten commands is negative; and as all negatives depend upon and must be measured by the truth of their contrary affirmative, I shall first consider what duties are here required, and then what sins are here forbidden.

This command has respect to *worship*, and REQUIRES four things:

1. That *we must have a God;* which, of course, is against atheism.

2. That *we must have the Lord Jehovah for our God;* which is against idolatry.

3. That *we must have the only true God, the Lord Jehovah alone, for our God;* and this is against polytheism, or the worshipping of many gods. It is opposed also to Samaritanism, or the worshipping of false gods together with the true, like those Samaritans spoken of, 2 Kings, 17 : 33, who feared the Lord and yet served their own gods; making a strange medley in religion, and blending those things together that were utterly irreconcilable: as if they intended not only to be partakers themselves with devils, but to make God so too; which is the greatest gratification that can be given to that proud and wicked spirit whose ambition it is to emulate and rival God in worship: for so the apostle tells us, that those "things which the Gentiles sacrifice, they sacrifice to devils, and not to God," 1 Cor. 10 : 20. Thus to join any other thing with God as the object of our worship, is infinitely to debase and disparage him; since it intimates that some-

thing besides God is excellent and perfect as himself. Therefore, in Zeph. 1 : 5, God severely threatens to cut off and to destroy those "that worship and that swear by the Lord, and that swear by Malcham."

4. It requires that *all our services and acts of worship to the true and only God be performed with sincerity and true devotion.* This is implied in that expression *before me* or *in my sight.*

And this is opposed both to profaneness on the one hand and hypocrisy on the other. For, since the most secret and retired apartments of the heart are all naked and bare in the sight of God, and our very spirits are as it were dissected and thus exposed to his view; it follows that to have no other god before him, denotes that our serving and worshipping him ought to be sincere and affectionate.

It is not enough to have no other god *before men;* not to fall down prostrate before any visible idol set up in a temple; but the law is spiritual, and searcheth the very thoughts and inward parts of the soul; and if there be any idol set up *in the heart,* although it be in the darkest corner of it; any secret lust or hidden sin, which is the soul's idol, and keeps it from being chaste and true to its God; any crooked ends and sinister respects in the worship of God; this is to have another god in the sight of Jehovah, and before him.

Indeed, we are very apt to rest contented if we can but approve ourselves before men, and carry a fair show of religion and godliness. But consider how weak and foolish this is : for, first, we deceive them with our appearances; and then we deceive ourselves with their opinions of us. It is not only before men, whose sight is terminated in the bark and outside of things, that we offer up our services; but before that God who is the searcher of the heart and the trier of the reins, who looks quite through us, and judgeth not according to outward appearance, but judgeth righteous judgment. For us to regard men, and seek to commend ourselves to them in the service of God, is as great a folly and irreverence as it would be for one who is to treat with a mighty prince, to regard and reverence only the images in the tapestry and hangings. Alas! men are but as so many blind images in respect to God; they cannot see the heart nor the affections; and those outward acts of worship which they do see and commend without the heart, are despised by God. He requireth truth in the inward parts; and is not delighted with the ostentation of performance, but with the sincerity of intention; for every one is delighted with that which doth most of all declare some singular excellency that is in himself; but it is God's excellency and prerogative to contemplate the heart, to weigh and consider the spirits of men; and therefore he is chiefly delighted in the unfeigned desires and breathings of the heart after him, because by these we own him to be an all-knowing God. But when we perform duties of religion only to be seen and applauded of men, we make God only our pretence, but men our idols; and set up as many gods before him as we have spectators and observers.

Thus we see what positive duties are required of us in this precept: that we should worship a God, and him the true God, and the true God only, and that in truth and sincerity, as doing all our services *before him*. So this first command respects *worship*.

It would be too long, and indeed almost endless, to insist particularly on ALL THE DUTIES included in the true and sincere worship of the true and only God. I shall therefore speak only of the three principal, and these are, the love of God, the fear of God, and the invocation and praise of God. In these three especially doth consist the having the Lord for our God.

I. This command requires of us *the most supreme and endeared love of God.*

Yea, indeed, the love of God is not only the sum of this command, but of all the commands of the first table; and therefore, as I have already said, when our Savior would give an abridgment of the law, he comprises all the *ten* under *two* great commands, Matt. 22 : 37-39, " Thou shalt love the Lord thy God with all thy heart, and with all thy soul, and with all thy mind. This is the first and great commandment. And the second is like unto it, Thou shalt love thy neighbor as thyself." From whence the apostle deduces that great conclusion, Rom. 13 : 10, that *love is the fulfilling of the law.* It is so, if not formally, yet virtually and effectively; for it will powerfully and sweetly sway us to yield a ready submission and obedience to what is required of us; and that not only as it is the dictate of divine and sovereign authority, but from the free spontaneous tendency of the soul itself, which, when it is once touched with this celestial and serene flame, must rebel against its own inclinations as well as against God's commands if it be not carried out towards that object in which alone it can find full acquiescence and satisfaction.

This love of God hath in it three acts or degrees; desire, joy, and zeal.

1. An earnest and panting *desire* after God. "As the hart panteth after the water-brooks, so panteth my soul after thee, O God. My soul thirsteth for God, for the living God:" oh, "when shall I come and appear before God?" Psalm 42 : 1, 2. As the poor imbossed deer that is closely pursued faints and melts with the heat of the chase, and hasteth to the known river where it was wont to quench its thirst, to find both safety and refreshment there, so doth the holy, amorous soul reach and breathe after God. He thirsteth after the *water-brooks*, the streams of his ordinances, wherein God doth pour out his grace and his Spirit to refresh the longing desires of his holy impatience; but, not being satisfied with this, he still makes up to the fountain, and never rests contented till he hath engulfed and plunged himself into God, and is swallowed up in beatitude.

2. From the fruition of the beloved object springeth *joy;* for joy is nothing else but the rest and acquiescence of desire; therefore, according to the measures of God's communicating himself to our souls, such proportionably will be the increase of our joy. Something we enjoy of God in this life, whilst we are absent from him in the body. He is pleased to give us transient glances of himself when he fills his ordinances and our duties with his Spirit; and yet these reserved communications are so ravishing that the soul is often forced by the agony of sweetness to cry out with holy Simeon, "Now, Lord, let thy servant depart in peace, for mine eyes have seen thy salvation." How overflowing then will our joy be when we come to heaven, where our fruition of God shall be entire and eternal! where we shall see him as he is, and know him as we are known by him! where the un-

veiled glories of the Deity shall beat full upon us, and we for ever sun ourselves in the smiles of God! Certainly the joy of such a state would be more than we could endure, but only that God who fills us will then likewise enlarge and support us.

3. If our fruition of God be hindered and obstructed, our love to him will then express itself in a holy *zeal*.

Zeal is the indignation of the soul, and a revenge that it takes upon whatsoever is an impediment to the obtaining of its desires. The earnest desire of a true saint is the enjoyment of God and the glory of God; of both which, sin is the only hinderance. Therefore a soul that is passionate for God, hath not so great an indignation against any thing as against sin. Can he endure to see that God, whom he loves dearer than his life, daily provoked and injured? to hear his name blasphemed? to see his ordinances despised, his worship neglected, his servants abused, and the most sacred truths of religion denied, and its sacred mysteries derided? He is the most meek and patient man on earth in his own concerns; unwilling to observe the wrongs that are done him, and much more to revenge them: but when God is injured, the dear object of his love and joy, he can no longer refrain: whatsoever may befall him, he rises up to vindicate his honor, and thrusts himself between, to receive those strokes that were aimed at God; and what he cannot prevent or reform, that he bitterly bewails.

This is true zeal; and he that saith he loves God, and yet is not thus zealous for him, is a liar.

Try, therefore, your love to God by these three things. Are your desires fervent and affectionate after him? Do you find a holy impatience in your spirit till you enjoy him? Will nothing else satisfy you but God? Can you say that there is none in heaven nor in earth that you desire in comparison with him; and if the whole world were thrown into your bosom for your portion, you would pluck it thence and cast it at your feet, resolving that you will not be put off with such trifles? Do you find a joy springing and diffusing itself through your hearts when you are engaged in communion with him? a sweet and potent delight, to which all the pleasures of sin are but flat and insipid? Are you jealous for the Lord of hosts? Are your anger and grief never so much kindled for any wrongs that are done unto yourself, as they are for the provocations that are daily committed against the great Majesty of heaven? Canst thou mourn and weep for these in secret; and if thou hast power and authority to do it, punish and avenge them openly? Then thou mayest for thy comfort conclude that certainly God hath kindled this heavenly flame of love in thy breast; a flame that aspires heaven-ward, and will at last carry up thy soul with it, and lodge it there, where the desire of love shall be satisfied, the joy of love perfected, and the zeal of love eternally rewarded.

So much for the love of God, the first principal duty required in this first command.

II. This command requires also *the fear of God*.

For certainly we cannot have the Lord for our God unless we supremely fear and reverence him. Yea, as the love, so the fear of God is made the sum of all the commandments, and indeed the substance of all religion: for, although it be but one particular branch and member of that worship and service which we owe to God, yet it is such a remarkable one, and hath such a mighty influence upon all the rest, that oftentimes in Scripture it is put for the whole; and generally, the character of a true worshipper and obedient servant of God is given by this periphrasis, that he is a man *fearing* God.

Now the fear of God is either *servile* or *filial*; and both are a strong bond to duty and obedience.

Those who are actuated only by a slavish fear, will beware how they stir up the dread wrath and severe justice of God against themselves by any wilful neglects or known transgressions.

And how much more those who are actuated by a principle of filial and reverential fear of God; who fear as much to offend as to suffer for it; and to whom mercy and goodness prove as powerful motives of fear, as wrath and fury! Yea, there is no attribute nor perfection in God but is very justly the object of our fear, for where this grace is true and genuine, it works in us rather a sedate awe and respect of God, a profound reverence of the soul, than any turbulent and tempestuous passions of affright and horror. And certainly if we acknowledge that there is a God, it is but reason that we should thus fear him according to his essential greatness and glory; for take away the fear of a Deity and a supreme power which is able to reward and punish the actions of men, and you open a floodgate for all villany and wickedness to rush out and overflow the whole world. And where this restraint of fear is taken off from the spirits of men, all laws given to curb their licentiousness are of no more force than fetters of air to chain up madmen; and therefore very fitly doth God enjoin the fear of himself in this first command, as that which will season and dispose the heart to obey him in all the rest.

III. Another principal part of worship required in this first command is *the invocation of the name of God in our prayers and praises.*

The two former, love and fear, respect the inward worship of God in our hearts; but this appertains to his outward worship, for by it we give express testimonies that we both love and fear him. It has respect to our prayers and praises, and they are the tribute and homage of religion. By the one we acknowledge our dependance upon him; by the other we own all our blessing and comforts to be from him; and to one of these two all external worship may be referred. Certainly such as neither *pray* to God nor *praise* him, cannot be said to have a God; for they acknowledge none, but are gods to themselves. For wherefore do we affirm that there is a God, if we make no addresses to him? If we have recourse only to our own power or policy to accomplish our designs, and when they succeed ascribe the success of them only to our own wisdom and conduct, we make these our idols and give them the honor which is due to God only. Therefore the prophet speaks of those who "sacrifice unto their net, and burn incense unto their drag; because by them their portion is fat, and their meat plenteous." Hab. 1 : 16.

Now as the love and fear of God are often used in Scripture for his whole worship and service, so likewise is this invocation and praise of his name. So we find it, Gen. 4 : 26, "then began men to call upon the name of the Lord:" that is, (as many learned expositors understand it, although some take it another way,) then began men solemnly and publicly to worship God in their assemblies; and Jerem. 10 : 25, "Pour out thy fury upon the heathen that know thee not, and upon the families that call not on thy name :" that is, those who do not worship nor serve thee. And the like we may observe in very many other places.

One thing more only I shall remark here; namely, that as this first command requires, in the general, that *the true God* should be truly worshipped, so the three next following commands prescribe *the means and branches of his worship, and the way and manner* how he would have it performed. The second commandment requires us to worship God, who is a spirit, without any visible image or representation of the Deity; for as it is impossible that there should be any true resemblance made of a spirit, so it is most impious to give any part of divine honor and reverence unto dumb idols: which, as to their materials, are but the creatures of God: as they are statues, but the creatures of art; and as they are images, but the creatures of fancy and superstition. The third commandment requires that we should never mention the name of the great God slightly and impertinently, but whensoever we have occasion to utter it we should do it with all prostrate veneration and serious affection. The fourth prescribes the time which God hath set apart and sanctified for his solemn worship. So you see each command of the first table is concerned in giving rules for divine worship; but the first, which enjoins it in the general, is the ground and foundation of the other three.

Thus much shall suffice concerning the *duties required* in this first command, THOU SHALT HAVE NO OTHER GODS BEFORE ME.

Next let us see what is FORBIDDEN in this command. As it requires, so it forbids four things. Thus it forbids atheism, or the belief and acknowledgment of no God; ignorance of the true God; profaneness, or the neglect of the worship and service of God; and idolatry, or the setting up and worshipping of false gods.

I. ATHEISM, or *the acknowledging of no god*, is forbidden and condemned by this command.

And well may this be reckoned the first sin forbidden; for certainly religion and worship will be found to be one of the most foppish vanities ever imposed on the credulous world, if either there be no God to whom we might direct our devotions; or only a god of Epicurus' and Lucretius' stamp, that sits unconcerned in heaven and loathes the fatigue of business, taking no thought nor care of human affairs. For if there be no god, or only such a one, what difference is there whether we pray or blaspheme? whether we lead holy and pious lives, or let loose the reins to all manner of lewdness and riot, and wallow in all the impure delights that vice and sensuality can recommend to our corrupted appetites? for if there be no God, there can be no future cognizance taken of either, no rewards nor punishments proportioned to either. Therefore it will be necessary here to show the folly and unreasonableness of atheism, and to convince men that there is a God, without which all religion and worship are but folly and madness.

Some perhaps may judge it altogether needless to insist upon such a subject as this among those who all acknowledge and worship the only true God, and Jesus Christ whom he hath sent. I heartily wish it were both unnecessary and impertinent; but truly, if we consider that usually the practices of men are guided and influenced by their principles, we shall find reason enough to suspect that there are some notions of speculative atheism that lie at the bottom of all that practical atheism which we may observe so generally to prevail in the world; for any considerate person would think it impossible that men should so daringly rush into all those prodigious crimes and villanies that every where rage and reign, were it not that they entertain loose and wavering apprehensions of the existence of a Deity, and encourage themselves in their vices by some unformed and vague thoughts that perchance all those truths which religion teaches concerning God and a future state are only politic devices and fictions.

Nay, indeed, our age has too many who, not only with the fool say in their hearts, but in desperate impudence even avow in express words, yea, dispute and argue it, that "there is no God."

I shall therefore confirm this great and primary truth, upon which depend all our religion and all our hopes, by some convincing and demonstrative arguments which I intend to make as plain and obvious as the matter will permit.

1. *The universal consent of all nations* strongly proves the being of a Deity.

For that which all agree in, must needs be accounted a dictate of nature; and what is such must needs be acknowledged to be a maxim of truth.

Next to the report of our senses we may credit the reports that nature and all mankind give concerning the truth and existence of things. Now if we should impannel all the nations of the world upon this trial, not only the more civilized, where custom or the authority of laws might be suspected to introduce this belief, but those that are the most rude and savage, they would all with one consent return this verdict, that *there is a God*.

Nay, although one part of mankind hath so strangely dissented from another about all other things, as concerning their laws, government and customs, yea, and manner of worship, yet those that differ in all things else, seem only to agree in these two; human nature and the belief of a Deity. Never was there any nation so wild and barbarous that acknowledged no God,* but their great fault and folly was that they acknowledged too many. And it is strange to think that the whole race of mankind in so many generations as have successively followed one another since the beginning of the world, (yea, and if there were no God, from all eternity,) should not have grown wise enough to free themselves from so troublesome an opinion as that of the existence of a God: an opinion that crosses their worldly interests, contradicts their sensual desires, damps their joys, torments their natural consciences, and which those who are wicked would give whatsoever is dearest to them to have utterly rooted out of their minds: it is strange, I say, that they should not all this while be able to deliver themselves from the tyranny and fetters of this fancy, were it only imposed upon them by false reports and surmises.

How could the world be so easily drawn into such several shapes and forms of religion, which among the heathen are almost infinite, and among others too various

---

* *Nulla gens est, neque tam immansueta nec tam fera, quæ, etiamsi ignoret vel eam habere Deum deceat, tamen habendum sciat.* Cicero.

and different, were there not a natural inclination in the souls of men to embrace some religion or other, and an indelible character of a Deity imprinted on their minds? Insomuch, that in the times of darkness, when the truth was not clearly revealed to the world, because they knew neither the true object nor the right way of worship, this restless notion of a Deity put them upon inventing divers vile, uncouth and ridiculous superstitions. But yet this is so far from invalidating, that it strongly confirms to us their belief of a Deity; in that they submitted themselves to observances, not only unreasonable, but many times barbarous and inhuman, if they thought them acceptable to the gods whom they worshipped. Yea, rather than they would be without a Deity, they would dig them gods out of their gardens; or consecrate dogs and serpents, and any vermin that first met them in the morning, and had the good luck thereby to creep into honor.

What then! is it likely that the world received this notion first by tradition; whereas, before, men generally believed there was no God? This cannot be; for would they in reason quit their former persuasion to receive this new false one, especially when it is the only thing that fills them with fears and torments, and a thousand affrights and horrors? Yea, those who would fain wear off this notion of a God, and persuade themselves to be atheists if they could, what violence have they offered to themselves to do it! And when they thought they had prevailed, yet this impression hath still returned when they have been startled with thunder, or earthquakes, or sickness, and the dreadful apprehensions of approaching death.

Possibly, some few may have been found in the world, who have dissented from the rest of mankind in this belief of a Deity; yet their dissent is not sufficient ground for us to conclude, that therefore it is not a dictate of nature. For how many are there that violate the laws of nature, and do those things which the innate light and reason of a man abhor and abominate! Yet none will from thence infer that there are no such things as natural laws; so neither, though some might have utterly razed out of their minds the notion and belief of a God, will it thence follow that this belief of a Supreme Being is not an impression of nature.

But suppose the number of atheists had been never so great, is it not far more probable that it should rather be a dictate of nature that there is a God, than that there is not; since the disbelief of his being would open a wide gap to all manner of licentiousness, yea, and to the bold commission even of those sins which are against nature itself? Shall men be thought to speak the sense of nature, whose opinion so directly tends to bring in sins contrary to the light and laws of nature? For, take away the belief of a Deity, and it is as much to be doubted whether the refined discourses of reason, and the consideration of decency, and the intrinsical rewards of virtue, will be of force sufficient to restrain men from the most enormous and unnatural vices. That, therefore, must needs be a dictate of nature, which is almost the only thing which gives authority to the law of nature; and such is the belief of a God.

2. Another convincing demonstration of the existence of a Deity, is taken from *the serious consideration and review of the frame and order of the universe;* in which there are as many wonders as there are creatures.

Certainly he must needs be very blind and stupid that

reads not God in every creature. Cast but your eyes upwards and contemplate the vast expanse of the heavens, which are the canopy of the world, the roof of this great house, the universe, the lid or cover put over all the works of nature. Behold how gloriously this canopy is studded! How many glittering lights are hung up in this roof to illuminate our inferior world, and to discover to our eyes all visible objects, and to our mind the invisible God! Who hath gilded the rays of the sun, or silvered the face of the moon? Who hath marshalled the huge host of heaven; and set the stars in such array, that not one of them hath broken its rank nor strayed out of its course and order? Whose hand is it that turns the great wheels of heaven; and makes them spin out days, and months, and years, and time, and life to us? Who hath ordered the vicissitudes of day and night, summer and winter, that these run not into one another and blend themselves and the whole world in confusion; but with a perpetual variety, observe their just seasons and interchanges? Do not all these wonderful works proclaim aloud, that certainly there is a great and glorious God who sits enthroned on high; and who hath thus paved the bottom of heaven with stars, and adorned the inner parts of it with glories yet to us unknown? Upon this very reflection the psalmist tells us, " The heavens declare the glory of God, and the firmament showeth his handy-work." Psalm 19 : 1.

But not to carry the atheist up to heaven, let us descend lower, through the vast ocean of liquid air, and there observe how the grosser vapors are bound together in clouds, which when the drought and thirst of the earth call for refreshment, dissolve themselves into small drops, and are as it were sifted into rain. How comes it to pass, and whose wisdom and providence hath so ordered it, that there should not fall whole clouds and cataracts, but drops and showers? that they should not tumble upon us, but distil? an effect so wonderful that there is scarce any other work of nature that the Scripture more frequently ascribes to God, as a demonstration of his power and government, than that he sendeth rain upon the earth. Yea, and these clouds, how often are they charged with thunder and lightnings; as though it were so ordered of purpose, that if their contexture cannot convince, yet their terror might affright the atheist! Who can give any satisfactory account how that artillery came there planted? or how those terrors of mankind are there generated? Let the atheist tell me how it comes to pass that such contraries meet together in one; and that the same cloud should be both a fountain of water and yet a furnace of fire, a wonder the prophet ascribeth particularly to God's almighty providence, Jer. 10:13, "He maketh lightnings with rain;" and accounteth it such a remarkable instance of the divine operation that he repeateth it again, chap. 51:16.

If we descend into the lowest story of this great building, the earth, what a shop of wonders shall we find there! That the whole mass and globe of it should hang pendulous in the air, without any thing to support it; and whereas small bodies of little weight fall through the air, yet that this great and ponderous body should be fixed for ever in its place, having no foundation, no support but that air which every mote and fly doth easily cut through; that this round ball of earth should be inhabited on every part; that the feet of other men should be opposite to ours, and yet they walk as erect and be as much upon the face of the earth as we are ; that the middle point of the earth should be the lowest part of it and of the universe, and whatsoever is beyond that be upwards : these and many others are such unaccountable mysteries to our comprehension, and yet are found so infallibly certain by experience and manifold proofs, that he must be an atheist out of mere spite, who shall seriously consider them and not be induced by that consideration to adore the infinite power and wisdom of their Author.

It would be too long to instance in the various sorts of creatures that we behold, how artificially they are framed, what an excellent configuration there may be observed in their several parts, what subserviency of one to another, and how all are suited to the offices of nature; what secret channels and conveyances for life and spirits, what springs of various motions are included even in the small body of a fly or of a mite. Certainly there is not the least thing that an atheist can cast his eye upon but it confutes him; but especially, if he shall seriously consider the wonderful structure of a human body, the excellent contrivance and use of all the parts, he cannot but, after he hath admired the artifice of the work, admire also the infinite wisdom of the Maker, and cry out with holy David, "I am fearfully and wonderfully made—and curiously wrought in the lowest parts of the earth." Psalm 139 : 14, 15. Yea, not only a David, but Galen, a heathen, one who it is thought was not over-credulous in matters of religion; yet when he had minutely inspected the many wonders and miracles that are contained in the frame of our body, he could not forbear composing a hymn to the praise of our all-wise Creator.

And therefore, as lord Bacon observes, (Essay of Atheism,) God never wrought a miracle to convince an atheist, because his ordinary works may convince him; and unless men will be wilfully and stubbornly blind, they must needs subscribe to that of St. Paul, Acts, 14: 17, God hath "not left himself without witness, in that he doeth good, and giveth us rain from heaven, and fruitful seasons, filling our hearts with food and gladness;" and, Rom. 1: 20, "The invisible things of God are clearly seen from the creation of the world, being understood by the things that are made, even his eternal power and godhead: so that they are without excuse." When we see footsteps evidently imprinted on the earth, shall we not easily collect that certainly some one hath passed that way? When we see a stately fabric built according to all the rules of art, and adorned with all the riches and beauty that magnificence can expend upon it, must we not presently conclude that certainly there was some skilful architect that built it? Truly every creature is *quoddam vestigium Dei*, some sign or evidence of Deity: we may observe his footsteps in it; and see how his attributes, his wisdom, his goodness and his power have passed along that way. And the whole world is a stately fabric; a house that God hath erected for himself: the magnificence and splendor of it are suitable to the state of the great King: it is his palace, built for the house of his kingdom and the honor of his majesty: and we may easily conclude that so excellent a structure must have an excellent architect, and that the builder and maker of it is God.

Now that which makes some proud spirits backward to acknowledge God in the works of nature is, that they think they can, by their reason alone, give a plausible account of those effects and phenomena which we see in the world, by deducing them from second and natural causes. And therefore many of those who are of an inquisitive and searching genius, when they find such effects depend upon and flow from such and such natural causes, applaud themselves in the discovery; and look no further nor higher, but neglect the first and chief cause of all, even God.

Hence some have thought that reason and philosophy are great enemies to religion, and patrons of atheism; but, in truth, it is far otherwise; and the atheist hath not a more smart and keen adversary, since he will not submit his cause to be tried by Scripture, than true reason and profound philosophy.

But if any, who seem to be knowing and learned men, are less inclined to the belief of a Deity, it is not their learning but their ignorance that makes them so. The same lord Bacon has well observed, that a little philosophy inclines a man's mind to atheism, but depth in philosophy brings it about again to religion. And I dare challenge the most learned men in the world to give a satisfactory account of the most common appearances in nature without resolving them at last into the will and disposal of the God of Nature. If I should ask them what makes the grass green, or a stone to fall downwards, or the fire to aspire upwards, or the sun to enlighten and warm the world? What answer can they give, but that it is the property of their natures; or what is altogether as insignificant and unintelligible? But, if I should question farther, how came their natures to be distinguished with such properties? they must either here be silent, or confess a First Cause, which endowed their natures with such properties and actions; for, although a man may, for some few successions of causes and effects, find one to depend upon another, yet they must all, at last, be resolved into and terminate in God.

3. Unless the being of a God be presupposed, *no tolerable account can be given of the being of any thing.*

We see innumerable beings in the world, different from each other both in kind and particulars. Now what rational account can the atheist give how these things came to have a being? There are but two ways imaginable: either that the world was formed by chance; or else, that it had its being from all eternity. And accordingly, as if it were still fatal for them to encounter the same inconsistencies for which they disavow religion, atheists are divided into two sects.

(1.) One is the *Epicurean* atheist, who affirms that the world indeed had once a beginning, but it was merely by chance: for, there having been from all eternity infinite particles of matter moving to and fro in an infinite space; these at last, meeting casually, linked one in another, and so, by mere chance, formed this world which we now see. A fancy so grossly ridiculous, that, were it not now again taken up by some who pretend to be great lights in reason and philosophy, I would not condescend so much as to mention it.

But, as Cicero saith, both judiciously and ingeniously, as soon shall they persuade me that an innumerable company of loose and disordered letters, being often shaken together and afterwards thrown out upon the ground, should fall into such exquisite order as to frame a most ingenious and heroic poem; as that atoms, straying to and fro at random, should ever casually meet together to make a world consisting of heaven, and of air, and sea, and earth, and so many sorts and species of living creatures, in the frame and structure of which we see such wonderful and inimitable skill.

Had Archimedes' or Posidonius' sphere, in which were imitated all the motions and changes of the sun, moon and planets, been presented to the most ignorant or illiterate nations under heaven, they could not be so grossly stupid as to think such a piece a work of mere chance, and not of accurate art and study. And shall any doubt, when he sees, in the great machine of the world, the same and many other phenomena exhibited in a more perfect manner than they can be represented in any such type, whether it be a work of uncertain chance, or the product of a most perfect mind and comprehensive understanding? For, certainly, if a strong and mastering reason be required only to imitate the works of nature; much more, then, to produce them. Cic. de Nat. Deor. lib. ii. 37, 34.

And why had not those atoms, that could thus fortuitously frame a world, why had they not built houses too, and cities, and woven us garments; that so, by very good chance, we might have found these necessaries ready provided to our hands, and been saved the trouble and labor of making them? Did ever any atoms fall into such exact order, and knit so artificially together, as to frame a clock, or a watch, or any other piece of ingenious mechanism? And will the atheist then be so silly as to believe that these little **dusts** of being should, by mere hazard, meet and join together to frame the whole world; and bestow such various forms and motions upon creatures as we daily see and admire? Look but upon the most contemptible worm that crawls, we shall find it a far more excellent piece of mechanism, a far more curious engine, than any that ever the art or wit of man could frame. And shall chance make these, yea, creatures of a more wonderful contexture, which yet could never make a watch, or a clock, or any of those engines which we have contrived for the use and service of life?

And what will they say to the accurate operations of sense and reason? Is it possible that one small dust should see or feel another? and, if not one, then not ten thousand put together. Shall their configuration give them this faculty, which their being and substance doth not? Which I shall then believe, when I shall be convinced that a statue, carved the most exquisitely that art can perform, can any more see, or taste, or feel, than it could whilst it was rude and unformed wood.

But, suppose that sense could be caused by mere matter put in motion; yet, what shall we say to the refined speculations and profound discourses of reason? Is it likely, or indeed possible, that little corpuscles should reflect and argue? that atoms should make syllogisms, or draw up parties between pro and con? Or will the atheist grant that there is no other difference between himself and a mere senseless block but only configuration of parts? and that when he disputes most subtilely for his cause, all his reasons and arguments are but a little dust that flies up and down in his brains? That the agitation of material particles should produce any sprightly acts of wit and discourse, is so monstrously abhorrent to true reason, that I doubt I shall never be persuaded to believe it, until some cunning man convince me that the highway too is in a deep speculation, and teeming with some notable discourse, whensoever the dust is stirred and flies about in it.

And yet, forsooth, men must now-a-days be atheists

that they may be rational; and think it a high demonstration of their parts and ingenuity to doubt of a Deity, and call all religion into question. Whereas, were there any thing in the belief of a God and the most mysterious points of our religion half so absurd and ridiculous as there is in atheism, I should most readily explode it and count it altogether unworthy to be entertained by any man that is ingenuous and rational.

(2.) Hence the other sect of atheists alluded to, the *Aristotelian*, being pressed with the huge and monstrous absurdities of this way of giving an account of the appearances of nature, hold that the world is from eternity, and never had any beginning at all. But,

It is altogether unreasonable to deny a God, and yet grant *that very thing for which alone they deny him.* The only reason that tempts atheists to deny a Deity, is because they cannot conceive a Being infinite and eternal. But when they yield the world to be so, what do they else but run into the same inconveniency which they would avoid; and, that they may not grant one eternal being, grant innumerable? So fatal it is for error to be inconsitent with itself and to confound its own principles.

If the world be eternal, there must of necessity have been passed *an infinite succession of ages.* Now, our understanding is as much non-plussed to conceive this, as it is to conceive an Infinite Being that should create the world; for, if the world had no beginning, then an infinite number of days and years, yea, of millions of years and generations of men are already actually passed and gone. And if they are passed, then they are come to an end; and so we shall have both a number that is actually infinite, and likewise something infinite and eternal that is come to an end: a very proper consequence for one that avoids the belief of a Deity because he would be rational and cannot conceive a being that is infinite!

If there have already been infinite successions of generations in the world, certainly those which are yet to come *will make them more;* and so we shall find a number greater than that which is allowed to be actually infinite. Or if, to avoid this contradiction, the atheist should affirm that the generations to Abraham and the generations to David were both equal because both infinite, he will thereby fall into two other gross contradictions: the one, that a number added to a number should make no addition; the other, that since the generations to Abraham were but a part of the generations to David, the part should be equal to the whole.

There is no one moment in succession which was not *once present;* and consequently, imagine a duration as long as you please, yet in it of necessity there must be some one moment which, when it was present, all the rest were future; and if all the rest were future, this moment was then the beginning. So that it is impossible there should be a successive duration without a beginning, and therefore impossible it should be from eternity.

In all the revolutions of generation and corruption that can be imagined, yet the life of animals must necessarily be *before their death:* for none can die till he hath lived; and none can live but he must pass some time before he dies. There was therefore a time before any animal died: consequently their corruption and death were not from eternity: neither before their death had they lived an infinite time, but only some few days or years; and therefore their generation and life were not from eternity.

FIRST COMMANDMENT.

These things I do but cursorily mention, to give you a taste of the folly and unreasonableness of atheism; nor perhaps, would it be proper to insist on them at large: but by these few arguments you may see how unreasonable it is for an atheist to boggle at the belief of a Deity; whereas, let him lay down whatsoever principles he will, he shall find his reason more puzzled and entangled by these absurdities that will necessarily follow upon them, than he shall by any difficulties that are consequent upon the belief of a God: which belief unless we entertain, we can give no tolerable account at all of the various beings that are in the world, for neither are they eternal, neither have they happened by chance, as I have demonstrated.

It is therefore absolutely necessary that there be some First Cause of all things which we behold, which is not itself caused, nor produced by any other: for if every thing were caused by some pre-existent being, then there never was a being before which there was not another; and so this gross absurdity will follow, That before there was a being, there was a being: a fit consequence for atheists, who pretend only to rational speculations, to swallow! Therefore we must necessarily rest in some First Cause, from which all other things have their origin, and which is itself caused by none: and that is the great God, whom we adore; the great Creator and Governor both of heaven and earth, and of all things visible and invisible.

And here I would add the argument of Bradwardine, which perhaps it would shrewdly puzzle the metaphysics of an atheist to answer, namely: It is possible that there should be such a being as should exist necessarily; since it is no more a contradiction to exist necessarily than to exist contingently, and a far higher and more absolute perfection. But if it be possible that there might be such a being, then it is certain that there is; because necessity of existence is included in the very essential conception of it, or else this contradiction would follow, that it is possible for that not to be, which yet is necessary to be. This being, therefore, must needs be eternal, independent, and self-sufficient; and that is the God whom we adore. De Causa Dei.

4. But, to leave these more abstruse and scholastic notions. If there be no God, then neither have there been *any miracles performed in the world, nor any prophecies or predictions of future events.*

(1.) There can be no *miracles* performed without a divine and infinite power.

For, certainly, if there be no being above nature, there can be no effects either above or contrary to the course of nature; for nature, when it is left to itself, cannot act contrary to its own laws.

Now that there have been miraculous works performed the atheist cannot deny, unless he will deny the truth of all records, and think it reasonable to make all faith and credit among mankind a sacrifice to his opiniativeness. All heathen authors, as well as the Scriptures, give abundant testimony to this; and although they deny the doctrine of the Scripture, yet there is no reason why they should disbelieve it when it only relates matter of fact. In this behalf we desire they would give it as much credit as they give to the histories of Livy or Tacitus, or any other author of approved honesty. And certainly it is but reasonable to credit the consonant depositions of several plain men, who all profess themselves to have been eye-witnesses of those things which they write. Yea, the Jews and heathens who lived in those very times, and were most inveterate and cankered enemies against the name of Christ, would have given whatsoever was dearest to them in the world, could they have proved any forgery in those miracles, or deceit in the relaters of them : but the evidence was so clear that they were forced to confess, even in spite of their own malice, that such strange works were done and really effected; and yet their spleen against the truth was such that they imputed them only to the power of magic and the operation of evil spirits. But will our atheist do so too? If so, he must needs acknowledge a God, by acknowledging a devil; if not, he hath as little reason to believe any thing in the world which he himself hath not seen, as to believe the truth of those reports which we have received from undoubted hands, delivered to us by the unquestionable testimony of those who have known and seen what they have reported.

Therefore, if ever there have been any such extraordinary effects as restoring sight to the blind, and feet to the lame, and life itself to the dead, and that by no other application than only a word's speaking, there must certainly be a God. For these things are not within the power of *second causes*, being so contrary to the course of nature, and therefore must be ascribed to a Supreme Deity, an infinite power, who is the author and great controller of nature.

(2.) As there could have been no miracles performed, so neither could there be any *prophecies* or predictions made of contingent events, unless we acknowledge a God who, in his infinite wisdom and counsel, foresees whatsoever shall come to pass, and "revealeth his secret unto his servants the prophets." Amos, 3 : 7.

We have many prophecies recorded which have already had their undoubted fulfilment. Not to instance all, l shall only mention two. The one is the prophecy of our Lord Jesus Christ concerning the final destruction of Jerusalem, Matt. 24 : 2, which received its full accomplishment about forty years after they had crucified the Lord of life and glory. And the other, the prediction concerning Cyrus, that he should rebuild Jerusalem, after it had been destroyed by the Babylonians, Isa. 44 : 28; and, to make this prophecy the more remarkable, it is said, chap. 45 : 4, that for Israel's sake God had called him by his name. This was a famous and very particular prophecy of a person named near two hundred years before he was born; and those things distinctly foretold of him which he should afterwards perform. The like we have, 1 Kings, 13 : 2, where the prophet declaims against the idolatrous altar and worship of Bethel, and foretells that Josiah should destroy it—calling him by his very name, three hundred and forty years before he was born: "O altar, altar! thus saith the Lord, Behold, a child shall be born unto the house of David, Josiah by name; and upon thee shall he offer the priests of the high places that burn incense upon thee, and men's bones shall be burnt upon thee;" which we read was exactly fulfilled by the same Josiah, 2 Kings, 23 : 20, for "he slew all the priests of the high places which were there upon the altars, and burnt men's bones upon them." Now let any atheist give a rational account how these future contingencies could be thus certainly and circumstantially foreknown and predicted, were there not "a God in heaven that revealeth secrets." Dan. 2 : 28. They could not certainly see such free and contingent events in the stars, especially so long before they were to be produced; or, if they might, yet certainly they could not read names there, nor spell the constellations into words and syllables. There is, therefore, a God who giveth knowledge, and declareth things to come, according as it pleaseth him to illuminate the minds of his servants the prophets, to whom and by whom he spake.

5. The fifth and last demonstration of the being of a God is this, *There is a conscience in man; therefore there is a God in heaven.*

Conscience could have no power at all unless it were given it from above. How comes it to pass that wicked wretches are still haunted with pale fears and ghastly horrors; that they are sometimes a terror to themselves and to all that are about them? They would, if possible, abandon themselves and run away from their own being, but only that they have a witness and a judge within them of all their crimes and impieties, and feel such secret stings and unseen whips lashing their souls, that the tortures they endure and inflict on themselves make them sometimes weary of their lives, and put them upon the desperate course of choking both themselves and their consciences too with a halter. Whence, I say, should this proceed, were there not a God, a just and holy Deity whom conscience reveres? These torments and regrets do not always proceed from fear of shame or punishment from men. No; but conscience hath a power to put them upon the rack for their most secret sins, which no eye ever saw, no heart ever knew but their own. Yea, and it forceth them sometimes themselves to confess and divulge their own infamy, and voluntarily to deliver up themselves to human justice. And whence is this, but only from that secret influence of a Supreme Being, that hath an awe and authority over conscience, and makes it review the sins of a man's life with horror, because it knows that the just and holy God will at last review them with vengeance.

So we find that those who in their prosperity have lived most regardless of a Deity, yet when their conscience hath been awakened by dangers, or sickness, or any surprising event, the apprehensions of a God have then strongly returned upon them, and filled them with amazement and confusion. Thus Suetonius, the historian, reports of the mad, wicked emperor, Caligula, who made an open mock and scorn of religion, that when it thundered he would creep under his bed to hide himself from the vengeance of that Jupiter whom at other times he would not spare to deride and threaten. And therefore, certainly, if there be any such thing as natural conscience in all men, it will necessarily follow that there must be a God; for, were there no God there would be no conscience.

Thus I have given you these several rational demonstrations that there is such a supreme and infinite being as a Deity. Many others might be added; but these I account sufficient to convince any atheist, who will indeed be swayed by that reason which he so much deifies and adores, *that there is another God besides and above reason.*

Well, then, what remains but that, as we have evinced the folly and unreasonableness of speculative atheism, so we condemn the impiety of *practical atheism*—the profaneness and irreligion of those, that, as the apostle speaks, live "without God in the world;" that live as though there were no God, nor devil, nor heaven, nor hell, nor future state, nor any distribution of rewards in it.

Indeed, every wicked man is, in this sense, an atheist; and such the apostle hath condemned, Tit. 1:16. "They profess that they know God, but in works they deny him, being abominable, and disobedient, and unto every good work reprobate." Did they really and cordially believe that there is a just and holy God that takes notice of all their actions; a great and terrible Majesty who will call them to a strict account for all their cogitations, all their discourses, and all their works; an almighty God, who hath prepared wrath and vengeance to inflict on all those who despise his authority and transgress his law; would they dare to profane his glorious and reverend name by impertinently using it in their trivial talk? would they dare to rend and tear it by their oaths and blasphemies, and hellish execrations and curses? Did they believe that he hath prepared "Tophet of old," that "the pile thereof is fire and much wood," and that all the wicked of the world shall be cast into it, and there be made an everlasting burnt-sacrifice to the incensed wrath of the great God; did men believe the horrors and torments, the woes and anguish of the damned in hell, which are as far from being utterable as they are from being tolerable, did they but as certainly believe these things, as it is certain that, if they believe them not, they shall eternally feel them, would they dare still venture on to treasure up to themselves wrath against the day of wrath? Would swearing, and lying, and stealing, and drunkenness, and uncleanness so generally reign among us as they do?

Indeed, we persuade ourselves that we do believe

these things: we profess that there is a God, and that God infinitely holy and infinitely just; and that he will recompense tribulation, anguish, and wrath upon every soul of man that doeth evil. But, alas, this is only a verbal belief, contradicted and borne down by a practical atheism! The little influence that the belief of a holy and just God hath upon us, to regulate our actions and to cause us to walk in a holy awe and dread of his Divine Majesty, clearly evinceth that we may possibly fancy these things, but do not believe them; for, if thou didst seriously and heartily believe that there is a great and a jealous God, who hath said "Vengeance is mine, I will repay," what is there in the world that could persuade thee to offend him?

Possibly, though thou believest that there is a God, yet thou art not fully persuaded that he is so holy or so just as his word declares him to be: not so holy in hating thy sins, nor so just in punishing them.

But if thou reliest on this confidence, yet know that this is only to hope in his mercy *in spite of his truth.* He hath sworn that he will take vengeance on all impenitent wretches, and "wound the hairy scalp of such a one as goeth on still in his trespasses." Ps. 68 : 21. And God will be true to his threatenings as well as to his promises, although thou, and ten thousand others like thyself, eternally perish.

Nay, if thou believest there is a God, and yet thinkest that this God will spare thee, though thou go on in the presumption of thy heart to add iniquity unto sin, thou art far *worse than an atheist;* for it is better to have no opinion of God at all, than to have such an opinion as is unworthy of him; for the one is but infidelity, the other is contumely. Even Plutarch, a heathen, could say that it were far less injurious to him if any should deny that there is such a man in the world as Plutarch, than if he should grant that such a one indeed there is, but that he is faithless, inconstant, cruel, or revengeful. So it is not so heinous an affront against the Divine Majesty to deny that there is any such Supreme Being, as to acknowledge that there is indeed a God, but that this God is not either infinitely holy in hating thy sins, or infinitely true to his threatenings, or infinitely just in punishing men's impenitency and disobedience. This is a degree of impiety worse than atheism; and yet of this are all ungodly sinners guilty.

Know then, O sinner, and tremble, that there is a God who sees and observes all thy actions; who writes them down in the book of his remembrance, and will call thee to a strict account for them. God will then judge thee out of thine own mouth, thou wicked servant. Thou believest that there is a God; why dost thou not then fear and serve him? Thou believest that there is a heaven and a hell, and an eternity to come; why then dost thou not live answerably to this belief? Either blot it out of your creed, and avow that you do not believe in God the Father Almighty, or else live as those should do who own so great and terrible, so pure and holy a God. For a speculative atheist to be profane and wicked is but consonant to his principles; for wherefore should not he gratify all his lusts and sensual desires, whose only hope is in this life, and who doth not look upon himself as accountable for any thing hereafter? But for thee, who acknowledgest a Deity, to live as without God in the world, to break his laws, to slight his promises, to despise his threatenings, is the greatest and most desperate madness: thou showest thyself hereby to be worse not only than an atheist, but worse than a devil; for the very devils believe and tremble; and yet thou, who professest thyself to believe, dost not tremble.

If therefore we would not be inexcusable, since we know God let us glorify him as God, yielding all holy obedience to his laws, and humble submission to his will; conforming ourselves to his purity, depending upon his power and providence, and trusting in his infinite mercy and goodness, till we, at last, arrive unto that state of perfect bliss and felicity where we shall fully know the ineffable mystery of the Deity, see him that is now invisible, and live there as much by sense and sight as here we do by faith and expectation.

Thus much for the first sin forbidden in this first commandment, which is atheism.

II. The second sin forbidden is, IGNORANCE OF THE TRUE GOD.

For this precept, which requires us to have the Lord Jehovah for our God, as well includes the having of him in our understandings, by knowing him aright, as in our wills and affections, by loving, fearing, and worshipping him. The right worship of God must, of necessity, presuppose the knowledge of the object to which we direct that worship; or, otherwise, we do but erect an altar to the Unknown God, and all our adoration is but superstition; yea, and we ourselves are but idolaters, although we worship the true Deity; for all that service which is not directed to the Supreme Essence, whom we conceive to be the infinitely and eternally holy, just, merciful and glorious beyond what we can conceive, is not tendered to the true God, but to an idol of our own making, shaped out in the ignorance and blindness of our minds. And therefore our Savior Christ lays this as a black brand upon the Samaritan worship, John, 4 : 22, "Ye worship ye know not what;" and that because with other gods they worshipped the true God under a confused notion of "the God of the land," without any distinct knowledge of his nature, will, and attributes. 2 Kings, 17 : 26.

It hath been a proverbial speech, that ignorance is the mother of devotion; but certainly such a blind mother must needs bring forth a blind and deformed daughter, a devotion more rightly called superstition than devotion, a devotion shaped only by the fancy, and imposed by irrational fear or humor.

Now because the being and existence of a Deity is a notion so common and natural to mankind, as I have already demonstrated—and we are strongly inclined to the worship of a God—it will be necessary rightly to know that God, to whom this homage of our souls and all our affection and veneration is due; for, while we remain ignorant of this, it is impossible but that we should be idolaters, giving that which is due to God alone to some vain created fiction of our own deluded understandings.

Idolatry, therefore, is a sin more common among us than we imagine; for as many ignorant persons as there are, so many idolaters there are, who, though they fall not down before stocks and stones, yet form in their minds uncouth ideas and strange images of God, that no more represent his infinite perfections and excellencies than those dumb idols that the heathens worship.

In prosecution of this general view I shall lay down these following propositions :

1. It is very hard and difficult to have *right and genuine conceptions of the Divine Majesty*, when we address ourselves to him to worship him.

I think I may here appeal to the common experience of christians, whether the most difficult part of their duties be not rightly to apprehend the object of them. Our fancy is bold and busy, and still ready to make too much use of its pencil, and to delineate a God in some shape or other, before whom we present our services: so that when we should be wholly intent upon our adoration we must necessarily be engaged in reformation, to pull down and break in pieces those false images that we had set up; and yet as soon as we have done this our imagination falls to work again, makes new pictures of a God, and sets them full before our eyes as so many idols for us to worship. And though both reason and religion endeavor to correct these bold attempts of fancy, yet it is a mighty distraction in our duty to be then disputing the object when we should be adoring it.

I shall instance this in one duty only, and that is prayer. How few are there that do not fashion God in some bodily shape when they come to pray to him! We are too apt to figure out his limbs, and to conceive him a man like ourselves. All the proportions that fancy hath to draw with are corporeal; and whensoever we frame a notion of angels, or God, or any spiritual substance, we do it by sensible resemblances. But this is infinitely derogatory to God, who is a spirit, and therefore cannot be represented in any form without a vast incongruity; and he is *the Father of Spirits*, infinitely more spiritual than spirits themselves, in comparison with whom angels and the souls of men are but drossy and feculent beings, and therefore cannot be worshipped under any form without idolatry; for that is not God which we can shape and mould in our imaginations.

We read how jealous God is lest any resemblance should be made of him. "Take ye therefore good heed unto yourselves (for ye saw no manner of similitude on the day that the Lord spake unto you in Horeb out of the midst of the fire,) lest ye corrupt yourselves, and make you a graven image, the similitude of any figure." Deut. 4 : 15, 16. And certainly if the erecting of a visible image of God be gross idolatry, it is no less than a mental and spiritual idolatry to frame an invisible image of God in our fancy and conceptions.

Therefore, although the Scripture frequently ascribes to God the members and lineaments of a man, as eyes, mouth, ears, hands, feet, &c. yet we must not be so stupidly ignorant as to believe that these are properly appertaining to the divine essence, (which was the old exploded heresy of the Anthropomorphitæ;) but these descriptions are given us only in condescension to our weaknesses and infirmities, and though they are spoken after the manner of men, yet they must be understood after such a manner as becomes the majesty of the divine nature. And by such expressions the Scripture only means, that all those powers and faculties which are in us are likewise to be found, although in an infinite and transcendent eminency, in the being of God. He hears and sees, and is able to effect whatsoever he pleaseth, and that without any configuration of parts or organs, which are utterly repugnant to the simplicity and spirituality of his essence. And therefore to shape and fashion out such a God in our thoughts when we pray unto him, is but to make and worship an idol; and unless faith and religion demolish such images which we set up in our fancy, the worship which we direct to them is hardly to be esteemed the worship of the true God, but rather worshipping the work of our own making and a creature of our own imagination.

And yet, unless we do represent God to ourselves when we worship him, it is very hard, if not altogether impossible to keep up the intentness of our spirit and to hinder our mind from straying. Therefore,

2. The right way to attain to a true notion and a sound understanding of the Divine Nature, is by *a serious consideration of his attributes*, for these are his very nature; and when we know them we know as much of God as can be known by us in this our weak and imperfect state.

These attributes of the Divine Nature are manifold; and commonly are distinguished into negative, relative, and positive. I shall enumerate only the chief of them, simplicity, eternity, unchangeableness, immensity, dominion, all-sufficiency, holiness, truth, omnipotence, omniscience, justice, and mercy. Of these the principal, and those which most respect us, are mercy and justice: all the others are declared in order to illustrate these. For the glory of these hath God created the world and all things in it, especially those two capital kinds of creatures, angels and men. For these hath he permitted sin, which is so odious and detestable to his infinite purity. For these hath he sent his Son into the world to taste of death for every man. For these hath he proclaimed his law and declared his Gospel; the threatenings of the one and the promises of the other. For these hath he appointed a day and will erect a tribunal of judgment, that he may make the glory of his mercy and of his justice conspicuous: his justice, in the eternal damnation of impenitent wretches, who are vessels of wrath fitted by their own sins for destruction; his mercy, in the salvation of penitent and believing souls, who are vessels of mercy fitted by his grace for eternal glory. All his other attributes, I say, serve to illustrate these two; and as we conjoin them either to mercy or justice, so they are most enforcing motives, either of hope or fear. It is a mighty support to our hope, when we reflect upon the mercy of God, accompanied with the attributes of eternity, immutability, truth, and omnipotence; and again it will affect us with a profound fear and dread of this great and glorious God, to consider that the same attributes attend on his justice; so that both are almighty, the one to save, the other to destroy.

If then we would conceive aright of God when we come to worship him, let us not frame any idea of him in our imaginations, for all such representations are false and foolish; but let us labor to possess our hearts with an awful esteem of his attributes; and when we have, with all possible reverence, collected our thoughts and fixed them upon the contemplation of Infinite Justice, Infinite Mercy, Infinite Truth, Infinite Power, and the rest, let us then fall prostrate and adore, for this is our God. So the apostle tells us, 1 John, 4 : 8, *God is Love:* not only loving, but love itself in the abstract. And, 1 John, 1 : 5, *God is Light.*

3. All the knowledge we have or can have of God here, is collected from what he hath been pleased to discover of himself, *either in his works or in his word.* We have but two books to instruct us; the book of the creation and the book of the Scriptures.

From the works of creation and providence we may come to know much of God; even his eternal being and godhead: and the lectures which are read out of this book are so convincing and demonstrative of many of the glorious attributes of God, that the apostle tells us the very heathen themselves were left without excuse because they did not worship him as God, when by the things which they saw they knew him to be God. Rom. 1 : 21.

But to us God hath vouchsafed more clear and lively discoveries of himself; declaring to us those attributes by his word, the knowledge of which we could never have attained by his works alone. Therefore the Scriptures are called the lively oracles of God, Acts, 7 : 38; and they are the *glass* wherein, with open face, we behold *the glory of the Lord.* 2 Cor. 3 : 18.

4. When we have improved and strengthened our understandings in the highest degree, it will still be *utterly impossible for us to know God as he is in himself.* He dwelleth in that light to which no mortal eye can approach. He hides and veils himself with light and glory. It is his sole privilege and prerogative, as to love, so to know himself; for nothing better can be loved, nothing greater can be known. God is incomprehensible to all his creatures, but is comprehended by himself; and that ever-blessed Essence, which is infinite to all others, is yet finite to its own view and measure.

All the discoveries we receive of God are not so much

to satisfy an inquisitive curiosity as to excite pious affections and devotion; for reason, which is the eye of the intellectual soul, glimmers and is dazzled when it attempts to look steadfastly on him who is " the Father of Lights;" and its weakness is such, that that light which makes it see doth also strike it blind. Yea, our faith, which is a stronger eye than that of reason, and given us that we might see "him who is invisible," yet here in this life it hath so much dust and ashes in it that it discerns but imperfectly, and receives the discoveries of a Deity refracted through the glass of the Scriptures, so allayed and attempered, that though they are not most expressive of his glory, yet they are fittest for our capacity.

The full manifestation of his brightness is reserved for heaven. This beatifical vision is the happiness and perfection of saints and angels on whom the Godhead displays itself in its clearest rays. There we shall see him as he is, and know him as we are known by him. Here we could not subsist, if God should let down upon us the full beams of his excessive light and glory.

Hence we read in Scripture what dreadful apprehensions the best of God's saints have had, after some extraordinary discoveries that God had made of himself to them. Thus Isaiah cries out, chap. 6 : 5, " Wo is me! for I am undone; because I am a man of unclean lips—for mine eyes have seen the King, the Lord of hosts." And when our Savior Christ put forth his divine power only in the working of a miracle, the glory of it was so terrible and insupportable, even to holy Peter, that he cries out, "Depart from me; for I am a sinful man, O Lord." Luke, 5 : 8.

Though God be the very life of our souls, and the manifestations of his love and favor better than life itself, yet such is our limited state here in this world, that we cannot see God and live. Frail nature is too weak to contain its own happiness, until heaven and eternal glory enlarge it; and then it shall see those inconceivable mysteries of the Trinity in Unity, the hypostatical union of the human nature with the divine: then it shall view and surround the incomprehensible God, and be able to bear the unchecked rays of the Deity beating full upon it. In the mean time we must humbly content ourselves with those imperfect discoveries that God is pleased to allow us; still breathing after that state where we shall enjoy perfect vision; and, in it, an entire satisfaction and happiness.

Let us then most earnestly covet the knowledge of God, and endeavor to make ourselves here, as like to what we hope to be hereafter, as the frailty of human condition will permit. This is the chief glory of a man; one of the highest ornaments and perfections of a rational soul; that which doth, in some sort, repair the decays of a fallen state, and renew those primitive characters which ignorance and error have obliterated in our souls. And, indeed, without the knowledge of God, we can never be brought to love him, to trust and confide in him, nor to serve him as we ought. And, though there may be a great deal of zeal in ignorant persons, yet zeal without knowledge is but a religious frenzy; it is religion frighted out of its wits. A man that knows not the bounds of sin and duty, is a fit subject for the devil to work upon, who will be sure so to manage him, that he shall do a great deal of mischief very honestly and with very good intentions.

III. A third heinous violation of this first command is by PROFANENESS.

Profaneness may be taken either in a more large and general, or in a more proper and restrained sense.

If we take it properly, it signifies only the neglect or despising of spiritual things; for, in a strict acceptation, he is a profane person who either slights the duties of God's service, or the privileges of God's servants.

But, in the larger and more common sense of the word, every ungodly sinner who gives up himself to work wickedness, and lives in a course of infamous and flagitious crimes, is a profane person. Indeed, he is profane in the highest degree, who not only neglects the more spiritual duties of religion, but the natural duties of moral honesty, temperance and sobriety; for, as there are but two things which practically make an excellent and accomplished christian, namely, religion and virtue, the one directing our worship towards God, the other our conversation towards men; so, on the contrary, the despising of religion and the neglect of virtue make up that consummate and accomplished profaneness which we see so common and prevalent in the world.

But, concerning the wickednesses which usually meet together, and are concerned in this sort of profane persons, I shall not now speak, reserving them to be treated in their proper place, when I come to insist on those commands which each of their sins transgresseth.

At present, I shall notice that only which is properly called profaneness, and speak of it as a distinct sin, distinctly prohibited in this precept. And here I shall first give you some account of the name, and then of the thing.

The word *profane* is supposed to have its etymology from *procul à fano*, which signifies "far from the temple."*

Now because their temples were the usual places wherein they solemnly worshipped, therefore the word profane is transferred to denote those who neglect and put far from them the worship of God. And so, according to this sense of the word, many others, besides lewd and debauched wretches, will be found to be profane. For, not only those who let loose the reins to all manner of villanies, but even those whose morality is unblameable, and perhaps exemplary; who lead a sober and rational life, and scorn a vicious action as a baseness below the nature and unworthy the spirit of a man; yet such grave, prudent, and honest persons do, too many of them, especially in these our days, deserve the censure and black brand of being profane. And therefore, that we may the better judge who are the profane, and on whom that imputation justly lies, let us consider what the sin of profaneness is, and what are the true and proper characters of a profane person.

1. *What profaneness is.*

In general, profaneness is the *slighting and neglecting of things holy and sacred; undervaluing and condemning those things that are spiritual and excellent.* And whosoever is guilty of this, let his outward demeanor in the world be as fair and plausible as morality or hypocrisy can adorn it, yet he is a profane person; and heinously violates this first command, which enjoins us to worship, reverence, and honor the most high God, whom we profess to own. Now spiritual and sacred things are,

(1.) *God himself*, in his *nature and essence*, whom we

---

* So Macrob. Saturnal. lib. iii. cap. 3.

profane whensoever we entertain any blasphemous or unworthy thoughts of him derogatory to his infinite perfections.

(2.) God, in his *name*, which we profane when, in our trivial and impertinent discourses, we rashly bolt out that great and terrible name at which all the powers of heaven and hell tremble. And how much more do we profane it by oaths and execrations, which are now grown the familiar dialect of so many, and are looked on only as a grace and ornament of speaking! Scarce can we hear any discourse from them but these flowers are sprinkled among it; and the name of God must be brought in, either as an expletive or an oath. And what doth sadly forebode the growing profaneness of the next age, how many children are taught, or suffered, to call upon God in their play, before they are taught to call upon him in their prayers!

(3.) God, *in his attributes*, which we profane when our affections or actions are opposite or unsuitable to them. We profane his holiness by our impurity; his omnipotence by our despondency; his omniscience by our hypocrisy; his mercy by our despair; his justice by our presumption; his wisdom by our sinful policy; his truth, by our security notwithstanding his threatenings, and our slothfulness notwithstanding his promises. And in this sense, every sin that we commit is a kind of profaneness, as it manifests a contempt of the infinite perfections and excellencies of the Deity; for there is no man whose heart is possessed with a reverential and due esteem of the great God, that can be induced by any temptations to sin against him and provoke him. Every sin is a slighting of God, either a slighting of his justice, or mercy, or holiness, or power, or all of them; for what doest thou else when thou sinnest, but prefer some base pleasure or some sordid advantage before the great God of heaven? The devil represents the delights of sin or the profits of the world to thee, to entice thee; but thy conscience represents to thee the everlasting wrath of the great God if thou consentest, his justice ready to sentence thee to everlasting torments, and his power armed to inflict them: now if thou yieldest, what dost thou but vilify and despise the Almighty God; as if his dread power and severe justice were not so considerable as to outweigh either the impure pleasures of a vile lust, or the sordid gain and advantage of a little transitory pelf?

Nay, couldst thou by one act of sin make all the treasures and delights of the whole world tributary to thee; should the devil take thee when he tempts, as he took Christ, and show thee all the kingdoms of the world, and the glory of them, and promise to instate it all upon thee —yet, to prefer the whole world before the authority of God, who hath strictly forbidden thee to think any thing in it worth the venturing upon his displeasure and the hazarding his wrath and vengeance, is a most notorious slighting and contemning the great God, and argues a profane spirit: how much more then, when we sin against God for nothing, and defy his wrath and justice without being provoked to it by any temptation! We find how heinously God takes it, and speaks of it as a mighty affront and indignity, that our Lord Christ should be so undervalued as to be sold for thirty pieces of silver; for it argued not only treason but contempt. Zech. 11:13. " A goodly price that I was prized at of them." And yet, truly, Judas was a very thrifty sinner in comparison with many among us, who not only betray Christ to the mocks and injuries of others, but crucify him daily, and put him to an open shame for far less.

Yea, there are many that would not suffer so much as a hair of their heads to be twitched off for that for which they will not stick to lie, and swear, and blaspheme. What should tempt the impious buffoon to deride religion, travest the Holy Scriptures, and turn whatsoever is sacred and venerable into burlesque and drollery, but only that he may gain a little grinning and sneering applause to his wit from a company of mad fools like himself? or what should tempt the cheap swearer to open his black throat as wide as hell, and to belch out his blasphemies against heaven and the God of heaven, but only that he fancies that a well-mouthed oath will make his speech the more stately and genteel? And are these matters of such consequence as to be called or accounted temptations? Certainly there can be nothing else in these sins besides a mere mad humor of sinning; which declares a most wretched contempt of God when we do that for nothing which his soul hates and his law forbids, and a most profane spirit in making that common and trivial which is infinitely holy and sacred.

Thus you see how God is profaned in his *nature*, in his *name*, and in his *attributes*. He is profaned also,

(4.) In *the time he hath set apart and consecrated for his own worship and service*. This we profane when we employ any part of it in the unnecessary affairs of this life, but much more in the service of sin. This is a sacrilegious robbing God of what is dedicated entirely to him; and that either by his immediate appointment, as the

Sabbath, or by the appointment of those whom God hath set over us, and intrusted not only to preserve our rights and property, but also his worship inviolate, as special days of joy or mourning, thanksgiving or humiliation.

(5.) In *the ordinances of Jesus Christ*. These we profane when we either neglect them, or are remiss and careless in our attendance on them. But of this I shall speak more anon.

Thus I have shown you what profaneness is. It is a slighting and despising of spiritual and sacred things: such as are holy originally, as God, his name and attributes; and such as are holy by institution, as his Sabbaths and ordinances. But we were to consider,

2. *What are the true and proper characteristics of a profane person;* and this, that we may the better look into our own hearts and lives, and both observe and correct that profaneness which resides there.

(1.) He then is a profane person who *thinks and speaks slightly of religion.*

Religion is the highest perfection of human nature. By it man differs more from brute beasts than he doth by his reason. For brute creatures have some notable resemblance and hints of reason; but none at all of religion: they glorify God as all the works of the creation do, by showing forth in their frame and production his infinite attributes, but they cannot adore nor worship him. This is a pre-eminence peculiar to the most perfect pieces of the creation, men and angels. For as it is a perfection of the Deity to be the object of worship, to whom all adoration both in heaven and earth ought to be directed, so it is the perfection of rational creatures to ascribe honor, and glory, and praise, and worship to Him who sitteth upon the throne, and to the Lamb for ever and ever. And therefore they who despise religion, despise that which is their own chiefest excellency, and profane that which is the very crown of their nature and being.

But alas, have we not many such profane persons among us, who deride piety and make a scoff of religion; who look upon it only as a politic invention to keep the rude and ignorant vulgar in awe?

Yea, and those who take up their religion, not by choice, but merely by chance; either as a patrimony left them by their fathers, or as a received custom of the country wherein they were born: never troubling themselves to examine the reasonableness and certainty of it. These likewise are profane-spirited men, who do not believe religion to be a matter of such concern as to require their exactest study and industry in searching into its grounds and principles, but think that any may suffice, whatsoever it be.

Again, those who secretly despise the holiness and strictness of others, and think they are too precise and make needless ado to get to heaven. But indeed they are not too precise; but these are too profane who thus contemn religion as unnecessary and superfluous.

(2.) He is a profane person who *neglects the public worship and service of God when he hath opportunity and ability to frequent it.*

And alas, how many such there are who yet think it foul scorn to have this black name fixed upon them; yea, and are the readiest in the world to brand others with it that are not of their way and sentiments! But let them be who they will that despise and forsake the solemn assemblies, they do thus despise and forsake God.

Now these are of two sorts: some absent themselves out of a wretched sloth and contempt of the word and ordinances of Jesus Christ; others out of a pretended dissatisfaction and scruple of conscience. Both are profane; but the one strangely mingles profaneness and hypocrisy, and the other is profane out of ignorance or atheism.

Some are *negligently profane.* These absent themselves from the ordinances of Jesus Christ and the solemn worship of God through mere sloth and reckless contempt. And how many there are of this sort, the thinness of many congregations doth too evidently declare. If we should search for them, should we not find them sleeping in bed, or idly lolling about the house, or walking or riding abroad for pleasure? spending their time in vain chat, eating and drinking, and sacrificing to their god, their belly, while they should be worshipping the great God of heaven. Possibly, a fair day, or want of other diversion, may sometimes bring them to church, yet this is so seldom that we may well suspect they come, not indeed for custom's sake, but rather out of novelty than devotion. But if it prove a wet or lowering day, these tender people, whom neither rain nor cold can prejudice at a fair or market, dare not stir out of their doors, nor step over their own threshold to go into God's house, lest they should hazard their health instead of gaining their salvation. What shall I say to such brutes and heathens, who not only deny the power, but the very form of godliness? Some of them may perhaps read what I here present, and may my word, nay, not mine, but the word of the living God strike them! God will *pour out his wrath* "upon the heathen, and upon the families that call not on his name."

But some again are *humorsomely profane;* and these are they who withdraw themselves from the public worship of God merely upon pretended scruple and dissatisfaction as to the mode of worship practiced by those with whom they might most naturally be expected to worship. Concerning such, I think it is no uncharitableness to say, that where scruple at the administration of ordinances is only pretended to color contempt of the ordinances, there religion is only made a mask and vizor for hypocrisy. And I would beseech them to account of all who preach the truth in Christ, that they are ministers of Christ, and stewards of the mysteries of God, although all do not observe the same *form* of worship; and if they cannot deny that they are such with whom they might be expected to worship, will they deny them audience when they come as ambassadors from the great King of heaven, to deliver his message to them in his name? Do not all who truly preach Christ, preach the same truths, and exhort to the practice of the same holiness? Do they not administer the same ordinances, wherein are represented to all believing partakers the benefits of the death of our Lord Jesus Christ?

(3.) He is also a profane person who neglects the performance of religious duties *in private.*

Every house ought to be a temple dedicated to God, and every master a priest, who should offer unto God the daily sacrifices of prayer and praise. But, alas, how many profane persons have we, and how many profane families, who scarce ever make mention of God but in an oath, nor ever call upon his name but when they imprecute some curse upon others! How many who wholly neglect the duty of prayer, and think they sufficiently discharge their trust if they provide for the temporal subsistence of their families, though they utterly neglect the care of their souls and their spiritual concerns! Such profane families as these God ranks with infidels and heathens, and devotes them to the same common destruction. Jer. 10 : 25.

Nor ought our family duties to be more seldom performed by us than morning and evening. In the morning, prayer is the key that opens to us the treasury of God's mercies and blessings; in the evening, it is the key that shuts us up under his protection and safeguard. God is the great Lord of the whole family both in heaven and earth : other masters are but, under him, intrusted to see that those who belong to their charge perform their duties both to him and themselves. One of the greatest services we can do for God, is to pray unto him and praise him. And how unjust and tyrannical is it for a master of a family to exact service to himself, when he takes no care to do service to his great Lord and Master, to whom it is infinitely more due!

Neither is there any excuse that can prevail to take off your obligation from this duty.

Not that thou art ignorant, and knowest not how to pray; for many are the helps that God hath afforded thee. Do but bring breath and holy affections; others have already brought to thy hands words and expressions proper enough for the concerns of most families. And besides, use and common practice will facilitate this duty; and, by an incessant conscientious performance of it, thou wilt, through the promised assistance of the Holy Ghost, be soon able to suit thy affections with pertinent expressions and to present both in a becoming manner unto the throne of grace.

Not the multiplicity and encumbrance of thine affairs. For the more and the weightier they are, the more need hast thou to ask counsel and direction of God, and to beg his blessing upon thee in them, without which thou wilt but labor in the fire and weary thyself for very vanity.

Not thy bashfulness and modesty. For will it not be a far greater shame to thee, that those whom thou governest and perhaps overawest even by thy rash and unreasonable passions, should be able to overawe thee from so excellent and necessary a duty? Be ashamed to sin before them; be ashamed to talk loosely, to profane the name of God, to be intemperate or unjust before them, to defile thy mouth and their ears with unclean and scurrilous discourse; be ashamed to neglect thy duty; but be not ashamed to pray, for our Savior hath told us, Mark, 8: 38, that "whosoever shall be ashamed of him in this adulterous and sinful generation, of him also shall the Son of Man be ashamed, when he cometh in the glory of his Father, with the holy angels."

And therefore, since there is no just reason why thou shouldst refrain prayer from the Almighty, whosoever thou art that doest so, be thy conversation in all other respects never so blameless (which yet it is not very probable that it should be when thou beggest not grace from God to direct it,) thou art a profane person; and declarest thyself to be so, by the neglect of the most holy and spiritual of all those duties wherein we are to draw nigh unto God.

(4.) He is a profane person that performs holy duties *slightly and superficially.*

All our duties ought to be warmed with zeal, winged with affection, and shot up to heaven from the whole bent of the soul. Our whole hearts must go into them, and the strength and vigor of our spirits must diffuse themselves into every part of them to animate and quicken them.

Hence the apostle commands us, Rom. 12:11, to be "fervent in spirit, serving the Lord." Sacrifices, which under the Jewish economy were the greatest part of God's solemn worship, were commanded to be offered up with fire; and no other fire could sanctify them but that miraculously sent down from heaven, or from the presence of God in the sanctuary, which was ever after kept burning for that very use. Lev. 9:24; 6:9. So, truly, all our christian sacrifices both of praise and of prayer must be offered up to God with fire; and that fire which alone can sanctify them, must be darted down from heaven: the celestial flame of zeal and love which comes down from heaven and hath a natural tendency to ascend thither again, and to carry up our hearts and souls upon its wings with it.

But indeed too often our duties are—

Offered up *with strange unhallowed fire*. They are fired by some unruly passion of hatred, or self-love, or pride and vain-glory. Like those choleric disciples that presently would command fire to come down from heaven to consume those who had affronted them by refusing to give them entertainment, only that God by such a severe miracle might vindicate their reputation and revenge the contumely that was done them. But this is a fire kindled from beneath, and therefore our Savior himself sharply checks their furious zeal, "Ye know not what manner of spirit ye are of." Luke, 9:55. And certainly, whensoever we pray thus in the bitterness of our spirits, devoting our enemies to destruction, and that because they are ours rather than God's; when we pour out a great deal of gall mingled with our petitions; such a prayer cannot be from the dove-like spirit of God, which is meek and gentle, and makes those so who are led and inspired by him. Every party and persuasion of men is very ready boldly to prescribe unto God those ways and methods by which he ought to be glorified; and if any shall but question their principles or oppose their rash and unwarrantable proceedings, their touchy zeal is straight kindled, and nothing less than solemn prayers must be made to devote such a one to ruin and destruction, as an enemy to God and to religion. Here is fire indeed! but it is wild-fire kindled from beneath; the fuel of it is faction, popularity, pride, contention, and vain-glory; and it sends forth a great deal of smoke from corrupt and inordinate passions.

Again, if there be none of the former incentives to heat them, then our duties are commonly very *cold and heartless*.

Our prayers are dull and yawning, and drop over our lips without any spirit or life in them: how often do we beg God to hear us when we scarce hear ourselves! and to grant us an answer when we scarce know what it is that we have asked! We make our requests so coldly and indifferently, as if we only begged a denial.

So likewise in our hearing of the word, we bring with us very slight and profane spirits to those holy and lively oracles. What else mean the vagrancy and wanderings of our thoughts; our lazy and unbeseeming postures, which would be counted rude and unmannerly to be used in the presence of some of those that are with us in our worship, were they any where else but in the church? What means our weariness; our watching every sand that runs; our despising the simplicity of the Gospel; our prizing the sound of words more than the weight of things; but especially our indulged sloth and drowsiness? a sin that I have observed is too common. What, cannot you watch with God one hour? Do we speak poppy and opium to you? Or do you expect that God will now reveal himself to you in dreams? Have ye not houses, have ye not beds to sleep in; or do you despise the church of Christ? Certainly God requires our most wakeful and vigilant attention when he delivers to us the most important things of his law and of our salvation. These, and many other things, which to particularize would perhaps be to descend below the majesty of this work, do too evidently declare that the precious truths of the Gospel are grown vile among us; that we have taken a surfeit of this heavenly manna, this bread of life, and now begin to loathe it. Beware lest this surfeit bring after it a famine.

It plainly argues much profaneness in our spirits when we bring only our outward man, our dull and heavy carcasses to attend upon God, while our hearts and minds are straying and wandering from him. This is a sign that we despise God, and account any thing good enough, the lame and the blind, to be offered to him. Against such God hath thundered out a most dreadful curse, Mal. 1:14, "Cursed be the deceiver, who hath in his flock a male, and voweth and sacrificeth unto the Lord a corrupt thing; for I am a great King, saith the Lord of hosts, and my name is dreadful." Thou, who sufferest thy thoughts, or thine eyes which are the index of them, to rove in prayer, or to be sealed up with sleep in hearing, thou despisest the great God before whom thou appearest, and thinkest it enough if thou affordest him thy bodily presence, although thy heart be with the eyes of the fool in the ends of the earth; for such a service is but mockery, and it is less reproachful to tender God no service than to perform it slightly and ceremoniously: the one is disobedience, but the other is contempt.

(5.) He is a profane person that performs holy duties *for worldly ends and advantage.*

For what greater contempt of God can there be than to make his service truckle under the base and low designs of this present life? This is to make religion tributary to interest, and God himself a homage to mammon. And this all hypocrites are guilty of: though they mask their designs with specious pretences, and draw the veil of religion over their sordid and wicked contrivances; yet they cry out, with Jehu, "Come, see my zeal for the Lord," when he drove on so furiously only for the kingdom.

Indeed, a hypocrite, though he be not commonly so esteemed, is the most profane wretch that lives. The gross, profligate sinner offers not half so much indignity to religion as he doth. For,

The hypocrite calls in God to be an accomplice and partaker with him in his crimes; and so makes God to be the patron of sin, who will be the judge and condemner of sinners.

All his injustice, rapine and rebellion are colored over with the fair pretence of the glory of God, the interest of the kingdom of Christ, the advancement of the power of godliness, reformation of idolatry and superstition, &c. and there is no act of fraud or violence, faction or sedition but he thinks it justified and hallowed by these glorious names: which is nothing else but to rob men and make God the receiver, who is the detester, and will be the punisher of such crimes. Now the open and flagitious wretch, although he hates God as much as the hypocrite, yet he doth not so much deride him: his wickednesses are plain and avowed, and every one may see from whence they proceed and whither they tend; that they come from hell, and directly tend thither: religion is not at all concerned to color but only to condemn them. And judge ye which doth most despise God and godliness; he who professeth it not at all, or he who professeth it only that he may abuse and abase it, and make it subservient to vile and sordid ends infinitely unworthy of it.

Again, *the wound religion receives from hypocrites is far more dangerous and incurable than that inflicted on it by the open and scandalous sinner.*

For religion is never brought into question by the enormous vices of an infamous person; all see and all abhor his sin. But when a man shall have his mouth full of piety and his hands full of wickedness, when he shall speak scripture and live devilism, profess strictly and walk loosely, this lays a grievous stumbling-block in the way of others; and tempts them to think that all religion is but mockery, and that the professors of it are but hypocrites; and so imbitters their hearts against it as a solemn cheat put upon the credulous world. Certainly such men are the causes of all that contempt which is cast upon the ways and ordinances of God; and their secret profaneness hath given occasion to the gross and open profaneness that now abounds in the world, and the hypocrisy of former years hath too fatally introduced the atheism of these.

Nay, a hypocrite must needs be an atheist; and in his heart deny many of God's glorious attributes, but espe cially his omniscience; and say within himself, as those, Psalm 73 : 11, "How doth God know, and is there knowledge in the Most High ?" For did they but believe that God looks through all their disguises; and that his eye, which is light unto itself, pierceth into their very souls : did they but seriously consider that all things are naked and open before him; that he knows our thoughts afar off, and is privy to our closest designs, they would not certainly be either so daringly wicked or so childishly foolish as to plot upon God, and seek to deceive and delude Omniscience.

This profaneness of the hypocrite, in seeking temporal things by spiritual pretences, is much more abominable than the profaneness of others who seek them by unjust and unlawful means; for the one only makes impiety, but the other piety itself an instrument of his vile and sordid profit, than which there cannot be a greater scorn and contempt put upon religion.

(6.) He is a profane person who *makes what God hath sanctified common and unhallowed.*

And have we not many such profane persons among us ? Many that abuse the holy and reverend name of God, which ought to be had in the highest esteem and veneration, about light and frivolous matters ? who only make mention of him in their idle chat, but are mute and dumb when any thing should be spoken to his praise ? Many that profane his Sabbaths; and although God hath liberally allowed them six days for the affairs of earth, yet will not spare the seventh for the affairs of heaven, but impiously invade what he hath set apart and consecrated for himself and his own immediate worship and service? Many that never speak scripture but when they abuse it; making the Bible their jest-book, and prostituting those phrases and expressions which God hath sanctified to convey unto us the knowledge of himself and eternal life, to the laughter and mirth of their loose companions? So that those very words which the Holy Ghost inspired into the penmen of the Sacred Scriptures for the edification of the church, the devil inspires into these wretches for their own damnation and the damnation of those that have pleasure in such horrid profaneness.

(7.) He is a profane person who *despiseth spiritual privileges and enjoyments.*

Upon this very account the Scripture sets that black and indelible brand upon Esau: "Lest there be any profane person among you, as Esau, who for one morsel of meat sold his birthright." Heb. 12:16. And why is Esau stigmatized as profane for selling his birthright, but because in those first ages of the world the first-born or eldest of the family was a priest, and that sacred function by right of primogeniture belonged unto him? and therefore we read that the tribe of Levi were taken by God to be his priests and ministers, in exchange for the first-born. Now, to slight and undervalue an office so holy and sacred, a privilege so eminent, a dignity so sublime and spiritual—to part with it only for the satisfying of his hunger—was a sign of a profane spirit; in preferring the god, his belly, before the God of heaven; and for ever renouncing his right of sacrificing to the true God, only that he might sacrifice one pleasant morsel to his impatient appetite.

And certainly, if it were so profane in Esau to slight and contemn the priesthood in himself, they are also profane who vilify it in others, and make those the objects of their lowest scorn and contempt whose office it is to stand and minister before God and Christ. Certainly, if a dishonor done to an ambassador reflects upon the prince that sent him, will not Christ account it as an affront and injury done to him, when you affront and injure those his messengers and ambassadors whom he hath sent to treat with you in his name, and about the concerns of his kingdom?

But, not to speak more of this, lest we should be thought to plead for ourselves; are not those profane who despise and contemn the high privileges and dignity of the children of God? who despise those whom God so highly honors as to adopt them into his own family, to admit them into near communion and endearment with himself, to make them his own sons, and give them the privilege of heirs of eternal glory? Doubtless, he who despiseth him that is begotten, despiseth him likewise that begetteth; and the common disrespect which is shown to the servants and children of God, argues a secret contempt of him who is their Master and their Father.

Now lay these things to your own hearts, and bring them home to your own consciences, and see whether you are in none of these particulars guilty of profaneness. Do none of you think slightly of religion; accounting it either a politic design or a needless preciseness? Are none of you negligent in the public worship and service of God, nor yet in private and family duties; or, if you perform them, is it not very carelessly and formally; or, if you seem zealous in them, is not your zeal excited by some temporal advantages, and low, base, worldly ends and designs? Do you not make that common and unhallowed which God hath made holy; either by abusing his name, polluting his Sabbaths, or vilifying his word in your ordinary raillery? And lastly, do none of you despise spiritual privileges and enjoyments, and those likewise who are invested with them? If so, how fair and specious soever your lives and actions may be, although you may think the rude debauched sinner at a vast distance from yourselves, and account him the only profane person; yet, certainly, this black style belongs as properly to you; and you are profane violators of this first command, which requires you to take the Lord for your God, and accordingly to honor and reverence him and whatsoever appertains to him.

IV. The fourth and last breach of this command is by IDOLATRY: *Thou shalt have no other gods before me;* which they are guilty of who set up any other god besides the Lord Jehovah.

Idolatry, according to its etymology and use, signifies a serving of images or idols. Now, an idol, though it properly signifies an artificial effigy or resemblance made to represent any thing or person; yet, in divinity, it signifies any thing besides the true God, unto which we ascribe divine honor and worship.

And, as an idol is twofold; one *internal*, in the fiction and imagination of the mind; another, *external* and visible, either the work of men's hands, as statues and images, or else the work of God's hands, as the sun, moon, and stars, or any other creature: so there is a twofold idolatry; the one *internal*, when in our minds and affections we honor and venerate that as God which indeed is not so, but is either a creature of the true God, or a fiction of a deluded fancy; the other *external*, which we are then guilty of, when we express the inward veneration of our souls by outward acts of adoration. As, for instance, whosoever shall believe the consecrated bread in the sacrament to be transubstantiated and changed into the true and proper body of Jesus Christ, and, upon this belief, shall in his mind revere and honor *it* as his God, as the papists do, he is guilty of *internal* idolatry : but if, to this internal veneration he add any external rites of worship, as prostration, invocation, &c. he is then likewise guilty of *external* idolatry.

It is the former of these two kinds of idolatry which is here prohibited in this first commandment, *Thou shalt have no other gods before me:* that is, thou shalt not give to any thing, either in heaven or earth, that inward heart-worship of affiance, love, fear, veneration, and dependance, which is due only to the true God, the Lord Jehovah.

The imperate acts, or outward expressions of this inward worship, are that which we call external idolatry, which is specially forbidden in the second commandment · of which I shall treat in its place and order.

Now concerning this *internal idolatry*, observe these following propositions :

1 *Whosoever acknowledgeth, and in his heart worshippeth another God, different from that God who hath revealed himself to us in his holy Scriptures*, is guilty of this internal idolatry, and the breach of this first commandment.

And therefore, not only are those idolaters who worship the devil; or those that have recourse to diabolical arts and charms; or those who worship men, whose vices were their apotheosis, and their crimes their consecration; as Bacchus, and Venus, and others of the heathenish gods; or those who worshipped men famous for their virtues, as the heathens did their heroes, and the papists do their saints; or those who worship any of the creatures of God, as the host of heaven, fire as the Persians, or water as the Egyptians, or the creatures of art, as statues and images, as if possessed and animated by their deities; in which respect Trismegistus called images the bodies of the gods;* (and with the same madness are the papists possessed, who are persuaded that God, and Christ, and the saints dwell in certain images made to represent them, and by those images give answers to their votaries, and perform many wonderful and miraculous works; whereas, if there be any spirit that possesseth them, as perhaps there may, we have reason to believe that, since their worship of them is the very same with the heathens, those spirits are likewise the same, viz. not God, nor saints, but devils and damned spirits;) I say, not only these are idolaters and transgressors of this first command, but those also who compound a God partly out of the figment of their own erroneous minds, and partly out of his own infinite attributes: and thus are all Arians, Socinians and Antitrinitarians guilty of idolatry; for they acknowledge one infinite and eternal Being, but, denying the persons of the Son and the Holy Ghost, they worship an idol, and not the true God,

---

* Aug. de Civ. Dei. l. viii. c. 23.

for the only true God is the Father, the Son, and the Holy Ghost.

2. Whosoever acknowledgeth, and in his heart worshippeth *more gods than the only Lord Jehovah*, is guilty of idolatry, and the violation of this first commandment

Thus was the idolatry of those nations which the king of Assyria planted in Israel, after he had carried away the ten tribes into captivity; for it is said "that they feared the Lord, and served their own gods." 2 Kings, 17 : 33. And upon this account also are all Arians and Socinians, who deny the natural divinity of Jesus Christ, justly charged with idolatry; for since they say that Christ is God, and worship him as God, and yet deny that he is of the same nature and substance with the Lord Jehovah, they must of necessity make more gods than one, and those of a diverse essence and being; and therefore they are not only guilty of blasphemy, but idolatry: of blasphemy, in robbing Christ of his eternal Sonship and the Divine nature; of idolatry, in attributing divine honor and worship unto him whom they believe to be but a creature, and not God by nature.

3. Whosoever doth *ascribe or render to any creature that which is proper and due only unto God*, is an idolater, and guilty of the transgression of this first commandment.

Now this attributing of the divine properties to creatures is either *explicit* or *implied;* explicit, when we avow the attributes of the divine nature to be in those things which are not capable of them, as those who hold the body of Christ to be omnipresent; implied, when we render unto any creature that inward worship, esteem and affection which is due only to the infinite perfections of the Deity.

And although our reformed religion be very well purged from the former idolatry, yet certainly the professors of it are not well purged from this latter idolatry; for, even among Protestants themselves, we shall find very many that are in this sense idolaters. For,

(1.) *Whosoever chiefly and supremely loves any creature, is an idolater;* because our chiefest love is due only to God.

Hence the *covetous* person is expressly called an idolater; and covetousness, idolatry. Col. 3 : 5. "Mortify your" earthly "members; uncleanness, evil concupiscence, and covetousness, which is idolatry." Likewise the *sensual* epicure is an idolater; his *belly*, saith the apostle, is his *god*. Phil. 3 : 19. The *proud* person is an idolater; for he loves himself supremely, sets up himself for his own idol, and falls prostrate before that image which he hath portrayed of his own perfections, in his own fancy and imagination. And generally all who love and admire any thing above God, or esteem any thing so dear that they would not willingly part with it for his sake, have set up another god before him, to which they give that service and respect which is due only to the great God of heaven.

(2.) *Whosoever puts his trust and confidence in any creature more than in God,* is guilty of this inward heart-idolatry.

As when we depend on interest, or power, or policy for our safeguard and success, more than on that God who is able both with and without created helps and means to relieve us. And that we do so, appears when we are secure and confident in the enjoyment of such created comforts and supports, but altogether diffident and dejected when we are deprived of them; for since

God is always the same, we should likewise have the same courage and spirit, did we place our whole trust in him.

(3.) He is an idolater, and a very gross one, *who sets up any creature in his heart, whether saint or angel, to pray to it, and to betake himself to it as a refuge in his straits and necessities.*

For invocation properly belongs to God alone, as an act of worship which he hath challenged to himself, and the highest glory that we can give to his Divine Majesty. And therefore he hath commanded us, Psalm 50 : 15, "Call upon me," not upon any saint or angel, "in the time of trouble, and I will deliver thee." And therefore papists are most gross and stupid idolaters, who direct their petitions, not to God, but to saints and angels: which is nothing else but to advance them into his throne, and to ascribe to them his infinite perfections; for prayer and adoration suppose the object of it to be omnipresent and omnipotent; omnipresent to hear, and omnipotent to save. or else they are in vain.

THE SECOND COMMANDMENT.

"Thou shalt not make unto thee any graven image, or any likeness of any thing which is in heaven above, or that is in the earth beneath, or that is in the water under the earth. Thou shalt not bow down thyself to them, nor serve them: for I the Lord thy God am a jealous God, visiting the iniquity of the fathers upon the children unto the third and fourth generation of them that hate me: and showing mercy unto thousands of them that love me, and keep my commandments."

IDOLATRY is twofold, either spiritual and internal, residing in the affections and disposition of the soul; or more gross and external, consisting in a visible adoration of any thing besides God. The former is forbidden in the First Commandment, as we have already seen; and the latter is particularly forbidden in this Second Commandment, to which our attention will now be directed.

In this Commandment we have two parts: the *Precept* itself, and the *Sanction* of the precept, each of which is twofold.

The *precept* runs negatively in two several prohibitions, both tending to the same end and effect; the one forbidding images to be *made*, "Thou shalt not make to thee any graven image, or any likeness of any thing;" the other forbidding them to be *worshipped*, "Thou shalt not bow down thyself before them, nor serve them."

The sanction contains a severe *commination* or *threatening* against those that shall presume to violate this command: "I, the Lord thy God, am a jealous God, visiting the iniquity of the fathers upon the children, unto the third and fourth generation;" and also for the encouragement of obedience, *a gracious promise,* of "showing mercy unto thousands that love God and keep his commandments."

I shall begin with the COMMAND, or PROHIBITION. And this, as I said, is twofold: Thou shalt not *make* images: Thou shalt not *worship* them. Not that the carver's or printer's art, but only the people's idolatry—not that the ingenuity in making, but the stupidity in worshipping those dumb representations—is here forbidden. The brazen serpent in the wilderness, the cherubim, and other resemblances in the temple, are a sufficient proof and evidence of this.

This prohibition, therefore, must be interpreted according to the subject matter here spoken of, and that being only divine worship, it is plain that it is not unlawful to represent to the eye any visible thing by an artificial image of it, but only when God saith, *Thou shalt not make,* and *Thou shalt not worship,* the meaning is, Thou shalt not make any thing with an intention of worship; and, Thou shalt not worship any thing which thou or others have made. But, concerning the prohibition of this command, I shall speak more hereafter.

For the more full and clear understanding of this precept, I must desire you to recall to mind one of those several general rules mentioned in the Introduction as helpful to instruct you in the due extent and latitude of the Commandments, namely, that *the negative commands all include the injunction of the contrary positive duties:* as, when God forbids the taking of his name in vain, by consequence he commands the hallowing and sanctifying of his name; where he forbids murder, he commands all lawful care and endeavor to preserve our own and the life of others; where, in the First Precept, he forbids the owning and cleaving to any other god besides himself, he enjoins us to acknowledge him as our God, to love, fear, and hope in him only. So, here in this Second Command, where he forbids the worshipping of images, by consequence he requires us to worship him according to the rules he hath prescribed us. Therefore, as under the First Command is comprehended whatsoever appertains to the *internal* worship of God; so, under this Second is comprehended whatsoever appertains to the *external and visible* worship of God.

Here I shall first speak of the *external and visible worship* of God; and then of *those sins which are contrary to it*, and condemned in this Commandment.

I. Concerning the WORSHIP OF GOD I shall lay down the six following propositions:

1. *The true and spiritual worship of God* IN GENERAL, *is an action of a pious soul, wrought and excited in us by the Holy Ghost; whereby, with godly love and fear, we serve God acceptably, according to his will revealed in his Word; by faith embracing his promises, and in obedience performing his commands; to his glory, the edification of others, and our own eternal salvation.*

This is the true spiritual worship of the true God, who is a spirit: and it comprehends in it, both the inward worship of our hearts and souls, and likewise the outward worship of holy and religious performances; of which I am now particularly to treat.

2. Therefore, this EXTERNAL *worship of God is a sacred*

action of a pious soul, wrought and excited by the Holy Ghost; whereby, with all reverence, we serve God both in words and deeds, according to his revealed will, in partaking of his sacraments, attending on his ordinances, and performing those holy duties which he hath required from us; to his glory, the edification of others, and our own eternal salvation.

This worship of God, although external, is nevertheless spiritual; for it proceeds from the Spirit of God exciting our spirits to the performance of it; and is directed by a spiritual rule, unto a spiritual end, the glory of God and our own salvation.

3. *The parts of this external worship are divers and manifold; whereof the most principal and essential are the celebration of the sacraments, solemn prayer, and solemn praise and thanksgiving.*

But, besides these, there are many other things which belong to the service of God; yea, as many as there are duties of religion and piety: such as a free, open, and undaunted profession of the truth; a religious vowing unto God things that are lawful, and in our own power; an invoking of the testimony of God to the truth of what we assert, or to the faithful discharge of what we promise, when we are duly called to do it by lawful authority; a diligent reading of the word of God, and a constant and reverent attendance on it when it is read and preached; and divers other duties, too numerous to be here particularly enumerated: some of which belong to the proper worship of God, immediately as parts of it; others, mediately, as means and helps to it.

4. *Although God doth especially delight in the acts of our internal worship, and principally regards the esteem and veneration that we have for his great and glorious*

Majesty in our hearts; yet this alone sufficeth not, without the performance of those parts of external worship and visible acts of piety and religion, which may to the glory of God express the devout dispositions of our souls.

The inward acts of piety are those of faith in believing; of hope, in expecting our reward; of charity, in loving both God and our neighbor; of fear, in reverencing him; of patience, in a contented bearing whatsoever burdens it shall please the all-wise providence of God to lay upon us; and of a cheerful willingness to perform all the duties of obedience which he enjoins us. These belong to the internal worship and service of God, and are especially pleasing and acceptable to him. And, indeed, without these, all outward acts of worship are both dead and unsavory: for, as the spirit of a man is his life, so the internal and spiritual piety of the heart, our love, fear, and reverence of God, is the life of all our duties, without which they are but as a dead carcass; so far from being a sweet-smelling savor, that they are not some and offensive to that God to whom we offer them.

Of this internal worship I have already spoken; and what we are now to consider, is the *external worship of God;* which also he hath absolutely required as we have ability and opportunity: for though there need be no overt actions to make the sincerity of our affections and intentions known to God; yet it is necessary, for his glory and a good example to others, to declare that to the world, by visible signs and expressions, which was before known to him in the secret purposes and thoughts of our hearts. And here I would remark,

(1.) *God hath no less strictly enjoined external worship, than internal.*

SECOND COMMANDMENT. 131

What can be more external than the ceremonial part of the evangelical law, the participation of Baptism and the Lord's Supper? Both of which are yet most expressly commanded. Matt. 28 : 19. "Go, teach all nations, baptizing them in the name of the Father, and of the Son, and of the Holy Ghost." Acts, 2 : 38. "Repent, and be baptized every one of you, in the name of Jesus Christ." And for the communion of the body and blood of Christ, see Luke, 22 : 19. "Do this in remembrance of me:" which command they violate, and refuse to give the most evident sign that they are christians, who either totally neglect, or else very seldom attend this most holy and spiritual ordinance.

(2.) *God doth severely both threaten and punish such as give external worship unto any other but himself.*

How often are the Israelites reproved for bowing the knee to Baal, for baking cakes to the Queen of Heaven! Yea, and very usually idolatry is set forth in Scripture by some of those visible actions by which some of these false worshippers used to express their devotion towards their false deities, as bowing the body to them. Josh. 23 : 16. "Served other gods, and bowed yourselves to them." Judges, 2 : 12, 17, &c. Kissing the hand unto them, in token of reverence. Job, 31 : 26, 27. "If I beheld the sun when it shined, or the moon walking in brightness; and my heart hath been secretly enticed, or my mouth hath kissed my hand, this also were an iniquity to be punished by the judge; for I should have denied the God that is above." So, likewise, bowing the knee to any idol, and kissing it. Hos. 13 : 2. "Let the men that sacrifice, kiss the calves." And so, when Elijah complained of the total defection of the Israelites from the service of the true God unto idolatry, God, to comfort and encourage him, tells him that he was not alone, but that there were "seven thousand in Israel, all the knees that had not bowed unto Baal, and every mouth which had not kissed him." 1 Kings, 19 : 18. And therefore, certainly, since he makes so punctual a computation of those who had not alienated their bodily worship to the service of an idol, he doth respect and accept those who in faith and sincerity tender it to himself.

(3.) *God hath created the whole man, both soul and body, for himself, and he sustains both in their being*, therefore he expects homage and service from both: from the soul, as the chief seat of worship; from the body, as the best testimony of it.

(4.) *Not only our souls, but our bodies too are redeemed by Christ*, therefore, both should be employed in his worship and service.

The whole man is bought with a price; the whole is justified; the whole is sanctified. Yea, our very bodies are said to be the temples of the Holy Ghost. 1 Cor. 6 : 19. And where should God be worshipped, or that worship appear, if not in his temple? And, therefore, on account of the purchase which Christ hath made of us to himself, the apostle draws this inference in the forementioned place : " Ye are not your own; for ye are bought with a price : wherefore glorify God in your body, and in your spirit, which are God's."

(5.) *The body as well as the soul is likewise to partake of the blessings of obedience;* and therefore it is but reasonable it should partake of the service of obedience.

Many blessings are promised to our outward man, here in this life; and hereafter it is to be made a glorious and incorruptible body, like unto the glorious body of our Lord Jesus Christ: it is to be clothed with light and crowned with rays; never more to suffer injuries without or diseases within; and therefore certainly duty belongs to it, since so many great and unspeakable privileges belong to it.

Thus you see how reasonably God requires from us the service not only of the inward but of the outward man; and therefore we are not to slight that outward reverence which is necessary to testify a due sense of his glorious presence when we come before him: neither must we rob him of any part, either of his service or of his servant, but sacrifice ourselves entirely to him; our bodies on the altar of our souls, hearts and affections; and both soul and body on that altar which alone can make both acceptable, even the Lord Jesus Christ. So much for this fourth proposition.

5. *All that outward reverence which we show towards God in his worship and service, must be measured and estimated according to the customs and usage of places and countries;* so that what they use as a sign and expression of honor to their superiors, they ought much more to use in the presence of the great God, the King of kings and Lord of lords. And, therefore, uncovering of the head, bowing of the body, an humble attitude and settled composure of the whole man, which among us are but fitting signs of respect and reverence when we appear in the presence of those who are much our superiors, ought likewise to be used by us in the presence of God, who is infinitely such: not indeed that they are essential parts of worship, but signs and testimonies of it.

6. *We ought not to worship God with any other external*

worship than what he himself hath commanded and appointed us in his holy word.

The Scripture hath set us our bounds for worship, to which we must not add, and from which we ought not to diminish; for whosoever doth either the one or the other, must needs accuse the rule, either of defect in things necessary, or of superfluity in things unnecessary; which is a high affront to the wisdom of God, who, as he is the object, so he is the prescriber of all that worship which he will accept and reward.

I well know that this rule hath given (I cannot say *cause*, but) *occasion* to many hot disputes about ecclesiastical rites and constitutions: some condemning whatsoever is prescribed or used in the service of God besides things expressly commanded in Scripture, as encroachments on the authority of God and additions to his worship, which he requires to be performed according to the pattern in the mount and the model he hath delineated for it; others again, maintaining the privilege and authority of the church, in ordaining some things for the more decent and reverent performing of the service of God, which are not particularly required in the holy Scriptures.

I shall not plunge myself into this controversy: only give me leave to say, and sadly to lament, that the seamless coat of Christ is rent in pieces among them, whilst some think it more decent to sew on loops and fringes to it, and others will have none. And truly I think our differences are of no greater importance in themselves, though too woful in their consequences. I shall clearly express my sense of this matter in a few words, without any reflection or bitterness, and so leave it to the judgment and discretion of all.

Things which belong to the worship of God may be considered either as *parts of that worship*, or only as *circumstances and modifications of it*.

Therefore whatsoever is imposed on us as a substantial part of the worship of God, if it be not expressly required of us in the Holy Scriptures, is to be not only refused but abominated; for this is a plain addition to what God hath commanded; and by it we lay an imputation upon him as though he wanted wisdom to ordain what is necessary for his own service.

Then, and then only, is any constitution of man imposed for a part of divine worship, when obedience to it is urged upon us not only from the authority enjoining it, but also from the necessity of the thing considered simply and nakedly in its own nature. For as it is with God's laws, some things are commanded because they are good, and some things are good only because they are commanded; so it is with laws and impositions of men about matters of religion and worship. Some things men command because they are in themselves necessary antecedently to their command, as enjoined before by God; and therefore this is no ordinance or doctrine of man, but of God, to which the magistrate, who is the guardian of both tables, doth well to add the sanction of secular rewards and punishments: other things are necessary only because they are commanded by the authority of those to whom we owe conscientious obedience in things lawful and indifferent. But we utterly deny that the imposition of any such things makes them any parts of worship, of which they are only circumstances; or that these observances are necessary to us, or acceptable to God antecedently to the command of authority; or that the worship of God would be imperfect, defective, unacceptable and invalid to the ends for which it is appointed, were not these observances commanded and performed.

Thus you see we put a vast difference between that which is a part of worship and that which is but a *circumstance* of worship: if any thing be commanded us by men as a part of worship which is not commanded us by God, we ought not to submit to it. And certainly, did we but rightly weigh what is required as a part of worship, and what only as a circumstance of worship, a great deal of heat, and contention, and uncharitable prejudice would be removed and prevented. It is true, our Savior, Matt. 15 : 9, condemns the Scribes and Pharisees, that taught *for doctrines the commandments of men:* that is, they taught those things which were but the traditions and ordinances of their elders, to be in themselves absolutely necessary to the serving and worshipping of God. But, certainly, this reproof falls not upon those who, though they do enjoin what they judge fit for order, yet do not teach them for doctrines, and are so far from thinking their commandments an essential part of worship, that they would abhor and anathematize all those that do so. Necessary they are to be submitted to and practised, because enjoined by that authority to which God hath committed the care of the first table as well as the second; but not necessary in themselves as any part of the worship and service of God, without which, although they were not imposed by men, it would be unacceptable to him.

And, now that I have delivered my judgment without bitterness, give me leave to make some few lamentations in the grief and bitterness of my soul. Is it not to be bitterly lamented, that in a reformed and orthodox church there should be such schisms, rents and divisions: altar against altar, pulpit against pulpit, and one congregation against another? And what is all this contention and separation for? Oh, they will tell you it is for the purity of religion; for the true and sincere worship of God; that they may serve him purely without human additions or inventions. Thus goes the cry, and well-meaning souls take it up and join with it, never examining the grounds of it; but conclude that those must be in the right who complain of corruptions and pretend to a happy and glorious reformation. Alas, my brethren, was there ever any schism in the world that did not plead the same? Do not others separate from their communion upon the same pretences on which they now separate from ours? And may not the same argument serve to crumble them into infinite fractions and subdivisions; till, at last, we come to have almost as many churches as men, and scarce a man constant and coherent to himself?

Is it then that we differ about mere accidents and circumstances? I confess we do; but assert, withal, that these things are not a just cause of separation and division.

If we look back upon the primitive times, we shall find that almost every church had its different rites and observances; and, yet, under that diversity they maintained unity and communion. Yea, and at this day the reformed churches observe different customs one from another, and yet they inviolably hold communion together. The Gallican, Belgic, Helvetian and German churches reject us not, nor we them; although we differ in rites and discipline, and in those things which are left to the prudence of every church to constitute as they shall judge most necessary for order and edification.

Now, certainly, if these different rites and observances be no ground for one national church to separate from the communion of another, they can be no ground for private persons to separate from the communion of the church to which they belong. Nay, although they might with reason dislike many usages either as frivolous or incongruous, yet it becomes the temper and modesty of a pious christian, in things merely circumstantial, to submit his practice to the judgment of those with whom and under whose watch he lives; and not to separate from the communion of the church, to forsake its assemblies, to disown its administration, only because he thinks some things might be more conveniently ordered, according to the model of his own or other men's apprehensions; which, in the folly and sad consequences of it, would be to act like him who took up a beetle and struck with all his force to kill a fly that he saw on his friend's forehead. What else were this but to rend the body of Christ by an angry contending about the fashion of its garments; and to tear away its limbs by a violent striving to strip off those clothes which they think indecent?

For my part, I freely profess that were my lot cast among any of the reformed churches beyond the seas, I would presently join in their communion, and not at all scruple to conform myself to their received customs; although, perhaps, in my own private persuasions I may judge some of them to be less serious and less reverent than those of the church to which I belong. I have ever venerated the advice of St. Ambrose to St. Austin: "If thou wilt neither give offence nor take offence, conform thyself to all the lawful customs of the churches where thou comest." Aug. ad Jan. Ep. 118.

But I will not farther enlarge on this subject: only I pray that our wanton dissensions about these less important matters may not provoke God to deprive us of the substance and essentials of our religion; and reduce us to a condition wherein we should be heartily glad could we enjoy the liberty of the Gospel and the ordinances of our Lord Jesus Christ under any form of administration. It were just with God to extinguish the light of his Gospel, when we use it not to work by, but all our study and strife is how to snuff it.—Thus much in general, touching the *external worship* of God required in this commandment.

II. As to the SINS FORBIDDEN by it, they are two: contempt of the worship of God, and superstition in performing it.

Of the former I have already spoken largely in giving the characters of a profane person. I shall therefore here speak only of *superstition*.

Concerning the etymology of the word, both Tully and Lactantius are agreed that it is derived from *superstites*, " survivors :" but about the reason of the notion they much differ. Tully saith, " *They* were called superstitious who immoderately prayed and sacrificed that their children might survive them." But Lactantius, not content with this reason, gives another: " *They* were called superstitious, not who desired that their children might survive them, for all desire this, but they who celebrated the surviving memory of the dead, or who surviving their parents, worshipped their images as their household gods." Cicero de Nat. Deor. lib. ii; Lactant. Instit. lib. iv. c. 28.

But, whatever be the etymology of the word, we may take this short description of it: that it is *a needless and erroneous fear in matters of religion*. And this is twofold, either negative or positive.

Negative superstition is, when men fearfully abstain from and abhor those things as wicked and abominable which God hath not forbidden, and which therefore are in themselves lawful and harmless. And they who are bigoted with this superstition, will be sure to cry out against all who observe such things as they condemn, as miserably seduced and superstitious souls. Like Diogenes, who is said to have trampled on Plato's pride with far greater pride, so these exclaim against superstition with far greater superstition. For superstition is not either the observing or not observing of such things; but the doing of either with an erroneous fear, lest God should be displeased and provoked if we did otherwise. He is, therefore, negatively superstitious who makes the not doing of that which is lawful and harmless, a matter of conscience and of religion.

Positive superstition is when men do fearfully observe and perform those things which either are forbidden or at least no where commanded by God. Or, if you will, it is a restless fear of the mind, putting men upon acts of religion which are not due or not convenient.

This positive superstition shows itself two ways: sometimes in giving divine honors to that which is not God; and sometimes in performing needless and superfluous services to the true God. Both are the effects of superstition, though commonly known by their proper names —the one being idolatry and the other will-worship,— and both are forbidden in this commandment.

1. *Idolatry* is a species of superstition.

So we find it expressly, Acts, 17 : 16, compared with verse 22. In verse 16, it is said that Paul's "spirit was stirred in him when he saw the city [Athens] wholly given to idolatry." And in verse 22 it is said that Paul reproved them as being *too superstitious*. Therefore, though all superstition be not idolatry, yet all idolatry is superstition; yea, and the blackest kind of it.

Now idolatry is nothing else but the giving of religious worship to an idol. And an idol is not only an artificial image or representation of any thing, whether real or fictitious, set up to be worshipped; but any creature of God, whether angels or men, sun or moon, or stars, &c. to which we give any religious honor and service, becomes to us an idol. The worshipping of any creature, whether in heaven above, or in the earth beneath, or in the water under the earth, is idolatry; which is particularly and by name forbidden in this commandment.

And indeed this is a sin so absurd and stupid, that it is a wonder it should ever be so bewitching as to inveigle the far greater part of the world. The prophet Isaiah very frequently derides the folly and madness of idolaters: especially chap. 44 : 16, 17. "He burneth part" of his wooden god "in the fire; he roasteth" his meat with it, "and is satisfied: he warmeth himself; and the residue thereof he maketh a god: he falleth down unto it, and worshippeth it, and prayeth unto it, and saith, Deliver me, for thou art my god." A most gross and bestial stupidity! as if there were more divinity in one end of a stick than the other. And yet a sin most strangely bewitching; after which all the heathen world ran a whoring; and from which all the remonstrances and threatenings which God makes to his own people of Israel could not restrain them. Yea, and so strangely besotting is it, that a very great part, even of those who profess the name and doctrine of Jesus Christ, are most foully guilty of it: I mean the papists; who, to hide their shame in this particular from the notice of the people, have covered it with a greater; and thought fit rather to expunge this second commandment than to leave their image-worship to be censured and condemned by it. For, in all their catechisms and books of devotion which they have published for the use of the vulgar, they have sacrilegiously omitted this second commandment; as fearing that the evidence of it would convict and condemn them of idolatry in the consciences of the most ignorant and illiterate that should but hear it rehearsed.

Let us now proceed to consider *who may be justly condemned of idolatry*, in the violation of this precept.

(1.) *He is an idolater that prays to any saint or angel;* for in doing this he ascribes that to the creature which is an honor due only to God the Creator. Our faith and our invocation ought to be terminated in the same object. Rom. 10 : 14. "How shall they call on him in whom they have not believed?" Therefore, if we cannot, without blasphemy, say that we believe in such a saint or angel; neither can we, without idolatry, pray to that saint or angel.

(2.) But the most execrable idolatry is *that of entering into league and correspondence with the devil; to consult and invoke him; and by any wicked arts implore or make use of his help and assistance.* Of this are those guilty in the highest degree who enter into any express compact with the devil; which is always ratified with some homage of worship given to him. And in a secondary and lower degree are those guilty of it who apply themselves to seek help from such forlorn wretches as use traditionary charms and incantations, or any vain observances to free them from pains and diseases, or other troubles that molest them. For all those things which have not a natural efficiency to produce that effect for which they are used, may very reasonably be suspected to have been agreed on formerly between the devil and some of his especial servants, and that all the virtue they retain is only from that compact; which as it was explicit in those that made it, so it is implicit in those that use them; for they still act in the power of that first stipulation and agreement.

(3.) *Whosoever bows down his body in religious adoration of any image, or other creature, is guilty of idolatry;* and doth most expressly transgress the very letter of this command, " Thou shalt not bow down before them, nor worship them."

And here is but a vain refuge, to which the Papists betake themselves when they excuse themselves from being guilty of idolatry, because, although they worship images, yet they worship the true God by them. For, in fact, they worship the images of very many creatures, both men and angels; nor is their evasion concerning *latreidouleia*, and *uperdouleia*, any other than a vain and frivolous distinction.

And whereas they pretend to worship the true God by an image, we reply, that it is most impious to attempt to represent God by any visible resemblance; and therefore much more to worship him, could he be so represented. For God, who is infinite, cannot be circumscribed by lines and lineaments; and, being invisible, cannot be resembled. Hence he again and again inculcates it upon the Israelites, that when he delivered the law to them, he appeared not in any shape, that they might not audaciously attempt to delineate him, and so be enticed to idolatry. " Ye heard the voice of words, but saw no similitude; only ye heard a voice." Deut. 4 : 12. " Take ye therefore good heed unto yourselves, (for ye saw no manner of similitude on the day that the Lord spake unto you in Horeb out of the midst of the fire,) lest ye corrupt yourselves, and make you a graven image, the similitude of any figure." v. 15. When therefore the Papists plead that they worship the only true God by images, this is no better than to excuse one horrid sin by the commission of another.

To worship the true and only God by an image, is gross idolatry. This the Papists deny, and place idolatry in the worshipping of images set up to represent *false* and *fictitious* gods; or else in worshipping them with a belief that they themselves are gods.

But if this be so, then upon the same account the Israelites were not idolaters in worshipping the golden calf. They were not so brutish as to believe that calf itself to be their God. Nay, it is most evident that they intended to worship the true God under that representation. See Exod. 32 : 4. " *These be thy gods, O Israel, which brought thee up out of the land of Egypt.*" They could not be so stupid as to think that that very calf which they themselves had made, had delivered them from Egypt; but they pretended to worship the true God who had given them that great deliverance, under this hieroglyphic sign and resemblance: which appears, verse 5. "*Aaron made proclamation, and said, To-morrow is a feast* TO THE LORD :" in the original it is Jehovah, the proper and incommunicable name of the true God. And yet, that this worship of theirs, although thus professedly directed to the true God, was horrid idolatry, the Scripture abundantly testifies. " Oh, this people have sinned a great sin." verse 31. " Neither be ye idolaters, as were some of them; as it is written, The people sat down to eat and drink, and rose up to play." 1 Cor. 10 : 7. "They made a calf in those days, and offered sacrifice unto the idol." Acts, 7 : 41.

And how was it with *Micah and his mother?* They were certainly guilty of idolatry in making and worshipping their images; and, yet, that their images were made to be symbolical representations of the true God, and erected to this very purpose that he might be worshipped by them, appears clearly from the history, Judges, 17 : 3. " I had wholly dedicated," saith she, " the silver unto the Lord, (Jehovah, Heb.) for my son to make a graven image and a molten image." Which when he had done, he hired a Levite to be his priest. And, in confidence of the reward of so much piety, he concludes, v. 13, that certainly now the Lord Jehovah would bless him, and do him good. Nothing can be clearer than that all this worship was professedly offered by him to the true and only God; yet, being performed by images, it was no better than rank idolatry.

And further, *If the Papists, in worshipping the true God by images, be not idolaters; then neither was Jeroboam, who made Israel to sin, an idolater, in setting up his calves at Dan and Bethel.* For whoever rationally considers the occasion and political grounds of this innovation must conclude that Jeroboam intended not to introduce a new God, which would have made the people to fall faster from him than tyranny and oppression did from Rehoboam; but only to set up some visible signs and representations of the true God; and to persuade the people that they need not go to Jerusalem to seek his presence and to offer their gifts and sacrifices, for the same God was as much present with them in those figures as he was at the temple of Jerusalem between the cherubims.* And therefore we find that the idolatry of Jeroboam is distinguished from the idolatry of those who worshipped Baal and other false gods : see 1 Kings, 16 : 31, where God speaks concerning Ahab, " as if it had been a light thing for him to walk in the sins of Jeroboam the son of Nebat, he went and served Baal, and worshipped him."

Nay, once more, although some among the heathen might be so grossly stupid as to suppose the images themselves to be gods, and so to worship them; yet their wise and learned philosophers were far enough from such a senseless error: yea, they were forced to use as many distinctions and subtle evasions concerning their worshipping of images as now the papists do; and truly most of those the papists use are the very same, and seem but borrowed out of the schools of the heathen.

But especially do the philosophers insist on this : that they venerated not their statues, as they were made of such or such materials, but only as they were the houses and bodies of God, where his presence resided, and by which his power was manifested: that they worshipped not the visible sign, but the invisible Deity by it.†

---

* Joseph. Antiq. Jud. lib. 8. c. 3.

† *Non hoc visibile colo ; sed numen, quod in illis invisibiliter habitat. Et qui videbantur sibi purgatioris esse religionis, dicebant: Nec si-*

SECOND COMMANDMENT. 147

And what do papists say more than this, viz. that they worship the images of God, not as if they were themselves God, but only as they are the visible signs and symbols of the divine presence: and so all their worship is directed unto God through them.

In respect to idolatry, therefore, I profess I can find no difference at all between heathens and papists: for, as the more learned papists do profess that they worship the true God by the image, so likewise did the more learned heathens.* And, for the ignorant and vulgar papists, I am very apt to suspect that they do, as the ignorant heathen, terminate and limit their worship in the very images before which they fall prostrate; esteeming them to have divine power and virtue of their own: for they are most grossly blinded and infatuated in this their image-worship, and may as well take a stone or a block to be a God as the great dragon to be a saint, as the poor woman did, who offered one candle to St. Michael and another to his dragon, that is, the devil.† And therefore, certainly, if the heathen world were ever guilty of idolatry, so is now the Popish Church; their worship, and all the reasons of it, being so exactly parallel.—Thus much concerning the first branch of superstition, which is idolatry.

2. The second is *will-worship*, of which I shall speak

---

mulachrum, nec dæmonium colo; sed, per effigiem corporalem, ejus rei signum intueor quam colere debeo. Arnob. lib. vi.

* Dio Chrysostom. Orat. 12 de Primâ Dei Notitiâ.—Τις γαρ ειμη παντη νηπι[Ο]΄ ταυτα ηγει τȣς θεȣς αλλα θεων αναθηματα και αγαλματα. Celsus: Orig. Cont. Cels. lib. vii. Where he likewise proves that it is lawful to make images of God, because, according to the doctrine of christians themselves, God made man according to his own image: the very argument urged by the Papists, and made use of by the Second Council of Nice.

† Estienne Apol. pour Herodote.

but very little, having already anticipated myself.

Will-worship is nothing else but the inventing and ascribing any other worship to God besides what he hath been pleased to command and institute.

God will not be worshipped according to our fancies, but according to his own appointment; for as we must have no other God besides the true, so that God must have no other service performed to him besides what himself hath required and prescribed: for this were to impute folly and weakness to him, as if, indeed, he would have servants, but knew not what service to enjoin them. Thus we have finished the prohibition, " THOU SHALT NOT MAKE UNTO THEE ANY GRAVEN IMAGE," &c.

Let us now consider the *sanction* of this precept; consisting, first, of a severe and fearful threatening against all those who should presume to violate it: *For I the Lord thy God am a jealous God, visiting the iniquity of the fathers upon the children, unto the third and fourth generation of them that hate me;* and, next, of a gracious *promise* of mercy to the careful and conscientious observers of this precept: *showing mercy unto thousands of them that love me, and keep my commandments.*

In the threatening we have these several particulars: Who it is that denounces it: " I, the Lord thy God." What it is that he denounces and threatens: " To visit the iniquity of the fathers upon the children." The persons against whom this threatening is directed: " Those that hate him;" and the duration and continuance of that vengeance which he will take upon them: It shall be to " the third and fourth generation." His wrath shall extend to their children, and their children's children.

SECOND COMMANDMENT.

I. Let us consider WHO IT IS that denounceth this threatening: " I, the Lord thy God, am a jealous God:" so most read the words as our English translation renders them. But others no less rightly read them thus: *For I, the Lord thy God, am strong and jealous;* for the word *El*, which is here used, signifies the *mighty* God.

And according to this acceptation, the words contain in them a description of God.

1. By *his relation to us:* The Lord *thy* God; a God who hath separated thee from all people of the earth, to be his peculiar treasure; who hath brought thee near unto himself, even into the bond of the covenant; who hath betrothed thee in righteousness, and is not only *thy Maker*, but *thy Husband*, as the prophet speaks. Isaiah, 54 : 5.

This God it is who commands thee faithfully to perform the marriage-vow that is between thee and him, and not to go a whoring after the vanities of the gentiles, nor to expose thy shame and nakedness before any false or idol-god; for idolatry is spiritual adultery, and is most frequently set forth under that name and notion in the holy Scriptures.

2. Thy God is described by *the mightiness of his power*. He is *El kana*, a strong and jealous God; able to revenge any dishonor that is done him by thy unchaste lewdness.

3. He is described by that violent passion which in men is called *jealousy:* I, the Lord thy God, am *strong and jealous*.

Jealousy is an affection or passion of the mind, by which we are stirred up and provoked against whatsoever hinders the enjoyment of that which we love and desire. The cause and origin of it is love; the effect of it is revenge.

Now God, to deter the Israelites from idolatry, sets forth himself as a strong and jealous God, that they might be assured not to escape punishment; for he is strong, and therefore *can* inflict it; and he is jealous, and therefore *will* inflict it if they shall dare to abuse and injure that love which he hath placed upon them

This jealousy is not to be ascribed to God, as if there were properly any such weak and disturbing passion in him; but only by way of accommodation and similitude, speaking after the manner of men. So is it to be understood, when God is said to be angry, to be grieved, to repent, &c. that is, his actions towards us are like the actions of one that is angry, or grieved, or repents: although the infinite serenity of the Divine essence is not liable to be discomposed or ruffled by the tempests of any such like passions as are incident to us mutable creatures.

Now the reason why God calls himself here a jealous God you will find in these following characteristics of jealousy:

(1.) Jealousy is *distrustful* and *suspicious*. It dares not rely upon the truth and fidelity of the person of whom we are jealous, but is full of misgiving doubts and fears. And so God (although, in propriety of speech, he can doubt nothing, nor fear any thing, yet) is pleased to express his jealousy by such language as intimates distrust and diffidence. And therefore, when the Israelites made that solemn promise to the Lord, Deut. 5 : 27, " All that the Lord our God shall speak unto us, we will hear it and do it," God returns answer as one that doubted the real performance of so fair a promise, ver. 28, 29, " I have heard the voice of the words of this people—they have well said all that they have spoken. O that there were such a heart in them, that they would fear me, and keep all my commandments always, that it might be well with them and with their children for ever!"

(2.) Jealousy is *searching* and *inquisitive*. It is hard to escape the discovery of a jealous eye; which is still prying and seeking after that which it would be loth to find. So the eye of the all-seeing and all-knowing God is continually upon us: he critically observes every look and every kind of glance that we cast upon ourselves: not the least motion of our hearts, not the least twinkling of our thoughts can escape his notice and censure. And, of all sins, there is none that God doth more jealously observe than that of idolatry; for this is the violation of that marriage-faith which we have plighted to him. Therefore we find that the idolatrous Israelites, as though they were conscious of the great abuse they offered to their *Maker*, their *Husband*, (as the prophet styles God, Isa. 54 : 5,) sought out dark and obscure groves to act their wickedness in; that, although they were not chaste, yet they might seem to be cautious. But in vain is it to draw the curtains of a thin shade about them: a few leaves could not cover their shame nor their nakedness from Him who is all eye every where, and whose eye is every where light to itself: "God is light, and in him is no darkness at all." 1 John, 1 : 5. It is not possible to conceal from him the prostitution of an unchaste and impudent idolatry. And therefore saith the Psalmist, "If we have forgotten the name of our God, or stretched forth our hands to a false god; shall not God search this out? for he knoweth the secrets of the heart." Psalm 44 : 20, 21.

(3.) Jealousy, as it is searching and inquisitive, so it is *angry and revengeful*. Solomon calls it "the rage of a man," Prov. 6 : 34, "therefore he will not spare in the day of vengeance." And, Cant. 8 : 6, "Jealousy is cruel as the grave; the coals thereof are as coals of fire, which have a most vehement flame." For as love is the most soft and tender affection of human nature, so jealousy, which is the sowering of love and turning it into vinegar, is the most wild and furious.

God is pleased to style himself a jealous God to express the heat of his wrath and indignation against sinners. So Deut. 29 : 20, "The Lord will not spare him, but the anger of the Lord and his jealousy shall smoke against that man, and all the curses that are written in this book shall lie upon him, and the Lord shall blot out his name from under heaven." See what dreadful effects this smoking jealousy hath when it breaks forth into a flame, Zeph. 1 : 18. "Neither their silver nor their gold shall be able to deliver them in the day of the Lord's wrath; but the whole land shall be devoured by the fire of his jealousy, for he shall make even a speedy riddance of all them that dwell in the land."

And of the signal revenge this devouring jealousy of the Almighty God hath taken upon sinners the whole world is full of sad instances. This fire hath kindled the eternal and unquenchable flames of hell. When the proud and rebellious angels aspired to be gods, God turned them into devils, and these devils into hell; for his jealousy could not endure to have rivals in his glory. All the ruins and calamities that have ever happened to persons or nations are but the effects of God's jealousy against sin. And of all other sins his jealousy takes most remarkable vengeance against idolatry, for this is spiritual whoredom, a provocation which the jealous God can least endure

See Deut. 32 : 16, 17, 19, " They provoked him to jealousy with strange gods. They sacrificed unto devils, not to God; to gods whom they knew not, to new gods that came newly up. And when the Lord saw it he abhorred them, because of the provoking of his sons and of his daughters." And verse 21, " They have moved me to jealousy with that which is not God : they have provoked me to anger with their vanities. A fire is kindled in mine anger, and shall burn unto the lowest hell, and shall consume the earth with her increase, and set on fire the foundations of the mountains." And so in the following verses God exaggerates those sore and heavy judgments which he would bring upon them in the fury of his jealousy, because of this heinous sin of idolatry. Thus we have seen in what respects God is said to be a jealous God.

What remains now but that expostulation of the apostle, 1 Cor. 10 : 22, "Do we provoke the Lord to jealousy? Are we stronger than he?" We, who are but as dust before the whirlwind, and as dry stubble before the consuming fire, shall we dare by our sins to affront and challenge that God who hath said, " Vengeance is mine, and I will repay" it? And yet such is the madness of every desperate sinner, that he rushes upon God's neck and upon the thick bosses of his buckler; and daily provokes him who is infinitely able to destroy both body and soul in hell-fire. Indeed jealousy of itself, without power to wreak vengeance, is but a weak and contemptible passion; but when it is armed with Almighty strength it is justly terrible. Now the Lord thy God is (Hebrew) *a strong and jealous God*. Every sin thou committest is a horrid wrong done unto him; and a violation of that faith which thou owest him. He hath wooed thy affections, sought thy consent, and yet thou perfidiously followest other lovers, and givest thy heart unto the world and the devil, which are God's greatest co-rivals. The highest indignity that can be done against love is to contemn and slight it, and to embrace those who are far more base and sordid: how notoriously then dost thou affront God, when thou despisest his love and thy own faith, to cast thyself into the embraces of every vile lust which now pollutes thy soul and will hereafter damn it! O foolish and unkind that thou art, to neglect the love of the great King of heaven and earth, and to make choice of the devil, who is but the slave of God, and solicits thee only to make thee his slave! Yet might it avail somewhat if thou couldst defend thyself, and maintain thy choice against the jealousy and wrath of the great God whom thou thus despisest and provokest: but assure thyself his wrath and his jealousy will smoke against thee; yea, kindle upon thee, till it hath burned thee down to the lowest hell: and that day is coming wherein he will expose thy nakedness and thy shame before men and angels, and upbraid thee with the folly as well as wickedness of thy choice; and then condemn thee to be an eternal companion with those devils whom thou hast preferred before himself. Believe it, it is a sad and fearful thing to fall into the hands of the living God; for he is "a jealous God," and "a consuming fire," as Moses speaks, Deut. 4 : 24.

II. The next particular is, WHAT JUDGMENT THIS STRONG AND JEALOUS GOD THREATENS TO INFLICT : and that is to "visit the iniquity of the fathers upon the children."

Visiting is a figurative expression: in the general, God

is said to visit, when, after a long space of time, in which he seemed to have forgotten or taken no notice of men, he declares by his providence that he hath still observed their ways and doings.

And this word *visiting* may be taken either in a good or in an evil part. In a good part, when God bestows great mercies and salvation upon his people, he is said to visit them: and thus it is frequently used in the Scripture. Exod. 3 : 16; Luke, 1 : 68, 28, &c. In an evil part, God is said to visit, when he rewards those sins at which he seemed to connive with deserved punishments. So Psalm 89 : 32, "I will visit their transgression with the rod, and their iniquity with stripes." And Jer. 5 : 9, "Shall I not visit for these things? saith the Lord: and shall not my soul be avenged on such a nation as this?"

And in this sense is the word to be taken here: *Visiting the iniquity of the fathers upon the children;* that is, punishing the fathers' iniquity in their children and posterity. And thus we have it interpreted, Jer. 32 : 18. "Thou recompensest the iniquity of the fathers into the bosom of their children after them."

Now here arise two important inquiries to be resolved: whether it be *just* with God, and consistent with the divine veracity, to punish the sins of the fathers upon the children; and whether God *doth always observe* this method of revenging the fathers' crimes upon their posterity and offspring.

As to the *former* inquiry there seems to be some difficulty in reconciling Scripture to itself in this particular, and in reconciling such a proceeding to justice and equity.

For sometimes the Scriptures do expressly mention the

punishment of parents' sins to be inflicted on their children. Exod. 34 : 7 ; Jer. 32 : 18, &c. And when God commands Saul utterly to destroy Amalek, he gives this reason of his injunction, 1 Sam. 15 : 2, "I remember that which Amalek did to Israel, how he laid wait for him in the way when he came up from Egypt." And yet almost four hundred years were passed between the journey of the Israelites from Egypt and the issuing of this command: so that none of those Amalekites who opposed them in their way could then have been alive to bear the punishment of that offence. Yea, and our Savior threatens the Jews of his time, Mat. 23 : 35, "That upon them should come all the righteous blood shed upon the earth, from the blood of righteous Abel unto the blood of Zacharias son of Barachias, whom they slew between the temple and the altar." That is, the sins of the progenitors, from the beginning of the world unto that very age when they murdered Zachary, the father of John the Baptist, in the court of the temple, shall be punished in this generation. Vide Baron. Annal. An. 1, Sect. 52, &c.

And yet again we read as expressly, Ezek. 18 : 20, "The soul that sinneth it shall die. The son shall not bear the iniquity of the father, neither shall the father bear the iniquity of the son; the righteousness of the righteous shall be upon him, and the iniquity of the wicked shall be upon him." And again, Jer. 31 : 29, 30, "In those days they shall say no more, the fathers have eaten a sour grape, and the children's teeth are set on edge. But every one shall die for his own iniquity." And indeed this seems most agreeable to the rules of justice, that the innocent should not be punished for the sins of the nocent and guilty.

To solve this difficulty therefore, and reconcile this seeming contradiction, I shall premise some distinctions; and then draw from them some conclusions satisfactory to the question propounded.

Punishments are either temporal—such as befall in this present life; or else eternal—such as are reserved to be inflicted on all impenitent and disobedient sinners in the world to come.

Again, children may be considered either as imitating the crimes and transgressions of their parents, or as repenting of them, and reforming from them, and so not walking in their fathers' steps, but in the ways of God's commandments.

1. Certain it is, *God never visits the iniquity of the fathers upon repenting and reforming children with eternal punishment.* And in this sense it is everlastingly true, that " the son shall not bear the iniquity of his father;" but " the soul that sinneth, it shall die;" and " every man shall bear his own burthen."

But some may say, " Are we not made liable even to eternal death by the sin of another? Hath not the sin of our first father brought condemnation upon all his posterity? And therefore how is it true that the son shall not, in this respect, bear the iniquity of his father?"

To this I answer. It is not his sin, considered personally as his, that hath made us obnoxious unto eternal death; but it was our sin as well as his; for in him we all sinned and fell. Adam was our federal head and common representative, and his sin was legally ours; even as his obedience would have been, had he persevered in it. But now the case of Adam is singular and much different from that of intermediate parents. They, indeed, are our natural heads; but not our federal heads, as Adam was. Their actions are only their own, and not ours, and have no influence at all upon the determining of our eternal state and condition; and therefore we shall not be accountable to God at the last day for what they have done, but only for what we ourselves have done in the body, whether it be good or evil. Yet,

2. *If the children imitate the wickedness and crimes of their fathers, it is but just and righteous with God to punish them with eternal death and damnation for them.* It is but fit that they should inherit their fathers' damnation, who inherit their fathers' transgressions. But in this case it must be observed that God punisheth them, not because they are their fathers' sins, but because they are their own.

3. *God may, and often doth, visit the iniquity of the fathers upon the children with temporal punishments, whether the children imitate the offences of the fathers or reform from them.*

And these temporal punishments are many times very sore and heavy: languishing diseases; racking and tormenting pains; loss of estate, sometimes ravished from them by violence, sometimes melting away insensibly. The father, possibly by his unjust oppression and extortion, entails a curse upon his estate; which, like a canker, eats it out and consumes it in his son's days; so that nothing is left in his hands but shame and poverty; although, perhaps, he might never know the sins for which God blasts him. Yea, we find that God doth inflict temporal death on the child for the offence of the parent: thus, 2 Samuel, 12:14, in Nathan's message to David, "Because by this deed thou hast given great occasion to the enemies of the Lord to blaspheme, the child also that is born unto thee shall surely die."

Thus God doth very frequently inflict temporal punishments upon the children for the fathers' transgressions.

Nor is it at all hard to reconcile this with the measures of justice and equity, because of the near relation which they bear to their parents: for certainly it is just with God to punish a sinner in all that is related to him. Children are part of their parents; yea, their parents live and survive in them; and therefore certainly God, in punishing them, may justly strike what part of them he pleaseth. And this even Plutarch, a heathen, could observe: speaking how God often inflicted grievous judgments on the posterity of lewd and wicked men, he tells us: "It is nothing strange and absurd for those who are theirs to suffer what belongs to them." De Sero Punitis.

But then another question is, *Whether God doth always observe this method of revenging the offences of fathers upon their children in temporal punishments.*

To which I answer, no, he doth not. Neither doth this threatening in the commandment oblige him to do it, but only shows what their sins deserve, and what he might justly do if he pleased to use his power and prerogative. Hence we read of the children of wicked parents who yet were both pious and prosperous: such were Hezekiah and Josiah, the one the son of Ahaz, the other of Amon. But most commonly we may observe in the course of Divine providence, that the posterity of wicked parents pay off their fathers' scores to divine justice in the temporal evils and calamities that are brought upon them. Yet, if they themselves be pious and holy, this may be for their comfort, that whatever afflictions they lie under shall be for their benefit and advantage; and they are not punishments to them, but only fatherly corrections and chastisements: for the very things which they suffer may be intended by God as a punishment to their ancestors, but a fatherly correction to themselves; and what to the one is threatened as a curse, to the other may prove a blessing and an advantage, as it gives them occasion of exercising more grace, and so of receiving the greater glory.

Suffer me to close up this with one or two *practical meditations*.

1. If it be the usual method of Divine Providence to visit the iniquity of the fathers upon the children, see then *what great reason parents have to beware that they do not lay up a stock of plagues and curses for their posterity; nor clog the estate which they leave them, with so many debts to be paid to the justice of God as will certainly undo them.*

Thou who, by fraud and cozenage, heapest together ill-gotten wealth, thinkest perhaps of leaving so many hundreds or thousands to thy children; but considerest not withal how many curses thou puttest into the bag, curses that, in time, will rot and eat out the very bottom of it. Thou who, by this or by any other way of wickedness, either swearing, or drunkenness, or uncleanness, provokest the holy and the jealous God, doth it nothing grieve thee to think that thy sins shall be punished upon thy poor children's back? Possibly thou art so fondly tender of them that thou art loth to chastise them when they really deserve it for their own faults; yet art thou so cruel to them as to abandon them over to the justice of God, to be severely scourged for faults which are not their own, but thine. Whose heart would not yearn, and whose bowels would not be turned within him, to go into a hospital and there view over all those scenes of human misery and wretchedness which are presented to us; the blind, the lame, the deaf, the dumb, the maimed, the distracted, the ulcerated and loathsome leper, and those several maps of man's woes and torments that are there exhibited? Think then with thyself, "This is the inheritance, this is the portion bequeathed them by their accursed parents:" and as thou wouldst have thine own children to be made the same sad spectacles of Divine wrath and vengeance, so go and sin them into the same condition. Certainly wolves and tigers are more merciful to their offspring than wretched man! It is thou thyself, O cruel man! who hast crippled, and maimed, and tormented, and beggared and undone thine own children: and perhaps every sin thou committest either murders or tortures a poor helpless infant, one whose greatest misery it is that ever he was born of thee. I beseech you, christians, think seriously of this thing; and as ever you would wish well to those dear pledges which are as your own bowels, so beware how ever you provoke the holy and jealous God by any known and wilful sin; who will be sure to repay it home, either in your own persons by his immediate judgments on yourselves, or that which will go as near the heart of every tender and compassionate parent, by his sore judgments on thy poor children and posterity.

2. *See here what great reason thou hast to render thanks and praise to God that thou art born of godly and pious parents; such as treasure not up wrath for thee, but prayers.*

Possibly they were but poor and low in the world; but yet they have bequeathed thee a rich patrimony; and made God executor, who will faithfully discharge his trust if thou discharge thy duty, and give thee a blessing possibly in this life, but certainly in the life to come. Let others boast their blood and their parentage, and reckon up a long row of monuments and ancestors : if they have been wicked, lewd and ungodly, but thine virtuous and the sincere servants of God, they possibly may be the last of their family, and thou the first of thine : howsoever know that it is far more noble to be born of those that have been born of God, than to be the grandchildren of the devil. Thou hast better blood running in thy veins, even the blood of them whom Christ hath judged worthy to be redeemed and washed with his own blood, whose names are written in heaven in the Lamb's book of life : a greater honor and dignity than if they were written in the worm-eaten pages of idle heraldry. And if thou followest their good examples, thy relations and portion too are greater and richer, for thou hast God for thy father, Christ for thy brother, and the whole heaven of stars for thine inheritance.—Thus much for the second particular, what is threatened in the commandment: viz. "*visiting the iniquity of the fathers upon the children.*" I shall be more brief in the two remaining.

III. Let us consider THE PERSONS against whom this threatening is denounced. " Visiting the iniquity of the fathers upon the children of those that hate me." And who those are is explained in the antithesis subjoined : " Keeping mercy for thousands of those that love me and keep my commandments."

If then those that keep God's commandments are lovers of God, (which our Savior expressly affirms, John 14 : 21, " He that hath my commandments, and keepeth them, he it is that loveth me ;") by direct consequence it follows, that those who transgress the commandments of God are haters of God. And what worse can be said of the very devil himself? Let them pretend never so fair, and speak words full of respect and reverence, yet bring them to this trial, do they observe and keep the commandments of God? If not, they are haters of God and goodness.

And indeed it is impossible that those who are disobedient and rebellious should love God. For can they love him who hath required from them what they do so extremely loath? Can they love him whom they must needs apprehend to be armed with wrath and vengeance to punish and torment them everlastingly for their sins? Can they love him who, if they have any conscience in them, they must needs know, hates them with a perfect hatred, and will be avenged on them in their eternal ruin and destruction? Certainly, if we love God because he first loved us, these cannot but hate him to whom their own consciences must needs attest that God hates both them and their ways.

IV. Consider *the duration and continuance of that vengeance which God will take upon those who thus hate him.*

On their own persons he will revenge himself eternally, and be ever satisfying his wronged justice in their insufferable torments; but on their posterity he will be avenged unto the third and fourth generation.

And yet, even in this very threatening, there is mercy contained. Mercy it is that such a wicked and accursed race are not cut off, and cast out of his sight and grace for ever; and that, where once the wrath of God hath seized on any family, it doth not burn down and consume the whole before it; but he graciously stops its course, and gives not way to all his fury. And, in this, mercy glorifies itself against judgment; in that he showeth mercy unto *thousands*, but visiteth iniquity only unto the *third* and *fourth* generation.

THE THIRD COMMANDMENT.

"Thou shalt not take the name of the Lord thy God in vain; for the Lord will not hold him guiltless that taketh his name in vain."

It is well known that all the precepts of the law respect either those duties which we owe immediately to God, or those which we owe immediately to man. The former constitute the First, the latter the Second Table.

The commands of the First Table are prescribed to regulate our worship of God; which is either internal and more spiritual, or external and more visible.

The internal worship of God, with the humblest veneration of our souls and most sincere affections of our hearts, is required in the First Commandment; as I have already shown.

The external, which we also entered upon in the Second, we are to consider still further here in the Third. And it consists of three parts: *Prostration* of the body; *profession* of the mouth; and the *observance of prefixed time*. Each of these hath a particular command to enjoin them. The first is required in the Second Commandment, of which I have spoken. The second, profession of the mouth, comes next to be considered. And to guide and regulate this, we have our rule prescribed in this third precept of this table: *Thou shalt not take the name of the Lord thy God in vain*, &c.

In these words we have both a *prohibition*, " Thou shalt not take," &c. and *a commination* or *threatening*, " For the Lord will not hold him guiltless," &c.

In the prohibition two things are to be inquired into : What is meant by the *name of God*, and what it is to *take God's name in vain.* Let us first inquire,

What is meant by the NAME of God. This hath sundry acceptations in the Scripture.

Sometimes it is taken for *the nature and being of the Deity itself.* Nor is it an unusual figure to put *name* for the thing or person that is expressed by it. As, Rev. 3 : 4, " Thou hast a few names even in Sardis, that have not defiled their garments, and they shall walk with me in white :" that is, thou hast a few persons in Sardis. So, likewise, we may observe it to be frequently used when the Scriptur speaks of God and Christ. Psalm 20 : 1, " The name of the God of Jacob defend thee :" that is, let the God of Jacob himself, who is the only true and almighty potentate, be thy shield and thy defence. Psalm 135 : 3, " Sing praises unto his name :" that is, offer your returns of thanks and praises unto that God from whom you have received your mercies and salvation. So, Psalm 115 : 1, " Not unto us, O Lord, not unto us, but unto thy name give glory :" that is, let the glory which is due unto thee be entirely ascribed unto thyself. And so concerning Christ, Luke, 24 : 47, " Repentance and remission of sins are to be preached to all nations in his name : that is, through him ; and John, 1 : 12, " He gave power to become the sons of God, to as many as believed in his name :" that is, to as many as believed in him. And thus it is used in innumerable places.

Again: Sometimes the name of God is taken for *the whole system of divine and heavenly doctrine revealed to us in the Scriptures.*

Thus the Psalmist, "I will declare thy name unto my brethren," Psalm 22 : 22, which the Apostle cites as spoken in the person of Christ, Heb. 2 : 12; and the meaning is, that Christ should declare and make known to the world a true spiritual doctrine and way of worship, and teach them a religion which should both perfect their reason and save their souls. And, as a testimony of the accomplishment of this prophecy, our Savior himself tells us, John, 17 : 6, "I have manifested thy name unto the men which thou gavest me." And ver. 26, "I have declared unto them thy name, and will declare it:" that is, I have instructed them in the true religion and right worship of the great God. And so it is taken likewise, Micah, 4 : 5, "All people will walk every one in the name of his god; and we will walk in the name of the Lord our God for ever and ever:" that is, we will walk in that way of worship and religion which is appointed and approved by the Lord our God.

And once more: The name of God is taken for *that whereby God is called, and by which his nature and perfections are made known to men.*

For names are imposed to this very intent, that they might declare what the thing is to which the name belongs. Thus, when God had created Adam and made him the lord of this visible world, he caused the beasts of the field and the fowls of the air to pass before him, both to do homage to their new sovereign and likewise to receive names from him; which, according to the perfection of his knowledge, did then aptly serve to express their several natures, and were not only names but definitions too. And so, when we read of the names of God in Scripture, they all signify some expressions of his infinite essence, in which he is pleased to spell out himself unto us, sometimes by one perfection and sometimes by another.

Now these names of God are either his *titles* or his *attributes*, concerning which I have formerly treated at large in expounding the first petition of the Lord's prayer, *Hallowed be thy name;* and therefore I shall here only mention them, and so proceed.

1. His *titles* are his name.

And these are some of them absolute: as those glorious titles of JAH, JEHOVAH, GOD, I AM. I AM *hath sent thee,* saith God to Moses. And these are names altogether incomprehensible and stupendous.

Others are relative, and have respect to us. So his name of *Creator* denotes his infinite power in giving being to all things. *Lord* and *King* signify his dominion and authority in disposing and governing all that he hath made. *Father* signifies his care and goodness in providing for us his offspring: *Redeemer*, his mercy in delivering us from temporal evils and calamities, but especially from eternal death and destruction.

These, and other such-like titles, God assumes to himself, to express in some measure, as we are able to bear, what he is in himself.

2. His *attributes* also are his name.

Some of these are incommunicable; as his eternity, immensity, immutability, simplicity, &c. which are so proper to the divine nature that they belong to no created being.

Others are communicable: as his mercy, goodness, holiness and truth. These are communicable, because some rays of them may be found in created beings: but yet, in the infinite degree and excellency which they have in God, they are incommunicable, and proper only to the Deity. Therefore, though angels or men may be said to be holy, or just, or good, yet none of them are so originally: none are so, infinitely and unchangeably; none are so, simply and in the abstract, but only God himself.

These then are the NAMES OF GOD. And here in the text, *Thou shalt not take the name of the Lord thy God in vain*, we must understand it concerning the name of God in this last acceptation; that is, for any name of his whereby he is pleased to reveal himself unto us, whether it appertain to his titles or to his attributes: neither of these must be taken in vain.

But we must now consider what it is to TAKE THE NAME OF GOD IN VAIN. And, first, to *take* the name of God is no other than briefly to make use of it either as the object of our thoughts or the subject of our discourse. And so we find this phrase used, Psalm 16 : 4, "I will not take up their names into my lips." And Psalm 50 : 16, " What hast thou to do—that thou shouldst take my covenant in thy mouth?" that is, that thou shouldst speak, or make mention of it. So that, to *take* God's name, is to *speak* or *mention* it.

And now, as to *taking God's name in vain*, we do so when we use it without propounding to ourselves a due end; or without due consideration and reverence; or in an undue and unlawful action.

I. WHEN WE USE IT WITHOUT PROPOUNDING TO OURSELVES A DUE END.

The end characterizes the action: if the end be vain, the action must be so too. There are but two ends that can justify and warrant the use of any of God's names—either his titles or his attributes—and they are, *the glory of God*, and *the edification of ourselves and others*. Whatsoever is besides these is light and frivolous, and can be no good ground to us to make any mention of his great and terrible name, which is so full of glory and majesty, that it should never be uttered but where the subject of our discourse is serious and weighty.

I will not now speak of those who vend the holy and reverend name of God with oaths and blasphemies; a sin by so much the more heinous and abominable, by how much less temptation there is to it, either of pleasure or profit. This is *an iniquity to be punished by the judge*. And, would to God laws were put in severe execution to cramp the black tongues of all such profane wretches, whose number so abounds and swarms that we can no where walk the streets without being assaulted with whole volleys of oaths and curses.

But for others who are of more blameless conversation, may it not be observed how their discourse and familiar tattle are filled up with the name of *God* and *Lord?* I beseech you, consider what end do you propound to your selves in thus using the great and terrible name of God? Are all your discourses so serious as to bear the burden of that great name? Are they all immediately directed to the advancement of his glory? Or do they all promote the benefit and welfare of those who hear them? If so, then indeed the name of God can never be more seasonably used. But if you make the name of the highest Lord serve only to express some small wonderment, or that of the great God only an expletive to fill up a gap in your speeches, certainly these are such low and mean ends that God will not hold thee guiltless. He accounts himself contemned when you mention his name to such idle purposes, and will revenge the dishonor that you do him by it.

II. The name of God is taken in vain, WHEN WE USE IT WITHOUT DUE CONSIDERATION AND REVERENCE.

Whensoever we make mention of him we ought seriously to ponder his infinite greatness and glory, and to bow our hearts in the deepest prostration before that name to which all the powers in heaven and earth bow down with most humble veneration.

But is it possible for those who speak of God promiscuously and at random, is it possible that they should utter his name with reverence, when all the rest of the discourse is nothing but froth and levity? Nay, if they be reproved for it, will they not allege for their excuse that which is their very sin, that they did not consider it? And what! will you dare to bolt out the great name of the great God *without considering it?* Is that a name to be sported with and to be tossed to and fro upon every light and vain tongue? The tongue of man is called his *glory*, Psalm 57:8, "Awake up, my glory." And shall the *glory* of man be the *dishonor* of God? Shall that, which was created to be a principal instrument of magnifying and exalting God's name, run it over without affection or reverence?

Those things which we most of all contemn and de

spise we use as by-words, and lay no great stress nor sense upon them. And truly when we speak of God, without considering how great, how glorious and excellent a being he is—how holy, just and powerful—we do but make him a by-word; which is the highest contempt and indignity that can be cast upon him.

And therefore the best means that can be used to secure us from the wicked habit many have of taking God's name in vain, is seriously to consider whose name it is, even the name of the great God, who is present with thee, and hears thee pronounce it; that God, to whom the greatest and most glorious things compared, are base and vile nothings; that God, who is jealous of his honor and will dreadfully revenge himself upon the contemners of it. And if thou hast but wrought these considerations into thy heart, and habituated them to thy thoughts, thou wilt for ever be afraid to speak of his majesty vainly and irreverently.

III. The name of God is taken in vain, WHEN WE USE IT TO AN UNDUE AND UNLAWFUL END; especially when it is brought to confirm a falsehood, either in perjury or heresy; which is a most horrid impiety.

Therefore it is observed that the same word which is here rendered *vain*, signifies also *false* or *deceitful*. So that this precept, *Thou shalt not take the name of the Lord thy God in vain*, may be rendered also, *Thou shalt not take the name of the Lord thy God in falsehood*. Not that this is the only unlawful way of using it, but that this is the chief and most notorious abusing of it. And indeed what greater sin can there be than to bring God to be a witness to our lie? to make him, who is truth itself, attest that which is falsehood and deceit? Therefore Agur prays against pinching poverty as well as superfluous riches: "Lest," saith he, "I be poor, and steal, and take the name of my God in vain." Prov. 30 : 9. That is, lest poverty compel me to steal, and fear of shame or punishment tempt me to swear by the name of the great God that I have not done it. This indeed is to take God's name in vain in the worst and highest sense.

Suffer me now to close this part of our subject with some *practical application* to your consciences.

1. Let your minds be *convinced of the greatness and heinousness of this sin, and be deeply humbled that you have been guilty of it.*

I well know that the commonness not only of God's mercies towards us, but of our sins against him, takes off much from our observation, and abates them both in our estimate. And because this is so common a sin, our ears are so beaten to it that we too little regard it. Possibly, should we hear a devil incarnate belch out some direful oath, we should start and tremble at it; but when we hear the name of the great God, and our only Lord, slip along in some trifling and impertinent discourse, this perhaps we take no notice of, and the commonness of the sin hath almost stifled all reproofs.

I beseech you, therefore, to consider,

1. *That we are not to weigh sins by the opinion of men, but by the censure and sentence of God.*

He hath no more allowed you to take his name in vain, than he hath to blaspheme it. The irreverent using of it is as expressly forbidden, as the abjuring and cursing of it. And when the law of God hath not given us liberty, it is most intolerable presumption that we should dare to take liberties ourselves.

2. Consider, also, thou that sportest away the name of God in thy ordinary prattle, *what wilt thou have to rely upon in thy greatest distresses?*

The Wise Man tells us, "The name of the Lord is a strong tower; the righteous runneth unto it, and is saved." Prov. 18:10. But, alas, what comfort canst thou find in the name of God in thy greatest necessities, since it is the same name that thou hast used and worn out before in the meanest and most trivial concerns? Thou hast already talked away the strength and virtue of it, and wilt hardly find more support from it in thy tribulation than thou gavest reverence to it in thy conversation. Let us then be more cautious than to spend so excellent a remedy against all fears, and sorrows, and afflictions, vainly and unprofitably. "Thy name," saith the spouse, "is as ointment poured forth." Cant. 1:3. But certainly, if, upon every slight occasion, we break the box and expose the name of God to common air, it will in time lose its fragrance and virtue; and when we have most need of it, we shall find no refreshment, no comfort in it.

3. This common and irreverent using of the name of God *will insensibly overspread us with a spirit of profaneness.* We shall by degrees arrive to a plain contempt of God, when we thus hourly and unnecessarily take his name into our mouths.

For what else is this, but to make ourselves rude and familiar with that infinite Majesty, towards whom the profoundest testimonies of respect and reverence must fall infinitely short of expressing our due distance? But by using his name vulgarly and promiscuously, what do we else but make it our sport, and blow it up and down with every idle breath, as children do bubbles in the air?

4. Again: *canst thou, in duty, easily compose thyself to reverence the holy and dreadful name of God*, when thou hast thus accustomed thyself to name him without any veneration or respect in thy common discourse?

Certainly it is the hardest thing imaginable to make the heart fall down prostrate before that God whom thou invokest in prayer, when once thou art used to invoke him slightly in thy ordinary converse.

Let me therefore beseech you, reader, as you regard his glory, of which he is jealous, that whensoever you speak of God, or but mention his name, you will do it with a holy awe and dread of his Divine Majesty; that you will seriously consider that that name, to which every knee bows, both of things in heaven, and things on earth, and things under the earth, whether they be angels or devils, requires from you more respect and honor than to be idly blurted out with every rash and foolish expression.

And you who are masters of families and have children and servants committed to your care, beware that, if they are addicted to it, you stop this growing sin in them betimes. It is the sin and shame of parents that they suffer little ones to lisp the name of God irreverently, and to learn the first syllables and rudiments of oaths and curses before they can well speak: whereby they lay a deep foundation for their future impiety, and thereby bring the guilt of the next generation upon us, who, by indulging them in these young sins, do but introduce those habits of wickedness in them which perhaps can never afterwards be rooted out.

IV. But there is also another kind of taking the name of God in vain, and that is in our DUTIES and HOLY PERFORMANCES.

One way this is done, is *when in our prayers we ask those things of God which are unlawful or unwarrantable.* As when we pray on the behalf of our lusts, to obtain provision to fulfil them: "Ye ask amiss, that ye may consume it upon your lusts." James, 4 : 3. When we pray out of envy, malice and revenge, that God would make himself a party in our unreasonable and angry quarrels; such prayers as these are vain; for what we thus desire either shall not be granted unto us, or, if it be, shall be granted unto us in wrath.

Another way is, *when we perform holy duties slightly and without affection:* whenever we do this we then likewise take the name of God in vain. Therefore, all hypocritical services, all heartless repetitions are vain, and God's name is not sanctified but abused in them. For, whatever we do in such a manner as we may be certain God will not accept it, is done in vain. God will accept of no performance which is not accompanied with the heart, and filled with most devout affections; and therefore they are performed in vain, and to no other effect but to increase our guilt and our condemnation. Such invocations are but scoffings of God; and all the motions of our lips, without the correspondent motion of our hearts, is no better than making mouths at God.

V. Beware also especially of another kind of profaning the name of God and taking it in vain, which is of a far higher and more heinous nature; and that is, by UNLAWFUL OATHS AND EXECRATIONS.

An oath, in the general, is a confirmation of our speeches, by calling in God to witness and attest the truth of them; called therefore by Tully, *a religious affirmation* De Offic. 1. iii. It is of two kinds, *assertory* and *promissory:* the former, when we assert that such a thing either hath been or is, the latter, when we engage that for the future it shall be, and be performed by us, which oath we do sufficiently and with a good conscience keep, if we use our utmost endeavors to accomplish what we have thus sworn, although the effect may be impeded by many invincible obstacles intervening.

Now because an unjustifiable scrupulousness hath seized on some persons, who think that every oath is unlawful, and the taking of the holy and reverent name of God in vain, and so a violation of this commandment; I shall therefore briefly allude to that much controverted question, *Whether at any time or in any circumstances it be lawful for a christian to assume the name of God in an oath;* and then I shall proceed to show *what oaths are unlawful and execrable sins.*

For the *first*, I assert,

1. That *an oath is so far from being always sinful, that it is sometimes a duty, yea, an act of religion and part of the service and worship of God;* and, therefore, not only lawful but necessary.

This we find, Deut. 6 : 13, " Thou shalt fear the Lord thy God, and serve him, and shalt swear by his name." Yea, the psalmist mentions it as a matter of exultation, as if some notable service were done by it unto God: " Every one that sweareth by him shall glory." Psalm 63 : 11. And if we consult the approved examples of holy men in Scripture, we shall frequently find them either ex acting oaths from others, or else themselves invoking the testimony of the most high God to confirm the truth of what they speak. The places are too numerous to be cited, and too well known to need it.

But because the great objection against these is, that they are only authorities produced out of the Old Testament, and we are now obliged by the precepts of a superior Lawgiver, the Lord Jesus Christ; therefore I say in answer, that the objection argues too great a vilifying and contempt of those sacred oracles which were given to the church by the hand of Moses; and that things of a moral nature, as an oath is, cannot in one age of the world be a duty, and in another a sin, when it is attended with the same circumstances.

And yet further, for their satisfaction, let us see what is spoken concerning oaths in the New Testament, or in the Old relating to it. In the Old we have a prophecy of what should be hereafter in the times of the Gospel: Isa. 45 : 23, "I have sworn by myself, the word is gone out of my mouth in righteousness, and shall not return, That unto me every knee shall bow, and every tongue shall swear." And again, Jer. 12 : 16, "And it shall come to pass, if they will diligently learn the ways of my people, to swear by my name—then shall they be built in the midst of my people." But yet, if neither of these will suffice, let us see some more immediate confirmation of this out of the New Testament itself. We find St. Paul himself more that once attesting the truth of those grave and weighty matters which he delivers in his Epistles, by calling God to witness, which is the very form and nature of an oath: so 2 Cor. 1 : 23, "I call God for a record upon my soul, that, to spare you I came not as yet unto Corinth;" and so again, Phil. 1 : 8, "God is my record, how greatly I long after you all;" and what other than a kind of oath is that vehement asseveration of the same Apostle, 1 Cor. 15 : 31, "I protest by your rejoicing, which I have in Christ Jesus, I die daily." And again, Rom. 9 : 1, " I say the truth in Christ, I lie not." And if you would yet have an example somewhat more perfect, we may see it in the practice of a holy angel: Rev. 10 : 5, 6, " The angel stood upon the sea and upon the earth, and lifted up his hand to heaven, and sware by Him that liveth for ever and ever, who created heaven— and the earth, and the things in them—that there should be time no longer." So that you do abundantly see, by all these instances, that it is not simply and universally unlawful to assume the holy name of God in an oath, and to call him in to be a witness to the truth of what we affirm.

The grand objection that lies against this, is taken from two places of Scripture. One is, Matt. 5 : 34–37, " But I say unto you, swear not at all : neither by heaven, for it is God's throne, nor by the earth, for it is his footstool: neither by Jerusalem, for it is the city of the great King. Neither shalt thou swear by thy head, because thou canst not make one hair white or black. But let your communication be, yea, yea; and nay, nay: for whatsoever is more than these, cometh of evil." Can any thing be more express against all manner of oaths than this; where we have a cautious enumeration of many of them which were most vulgar and common ?

The other place is James, 5 : 12. " But above all things, my brethren, swear not ; neither by heaven, neither by the earth, neither by any other oath; but let your yea be yea, and your nay nay, lest ye fall into condemnation." Can any thing be more express, or more commanding than this, "above all things, my brethren?" and, "lest you fall into condemnation?"

But, for answer to this, we must know that our Savior and his Apostle do not here simply and absolutely condemn all oaths, but only that common and profuse swearing which the scribes and pharisees taught corruptly to be no sin. For in this point of oaths they had divulged among the people three false traditions.

One was, that it was lawful for them to swear commonly, and without restraint, by any creature. Another was, that there was no binding oath wherein the name of God was not expressly used; and therefore, though they should swear by creatures, yet they were not perjured, although they should not perform what they thus uttered, except some few cases, wherein interest made them conscientious. This we have, Matt. 23 : 16, 18, "Wo unto you, ye blind guides! which say, whosoever shall swear by the temple, it is nothing. And whosoever shall swear by the altar, it is nothing." That is, they taught that such an oath was not obligatory, because it was only by creatures. And yet, even here, they excepted such oaths as were conceived and uttered by the gold of the temple, or the gifts on the altar, out of a politic covetousness, that by so great a reverence shown to the gifts that were offered the people might be induced to offer more freely, and by that means their share of them might be the larger.

A third false doctrine that they taught was, that common swearing was no sin, although it were by the great God, if what they sware were true. And by this they gave scope and liberty to confirm all that they said with an oath, if they only took care to utter nothing that was false.

Against these three corrupt traditions are our Savior's and the apostle's words directed.

(1.) For it is perjury to violate an oath conceived by creatures, and that because of the near relation that all creatures have to God, the great Creator. This reason our Savior mentions in the fore-named place: "Swear not— by heaven, for it is God's throne; nor by the earth, for it is his footstool; nor by Jerusalem, for it is the city of the great King." And, more expressly, Matt. 23 : 21, 22, "He that shall swear by heaven, sweareth by the throne of God, and by him that sitteth thereon," even as he who "shall swear by the temple, sweareth by it, and by him that dwelleth therein." And so, by the same proportion of reason, whoever shall swear by any creature doth also virtually swear by the Almighty Creator of it; and therefore it is as much perjury to falsify an oath made by any creature as if it were made by the great God himself; because creatures are all of and from God. And,

(2.) Although it be perjury to falsify an oath taken by any creature, yet it is a sin likewise, and utterly unlawful, to make any such oath, insomuch as it is an idolatrous ascribing of religious worship unto the creature which is due to God only. And in this sense, especially, I understand these words of our Savior, *Swear not at all;* that is, not *by any creature.* And this, the following enumeration of *heaven,* and *earth,* and *Jerusalem,* and their *head,* which were the usual forms of their oaths, and by which our Savior forbids them to swear, doth clearly prove to be his true meaning.

(3.) These places teach that it is a sin to swear at any time, or by any thing, although the great God himself, unnecessarily and arbitrarily: therefore swear not at all unless some just reason and cogent necessity constrain you to call in so great a testimony to confirm the truth of what you speak; for common and daily swearing is a high contempt and irreverence shown to the majesty of that God whom we bring in to attest to every trifle and frivolous thing we utter.

And this I take to be the true sense and meaning of these places of Scripture; and that they do not simply and absolutely condemn all manner of oaths, but the corrupt doctrine of the scribes and pharisees, and the corrupt practice of their disciples, who thought it no sin to swear familiarly if they did not swear falsely. So that the meaning of *Swear not at all*, is, swear not unnecessarily and voluntarily.

2. To make an oath lawful it must have these three qualifications mentioned by the prophet, Jer. 4 : 2. " Thou shalt swear, The Lord liveth, *in truth, in judgment, and in righteousness.*"

A warrantable oath must be accompanied with *truth*. For it is taken in the name of the God of truth. Isaiah, 69 : 15. *He that sweareth in the earth shall swear by the God of truth.* Therefore it behoves him to consider whether what he deposeth be truth or not. Yea, moreover, we must be fully certain that the thing is as we attest it; for a man may be guilty of perjury in swearing that which is true, if he either believe it otherwise, or be doubtful of it. Hence he that is called to give his oath must look to these two things: that *his words agree with his mind*, and that *the thing agrees with his words*. He who fails in the second is a *false swearer:* he who fails in the first is a *forswearer;* and in both is a perjured person.

A lawful oath must be taken in *judgment;* discreetly and deliberately; advising and pondering with ourselves before we swear. And here we must consider both the *matter*, whether that be right and good; and the *ends*, whether they are duly propounded by us. Now there are but two ends that can warrant an oath: one is the benefit of ourselves or others, the other is the glory of God. And whosoever shall swear without a due consideration of these ends, and a holy and sincere desire to accomplish them by his oath, he swears rashly and unwarrantably.

A lawful oath must be taken in *righteousness* and *justice.* Hence it is very wicked to bind ourselves by an oath or vow to do things that are either impossible or sinful.

1. The matter of a just oath ought to be *possible.* Thus we see how cautious Abraham's servant was when his master made him swear to take a wife for his son Isaac of his kindred, Gen. 24 : 5. *Peradventure the woman will not be willing to follow me unto this land.* And so should we, in all our promissory oaths, caution and limit them with those reasonable exceptions, of as far as we know, and can lawfully endeavor.

2. The matter of a just oath must be not only possible but *lawful* and *honest* too. For if it be unlawful we are necessarily ensnared in sin: for either we must violate God's command or our own oath. Thus it was a most wicked oath in the Jews who combined together against Paul, and bound themselves under a curse that they would neither eat nor drink till they had killed him. And so every oath which engageth men to sedition, disturbance of government, and rebellion, is in itself an unlawful oath, and obligeth them to nothing but to repent of it and renounce it.

According to these three qualifications therefore must every oath be regulated, else it is not a lawful oath, but a horrid contempt of God and taking of his name in vain.

But, to speak no more concerning lawful oaths, let us now consider those which are but too common among us: I mean *unlawful and sinful oaths.*

Two things make an oath unlawful: *falsehood* and *rashness.*

1. When it is *falsehood.*

This, indeed, is a most desperate sin, to vouch a lie upon God's credit, and to father a falsehood upon him who is the God of truth, yea, truth itself. This manifests the highest contempt of God, when we call him to witness that which the devil prompted us to speak. Should not we ourselves take it for a high affront and indignity, to be made vouchers of other men's lies to put off their falsehoods? How much more, then, is it a most hellish wickedness committed against the great God, to assert a known lie and then call in God to attest it for a truth! which is no other but to father a brat of the devil, who is a liar and the father of lies, upon God, who hates liars, and hath appointed severe torments for them. See how dreadfully God is incensed by this sin, Jer. 7 : 9, 15, 16, where he speaks of it as almost an unpardonable offence: " Will ye steal, and murder—and swear falsely? Therefore I will cast you out of my sight, as I cast out your brethren. Pray not thou for this people; neither lift up a cry nor prayer for them; neither make intercession to me, for I will not hear thee." And so, Zech. 5 : 4, speaking of the curse that should go forth over the face of the whole earth : " I will bring it forth, saith the Lord of Hosts, and it shall enter into the house of the thief, and into the house of him that sweareth falsely by my name; and it shall remain in the midst of his house, and it shall consume it, with the timber thereof, and with the stones thereof."

2. As false swearing is a notorious profaning of the name of God, so likewise is *rash swearing* in our common and ordinary discourse.

This is a sin that greatly abounds and prevails, and often we may see the very soot of hell hang about men's lips. Nay, this is the sin not only of more lewd and profligate wretches, who mouth their oaths with sound and cadence; but of those, too, who would be thought to be of better character. And indeed all oaths which are conceived by any other thing besides the great God, how modest soever they may be in their sound, yet are more impious in effect than those louder ones which immediately call God himself to witness; and therefore the prophet speaks of it as a most heinous and almost unpardonable sin, Jer. 5 : 7, " How shall I pardon thee for this? Thy children have forsaken me, and sworn by them that are no gods." For since an oath is sacred, and a part of divine worship, those that swear by any created thing, as their *faith*, and *truth*, and *conscience*, are guilty not only of vain swearing, but of idolatry too.

But some will say, *What so great evil can there be in an oath so long as it is truth which they assert by it?* This I know is the common reply and excuse of those who are guilty of this sin and reproved for it. To this I answer,

1. Although what they speak may be true, yet it is a most provoking sin so far to debase the holy and reverend name of God as to bring it to attest every trivial and im-

pertinent thing they utter; and if they swear by any creature, it is by so much the worse. No oath is in itself simply good and voluntarily to be used, but only as medicines are, in case of necessity. But to use oaths ordinarily and indifferently without being constrained by any cogent necessity, or called to it by any lawful authority, is such a sin as wears off all reverence and dread of the great God; and we have very great cause to suspect that where his name is so much upon the tongue there his fear is but little in the heart.

2. Though thou swearest what is true, yet customary swearing to truths will insensibly bring thee to swear falsehoods. For when once thou art habituated to it, an oath will be more ready to thee than a truth; and so when thou rashly boltest out somewhat that is either doubtful or false, thou wilt seal it up and confirm it with an oath before thou hast had time to consider what thou hast said or what thou art swearing; for those who accustom themselves to this vice lose the observation of it in the frequency; and if you reprove them for swearing, they will be ready to swear again that they did not swear. And therefore it is well observed by Augustine, "We ought to forbear swearing that which is truth, for by the custom of swearing men oftentimes fall into perjury, and are always in danger of it."

But now further to *dehort you from this sin of common swearing*, consider,

1. *It is a sin which hath very little or no temptation to commit it.*

The two great baits by which the devil allures men to wickedness, are profit and pleasure.

But this common rash swearing is the *most unprofitable, barren sin in the world*. What fruits brings it forth, but only the abhorrence and detestation of all serious persons, and the tremendous judgment of God? The swearer gains nothing by it at present, but only the reputation of being a devil incarnate; and, for the future, his gains shall be only the torments of those devils and damned spirits whose language he hath learned and speaks. He that sows the wind of an oath, shall reap the whirlwind of God's fury.

Again: what *pleasure* is there in it? Which of his senses doth it please and gratify? "Were I an epicure," saith one, "I would hate swearing." Were men resolved to give themselves up to all manner of sensual delights, yet there is so little that can be strained from this common sin, that certainly unless they intend to do the devil a pleasure rather than themselves, they would never set their black mouths against heaven, nor blaspheme the great God who sits enthroned there.

Ask them why they indulge themselves in such a provoking sin: some cannot forbear *out of mere custom;* and others are pleased with the *lofty sound* and *genteel phrase* of an oath, and count it a special grace and ornament of speaking. And, what! Are these temptations? Are these such strong and mighty provocations that you cannot forbear? Shall the holy name of the great God be torn in pieces by you, only to patch and fill up the rents of your idle talk? If this be the motive and inducement that makes you commit so great a sin, as commonly there is no other, know that you perish as fools perish, and sell your souls to damnation and eternal perdition for very nothing.

Others, perhaps, will plead for their excuse, that they never use to swear but when they are *vexed* and *put into a passion*. But what a madness is this, when men anger thee, to strike at God, and to provoke him far more than others can provoke thee! If thou art never so highly incensed, why shouldst thou throw thy poisonous foam in God's face? Hast thou no other way of venting thy passion, but to fly in God's face and to revenge thyself on him when men have injured thee? Certainly thy passion can be no more a temptation to do this, than it would be to stab thy father because thine enemy hath struck thee.

2. *It is a most foolish sin*, because it contradicts the very end for which they commit it.

The common swearer perhaps thinks that he shall be much the sooner believed for his oaths; whereas, with all serious and judicious persons, there is nothing that doth more lighten the credit of his speeches than his rash binding and confirming the truth of them by swearing. For what reason have I to think that man speaks truth who doth so far suspect himself as to think what he relates is not credible unless he swear to it; and certainly, he that owes God no more respect than to violate the sanctity and reverence of his name upon every trifling occasion, cannot easily be thought to owe the truth so much respect as not to violate it; especially considering that there are far stronger temptations unto lying than unto swearing.

3. *Consider that the devil is the author and father, not of lying only, but of swearing also.* "Let your yea be yea, and your nay, nay," saith our Savior; "for whatsoever is more than these, cometh of evil," Mat. 5 : 37, *ek tou ponerou esti*, that is, cometh of the evil one, who is still

prompting the swearer and putting oaths upon the tip of his tongue.

And now to conclude this subject, I shall give you some *rules and directions*, by the observance of which you may avoid this too common sin.

1. *Beware of the first rudiments and beginnings of oaths.*
And such are a company of idle words frequently used in the mouths of many, which formerly were bloody oaths, but are now worn to rags and disguised into imperfect sounds and nonsense. Few that speak them know what they mean; but if they did, certainly they would tremble at such execrable words that hide and dissemble the most horrid oaths that can be uttered: some of them being blasphemous, as those that are conceived by the limbs of God; and others being idolatrous, as those which are conceived by creatures; as in that ordinary by-word of " Marry," which is no less than swearing by the Virgin Mary. And it is a notable artifice of the devil to bring such foolish and masked words into common use, that both they may swear that use them, although they know it not, and that, by using themselves to unknown oaths, they may be brought in time to take up those that are known.

So also all vehement asseverations have in them somewhat of the nature and are dangerous beginnings of oaths; and those who accustom themselves to them will in time think them not forcible enough to confirm their speeches, and so be brought to attest them by oaths. Make nothing, therefore, the pawn and pledge of a truth, but speak it out simply and nakedly as it is in itself; and this will sooner conciliate belief than the most strong and binding asseverations that thou canst invent. This sin of swearing is strangely growing and thriving; for, by a customary using of asseverations, we shall insensibly upon every occasion be tripping upon an oath; and a custom of swearing will at length bring in perjury; and a custom of perjury, blasphemy; and make them deny that God by whom they have so often forsworn themselves, and yet gone unpunished. Beware, therefore, that you allow not yourselves any form of asseveration; but *let your yea be yea, and your nay, nay:* proceed no further, for Christ hath allowed you no more.

2. *Subdue, as much as you can, all inordinate passion and anger.*

For anger is, usually, the cause and provocation of oaths and blasphemies. Anger is a fire in the heart; and swearing is the smoke of this fire, that breaks forth at the mouth; and those who are violently hurried with this passion usually find nothing so ready at hand as an oath; which, if they cannot be revenged on him whom they conceit to have done them the injury, they fling against heaven itself, and thereby seem to take an impious revenge upon the Almighty God.

3. *Labor to possess thy heart, and overawe it with the most serious considerations and apprehensions of the greatness and majesty of God.*

This will be a good preservative to keep thee from abusing and profaning his name in common and rash swearing. Is he the great and terrible God of heaven and earth? and shall I put such indignity upon him as to call him from his throne to witness every vanity and trifle that I utter? Would I serve any mortal man so, whom I respect? or would not he account it an affront and injury done him? How much more, then, will the great God be provoked, who is so great and glorious that it tires the conceptions of angels to apprehend his majesty! How much more will he be provoked to have his name, which he hath commanded to be sacred and reverend, daily rubbed and worn out between those lips that talk so many light, foolish and impertinent vanities!

There are several other violations of this Third Commandment: as *blasphemy, rash vows, unnecessary lots,* &c. which being chiefly to be condemned upon the same account as swearing and a vain irreverent invoking the name of God, I shall not here treat of particularly, but leave the sin and guilt of them to be estimated in connection with a due consideration of the several circumstances that attend them. Indeed the great positive duty required in this command, is, the reverencing and sanctifying the name of God whensoever we make mention of him, or of any thing that relates unto him. But because I have in a former treatise* spoken concerning that subject, I shall therefore wave it at present, and here close the exposition of this Third Commandment.

---

* On the Second Petition of the **Lord's Prayer**

THE FOURTH COMMANDMENT.

"**Remember the Sabbath-day, to keep it holy. Six days shalt thou labor, and do all thy work. But the seventh day is the Sabbath of the Lord thy God: in it thou shalt not do any work, thou, nor thy son, nor thy daughter, nor thy man-servant, nor thy maid-servant, nor thy stranger that is within thy gates. For in six days the Lord made heaven and earth, the sea, and all that in them is, and rested the seventh day: wherefore the Lord blessed the Sabbath-day, and hallowed it.**"

We are now arrived to the Fourth and last Commandment of the First Table, and with the exposition of this I shall finish the consideration of those duties which immediately concern the worship and service of God.

We have already observed, as a great deal of wisdom and excellency in the matter of each command, so a great deal of heavenly art in the method and digestion of them. And, upon serious reflection on both, we may very well conclude that they are as well the contrivance of the divine understanding as the engraving of his finger.

The first requires that which is first and principally to be regarded, the inward veneration of the true God, in the dearest love and highest esteem and choicest affections of a pious soul.

The second enjoins the external expression of this reverence, in the prostration of the body and other acts of visible worship. For although God chiefly regards the heart and the frame and disposition of the inward man, yet he neglects not to observe the due composure of the body as a testimony of the soul's sincerity.

And as this requires us to honor the majesty of God in

our gestures, so the third requires us to glorify the holy and reverend name of God in all our speeches and discourses: never to make mention of it but with that prepossession of holy awe and dread that might compose us into all possible gravity and seriousness.

And because every thing is beautiful in its season, therefore we have subjoined to all these a particular command concerning the time wherein God prescribes all these to be more especially tendered unto him. And this is the precept which we have now under consideration: REMEMBER THE SABBATH-DAY, TO KEEP IT HOLY.

In these words we have a *command*, and the *enforcement* of it.

The *command* is, to *sanctify* the Sabbath. And here this is justly observable: that, whereas all the rest are simply either positive or negative, this is both. *Remember to keep it holy:* and, *in it thou shalt not do any work.* As if God took an especial care to fence us in on all sides to the observance of this precept.

The *enforcement* also is more particular, and with greater care and instance than we find in any other command. For God hath here condescended to use three cogent arguments to press the observance of this law upon us.

The first is taken from his own example, whom certainly it is our glory as well as our duty to imitate in all things in which he hath propounded himself to be our pattern: *The Lord rested the seventh day*, and therefore rest ye also.

The second, from that bountiful and liberal portion of time that he hath allowed us for the affairs and business of this present life: *Six days shalt thou labor, and do all thy work;* and therefore it is but fit and equitable that the seventh should be given to God, who hath so freely given the rest to thee.

The third, from the dedication of this day to his own immediate worship and service: *The Lord blessed the Sabbath-day, and hallowed it.* So that it is no less a sin than sacrilege, and stealing of that which is holy, to purloin any part of that time which God hath thus consecrated to himself, and to employ it about either sinful or secular actions.

I shall begin with the COMMAND, REMEMBER THE SABBATH-DAY, TO KEEP IT HOLY.

The word *Sabbath* signifies *rest* and cessation from labor, and is applied to several things.

Thus it signifies the *temporal Sabbath*, or the recurring seventh day or year, which we are now treating of. And because this was the principal day of the week, therefore we find that the whole week is denominated from it a Sabbath. Luke, 10 : 12 ; Mat. 28 : 1.

It signifies also a *spiritual rest*, a rest from the slavery and drudgery of sin, and those sordid labors which the devil, our grievous taskmaster, exacts of us. And of this spiritual Sabbath the temporal one is a sign and type. So Exod. 31 : 13, "My Sabbaths ye shall keep; for it is a sign between me and you, that ye may know that I am the Lord that doth sanctify you."

Again: it is used likewise to signify the *eternal rest* of the blessed in heaven, where they rest from all their labors and from all their sorrows, in the full fruition of the ever-blessed God and of all blessedness in him. So the apostle, Heb. 4 : 9, "There remaineth a rest unto the people of God." The word is σαββατισμος, there remaineth *a Sabbath*, or *the celebration of a Sabbath*, unto the people of God.

It is only of the first of these, the *temporal Sabbath*, that I am now speaking.

And here neither shall I speak of the *Sabbath of years*, when the land was every seventh year to rest from the labor of tillage and husbandry, as we find, Lev. 25 : 4, " The seventh year shall be a Sabbath of rest unto the land;" nor yet of the greater *Sabbath of the jubilee*, observed every fiftieth year, at the period of seven sabbatical years, wherein all possessions and inheritances which had been sold or mortgaged were again to return to the first owners, which Sabbath you have described, Lev. 25 : 8, &c. But I shall only treat of the *Sabbath of days*, which this commandment doth principally respect.

And the general heads upon which I shall proceed are these four: its primitive institution; its morality and perpetual obligation; its change from the last to the first day of the week; and the manner how God hath required it to be sanctified by us.

I. *Its primitive institution.*

When the Sabbath was instituted there is some difference between learned men.

Some date it late, and refer its beginning to the promulgation of the law, or at farthest to the sending of manna to the Israelites. And they ground their assertion on this: that before that time we read not in all the history of the patriarchs and first ages of the world of any Sabbath that was observed and sanctified by the holy fathers who then lived, which doubtless they would not have neglected had any such command been given them.

Others, who I believe concur with the truth, date its original as high as the creation of the world; grounding their opinion upon that unanswerable testimony, Gen. 2: 2, 3, "On the seventh day God ended his work, which he had made; and God blessed the seventh day, and sanctified it." Now, that there cannot in these words be understood any prolepsis, or anticipation, declaring that as done then which was done many ages after, appears plainly, because God is said to sanctify the Sabbath then, when he rested: but he rested precisely on the seventh day after the creation; therefore that very seventh day did God sanctify, and made it the beginning of all ensuing Sabbaths. So that you see the Sabbath is but one day younger than man; ordained for him in the state of his uprightness and innocence, that his faculties being then holy and excellent, he might employ them, especially on that day, in the singular and most spiritual worship of God his Creator. And although we find no more mention of the Sabbath until Moses had conducted the children of Israel into the wilderness, which was about two thousand four hundred and fifty years after the creation; yet it is not to be supposed that among the people of God, who were very careful, as in observing the law of God themselves, so in delivering it likewise to their posterity, that the observance of this law or of this day utterly failed; but it was doubtless continued among those that feared God, till it was again invigorated with new authority by the promulgation of it from Mount Sinai—Thus much for the *institution*.

II. The MORALITY of the Sabbath. Concerning this there is a greater controversy, and of far greater moment.

Some loose spirits contend that it is wholly *ceremonial*, and so was utterly abolished at the coming of Christ; and therefore they will not be under the restriction of their liberty in observing any days or times. Others again make it wholly *moral;* and affirm that the observance of the very seventh day from the creation is a law of nature and of perpetual obligation; and therefore think themselves bound to keep the Jewish Sabbath.

That I may clearly state this obscure and difficult question, I shall only premise, that those things are said to be moral and of the law of nature which are in themselves rational and fit to be done, although there were no express command to enjoin them. So that where there is a great equity in the thing itself, enough to sway a rational and honest man to the doing of it, that is to be accounted moral and authorized by the law of nature. That is of positive right which is observed only because it is commanded, and hath no intrinsical goodness or reason in itself to commend it to our practice, but obligeth only upon the injunction and authority of another. As for instance: it is naturally good to obey our parents, to abstain from murder, theft, adultery, &c. to do to others as we would be content to be dealt with; these things we are obliged to by the very light of reason and the principles of nature, although there had been no written law of God to impose them. But then there were other things to which God obliged some of his people, that had nothing to commend them besides the authority of his command; and such were the various ceremonies under the law; yea, and in innocence itself, the prohibition given to Adam not to eat of the tree of the knowledge of good and evil. The former sort are moral and natural commands;

the latter positive and instituted. The former are commanded, because good; the latter are good, because commanded.

1. *Certain it is that a convenient portion of our time is due to the service and worship of God by natural and moral right.* For certainly it is but fit and just that he should have a large share of our life and time, who hath given us life and time here upon earth, and hath created us to this very end, that we might serve and glorify him. Yea, had it been propounded to ourselves how much we would have allowed for God, could we, without shame and blushing, have set apart less time for his service from whom we have all, than himself hath done? This I think is by all agreed to.

2. *The law of nature doth not dictate to us any particular stated days to be set apart for the worship of God, one more than another:* indeed there is no evident natural reason why this day more than that; why every *seventh* day rather than every sixth, or fifth, or fourth; for all days being in their own nature alike, reason can find no advantage to prefer one day before another. But that which is obligatory by the law of nature, ought to be plain and evident to all men, or else evidently deducible from some natural principles. Now, if we lay aside the positive command of God, there is no one day in itself better than another; and therefore there is a *memento* prefixed to the command, *Remember that thou keep holy the Sabbath-day*, which is not added to any other precept; intimating to us that the observance of a special day is not a dictate of nature, but only an imposition of God, which he requires us to remember and bear in mind.

3. *That the seventh day should be especially consecrated*

to *the service and worship of God is from his positive will and command,* and therefore is as binding and forcible as if it were a law of nature engraven on our hearts; unless the same authority alter it that did first enjoin it. For this being a positive law, is therefore good and necessary, because commanded. And if it had not been revealed to us, we should never have been obliged to this observance, nor made obnoxious to punishment for failing in it. Yet again,

4. *This declaration of the will of God concerning the sanctification of the Sabbath is attended with a moral reason;* and therefore is not merely and barely positive, as ceremonial laws are. The reason is, that God rested on the seventh day; and therefore we ought so to do. Now, although this reason carries not such a natural evidence in it as to have obliged us, unless it had been revealed; yet, being revealed, we may discern a certain aptitude and fitness in it to oblige us to the observance of the seventh day rather than any other; since piety and religion require that we should imitate God in those things wherein he would have us imitate him. So that I account this command to be *moral-positive: moral,* in that it requires a due portion of our time to be dedicated to the service and worship of God: *positive,* in that it prescribes the seventh day for that especial service which the light and law of nature did not prefix; and *mixed of both,* in that it gives a reason of this prescription, which hath somewhat of natural equity in it, but yet such as could not have been discovered without special and divine revelation.

Now, because the observance of a Sabbath hath thus much of morality and of the law of nature in it, it is most certain that we are bound to *keep a Sabbath* as much as the Jews were : although not to the circumstance of the duty. For,

(1.) *This command was obligatory, even in paradise it self,* in the state of innocency; and therefore contains nothing in it unworthy the state of a christian. It is no ceremonial command, nor to be reckoned amongst those things which were typical, and prefigured Christ to come in the flesh, and therefore, neither was it abolished at his coming; but still there lies a strict and indispensable obligation upon us to observe a Sabbath holy unto the Lord.

(2.) *The reasons of this command are all moral and perpetual;* and therefore such is the obligation of it to us christians. The equity is the same to us that it was to them; namely, that we should allow one day in seven to the worship of that God who so liberally allows us six for our ordinary affairs: the ease and refreshment of our bodies from the labors of our callings is as necesary as then it was; and we are still as much obliged with thankfulness to remember and meditate upon the great mercy of our creation as they were. And, therefore, if these were sufficient reasons why the Jews should observe a particular Sabbath, they are still as forcible and cogent with us. Again,

(3.) Our Savior, foretelling the destruction of Jerusalem, bids his disciples "*pray that their flight might not be in the winter, nor on the Sabbath-day.*" Mat. 24 : 20 And yet the destruction of that city happened about forty years after the death of Christ; and therefore, certainly those who were his disciples lay under an obligation of observing a Sabbath-day; because our Savior intimates that it would prove a heavy addition to their affliction if they should be forced to take their flight on the Sabbath, when they ought and desired to be employed in the spiritual exercise of devotion and holy duties proper to that day.

But although the sanctifying of a Sabbath be thus obligatory to christians, yet it is not the same Sabbath-day to the observance of which the Jews and the people of God, before Christ's coming into the world were bound. But it is, with good ground and upon good authority, changed from the last to the first day of the week; from Saturday to Sunday; called now *the Lord's day*, because it was that day of the week on which our Lord and Savior rose from the dead: in memory of which, and in a thankful acknowledgment of the great mercy of our redemption fully completed by his resurrection, the Sabbath has been translated to this day; and is now rightly celebrated on this day by all the churches of Christ throughout the world.

III. This CHANGE of the Sabbath is the third head which I promised to speak of.

As the first institution of the Sabbath was by divine authority; so likewise is the change of it. For as God rested from his labor on the last day of the week; so Christ rested from all his labor, sorrows and afflictions on this day, in which he fully completed the work of our redemption, and manifested it to be perfected by his resurrection from the dead. Therefore, as the *Jewish Sabbath* was sanctified because of the finishing of the *work of creation;* so was the *christian Sabbath* because of the finishing of the *work of redemption;* which is of far greater importance, and therefore deserves more to be celebrated than the other. Christ sanctified this day by his resurrection; and the Apostles confirmed the observance of it, both by their writings and uniform practice; and it hath such an inviolable stamp of divinity upon it, that now it is no more alterable to the end of the world.

Nor is it needful that an express command of Christ should be brought for this change out of the New Testament. It is sufficient, if, by necessary consequence, it may be deduced from Scripture. And yet,

1. *We have express places of the Scripture thus far, that the first day of the week is mentioned as the stated time for christians to meet together, to preach, to hear, to break bread in the Lord's supper, and to perform other duties of religion.* So, Acts, 20:7; "Upon the first day of the week, when the disciples came together to break bread, Paul preached unto them:" which plainly declares that the solemn meetings and assemblies of christians were then on this day; the Jewish Sabbath beginning to wear out, and the christian Sabbath, or the Lord's day, coming into its place and stead.

Again: *The public collections* for the poorer saints were ordained by the apostle to be made on this day. "Now concerning the collection for the saints—upon the first day of the week let every one of you lay by him in store, as God hath prospered him." 1 Cor. 16:1, 2. And this very rule and custom the apostle says he had before established in the church of the Galatians. And why should this day be chosen for their collections, but only because the assemblies of christians were held on this day; and so gave a better conveniency to gather their charity than at any other time?

Again: St John saith of himself, that he *was in the*

Spirit on the Lord's day; Rev. 1 : 10; which is no other but this our christian Sabbath that hath received this title and denomination from our Lord Christ. For what some say, that St. John by the Lord's day means no more than the day of the Lord's appearing to him and revealing those many mysterious visions, is vain and scarce agreeable to the sense and gravity of Scripture expression. It signifies, therefore, this day; wherein the apostle being, in all likelihood, taken up with spiritual meditations, God was pleased to gratify him with the revelation of those great things which were afterwards to take their effect and accomplishment.

Put the force of these Scriptures together, and they will certainly amount to the full proof of the institution of this first day Sabbath. It is called the Lord's day: it was appointed and used for the assemblies of the saints; for the preaching and hearing of the word, and the administration of the Lord's supper; for the collection of alms for the relief of the poor; and this not in one church only, but in other churches of the saints; and that likewise not at some solemn times only, but weekly. Put these together, and what more plain and evident proof can a thing of this nature admit of?

2. A second argument to prove this change is, *the constant and uninterrupted practice of the church in all ages, from the time of man's redemption by the death and resurrection of Christ to this very present day.*

Christ himself began the sanctification of it by his resurrection; on the same day he appeared to his disciples; and he himself informs them of his resurrection, John, 20 : 19.

I have already spoken of the practice of the Apostles;

and for the practice of the primitive church immediately after the Apostles, all ecclesiastical histories with one consent testify that the solemn assemblies of christians were held on this day: which unvaried custom and observance of the church of Christ ought to be of great weight with all solid and serious christians. And if we add to this likewise the unanimous consent of the most holy and spiritual men, who are generally found to be the most strict observers of the Lord's day; and lastly, the great blessing that God hath poured out upon his people in the plentiful effusion of his grace and Spirit on them in his holy ordinances celebrated on this day; it will be past all question that "this is the day that the Lord hath made" for himself, and therefore "let us be glad and rejoice therein."

We have thus considered the *institution, morality* and *change* of the Sabbath.

IV. It remains now only to consider THE SANCTIFICATION OF THE SABBATH.

In treating this I shall observe the same method as above, and satisfy myself in laying down positively what Scripture and reason dictate, without engaging in those tedious disputes about it which might make this discourse both unpleasing and unprofitable.

This commandment speaks of a *twofold sanctification* of this day; the one, which it hath already received from God; the other, which it ought to receive from man; and the former is given as a reason of and motive for the latter.

1. *God hath sanctified the Sabbath-day.*

So we have it, verse 11, "*The Lord blessed the seventh*

day and hallowed it; where these two words *blessed* and *hallowed* are only exegetical one of the other, and carry in them the same sense common to both.

Now God blessed and hallowed the Sabbath-day, not by infusing any inherent quality of holiness into it; for neither days, nor places, nor any inanimate things are subjects capable of real holiness; but, *by separating that day from others,* bestowing a higher dignity and privilege upon it, as the day whereon both himself chose to rest from the works of creation, and the day whereon he requires that we also should rest from the works of our ordinary vocations.

For, to hallow and sanctify, is to set any thing apart from profane and common to sacred and spiritual uses. God therefore sanctified the Sabbath, when he selected it out of the course of other days, and set it apart from the common employments and services of life; ordaining that the spiritual concernments of his glory and our salvation should be therein especially transacted. And this is the blessing which God hath conferred upon this day; for what other benefit is a day capable of, but only that when the other six days, like the unregarded vulgar of the year, were to be employed in the low and sordid drudgery of earthly affairs; this seventh day God hath raised from the dunghill and set upon the throne, appointing it, according to Ignatius' phrase, *ten basilida, ten upaton ton emeron,* "The prince and sovereign of days:" exempting it from all servile works; and designing it for such spiritual and celestial employments, that were it observed according to God's command, eternity itself would not have much advantage above it, but only that it is longer. So that in the ring and circle of the week the

Sabbath is the jewel, the most excellent and precious of days.

Again: God hath blessed and sanctified it, not only in this relative but also in an effective sense, *as he hath appointed it to be the day whereon he doth especially bless and sanctify us.* Yea, and possibly he makes the means of our sanctification to be more effectual on this day than when they are dispensed on any other common days. God doth then especially give out plentiful effusions of his Spirit, fills his ordinances with his grace and presence; and we may with a more confident faith expect a greater portion of spiritual blessings from him when both the ordinances and the day too are his, than when, though the ordinances be his, yet the day is ours. In this sense God may be said to bless and sanctify the Sabbath-day, because he blesseth and sanctifieth us on that day. As the Psalmist most elegantly and in a high strain of poetry saith that God "crowneth the year with his goodness," Psalm 65 : 11; not that the plenty and fruitfulness of the year is any blessing unto it; but it is a blessing unto men, whose hearts God then filleth with food and gladness. In both these senses God may be said to bless and sanctify the Sabbath.

2. As God sanctified the Sabbath, so *man is commanded to sanctify it also;* verse 8, "Remember the Sabbath-day to keep it holy." We sanctify and hallow a day when we observe it holy to the Lord; sequestering ourselves from common affairs to those spiritual exercises which he hath required us to be conversant about on that day. God sanctifies it by *consecration*, we sanctify it by *devotion*. He hath set it apart for his worship, and on it we ought to set ourselves apart for his worship, and to be taken up

only with those things which he hath either allowed or prescribed us. And therefore God doth lay an especial claim to this day. For although he be the Supreme Lord of all, and doth dispense and as it were draw out the thread of time, and days, and years for us, out of the infinite bottom of his eternity, yet he doth not so particularly challenge any part of it to himself as he doth this seventh day. Whence it is said, verse 10, *The seventh day is the Sabbath of the Lord thy God.* The six foregoing days of the week are thine, and thou mayest dispose of them in the honest works of thy calling, as prudence and convenience shall direct; but this day God challengeth to himself, as his peculiar portion of our time, because he hath ordained it for his worship and service, and therefore it is called his. And when we devote ourselves to his service and worship, meditating on his excellency, magnifying and praising his mercy, and invoking his holy name, we then hallow this day, and give unto God that which is God's.

Thus you see what it is to sanctify the Sabbath; both as God hath done it by dedication, and as man ought to do it by observance.

But the great question is IN WHAT MANNER the Sabbath ought to be sanctified and kept holy: whether we are bound to the same strict and rigorous observance of our christian Sabbath as the Jews were of theirs under the economy of Moses.

And on this I observe in general, that as our Sabbath is not the very same with theirs, but only the same analogically, bearing a fit proportion to it; so likewise our sanctification of the Lord's day, (for thus I would rather call it than the Sabbath) is not, in all particulars, the same that was required from the Jews, but bears a proportion to it in those things which are not ceremonial nor burdensome to our christian liberty.

But more particularly: the sanctifying of this day consists partly in abstaining from those things whereby it would be profaned; and partly in the performance of those things which are required of us, and tend to promote the sanctity and holiness of it. And,

1. Here I shall lay down this: that, in order to our due sanctifying of the Sabbath, we ought to *abstain from the common and servile works of our ordinary callings and vocations.*

So we have it expressly, verse 10, *In it thou shalt not do any work.* And this God prohibits, not that rest and cessation is in itself acceptable to him, or any part of his worship and service, but only because earthly employments are an impediment and distraction to that heavenly frame of spirit which we ought to maintain in all the parts and duties of this day. The works of our callings are not evil in themselves, but lawful and good; and such wherein on other days we serve God, and whereon we may expect a blessing from him; but yet our mind is so narrow and stinted, that we cannot at once attend them and the service of God with the zeal and fervor that he requires; and therefore, that we may be wholly employed in *his* work, he hath taken us off from *our own.*

This prohibition of working on the Sabbath is strongly enforced by the concession of six days for our ordinary labor: a concession, I call it, considering the indulgence granted to us. But yet it is not merely a concession, but a command too: *Six days shalt thou labor, and do all thy work; but the seventh day is the Sabbath of the Lord.* That exceptive particle *but*, intimates that none of that work which is lawful to be done on ordinary days ought to be performed by us on the Sabbath.

I know it is a question whether these words " Six days shalt thou labor," be a *precept* or a *permission* only. To me they seem preceptive, requiring us diligently to attend that vocation and state of life in which the Divine providence hath set us, and to perform the offices of it with care and conscience; for it is said thou *shalt* labor, not only thou *mayest* labor. And those who contend that the words merely signify a permission of the daily works of our callings, open too wide a gap for sloth and idleness to creep in, without violating any commandment, or being censured and condemned as sin.

But I shall not trouble you with the disputes about this. Only let me notice the weakness and inconsequence of one inference commonly drawn from it: that if it be a divine precept that we ought six days to labor, then we cannot by any constitution whatsoever be taken off from the lawful works of our callings, nor be obliged religiously to observe any other days besides the Sabbath; for God's laws do not contradict themselves, and whereinsoever human laws contradict the divine, they are of no force nor validity.

But this argument fails in its deduction. For the command, " Six days shalt thou labor," is not to be understood *absolutely* and *unlimitedly*, but with a *just restraint* and *exception:* that is, Thou shalt labor six days ordinarily, unless any of them be set apart, either by thine own private devotion or by public authority, for the immediate worship and service of God.

And that this is of necessity to be so understood, ap

pears, if we consider how many days in the week God himself dedicated in those feasts which he commanded the Jews strictly to observe, notwithstanding that they were enjoined six days' labor. Besides every new moon, there was the passover, in remembrance of their deliverance from the bondage of Egypt, and a type of Christ, who, as a lamb without spot, was offered up to God for us. Then the pentecost or the feast of weeks, fifty days after the passover; a memorial that the law was given to them from Mount Sinai fifty days after their departure out of Egypt; typifying likewise the sending of the Holy Ghost to inspire the apostles with heavenly truth, and to enable them to preach the Gospel, which is the law of Jesus Christ, which was accordingly fulfilled fifty days after Christ our great Passover was sacrificed for us. Then, thirdly, the feast of atonement or expiation, which was celebrated on the tenth day of the seventh month, whereon the high-priest was solemnly to confess unto God both his own sins and the sins of the people, and to make atonement for them; typifying thereby the full expiation and atonement of our sins made by our High-priest Jesus Christ. And lastly, there was ordained likewise the feast of tabernacles, on the fifteenth day of the same month; and this was to last not only one day, but a whole week together, and was instituted to be a memorial to them of their journey through the wilderness, wherein for forty years they lived in tents and tabernacles. All these feasts we find appointed by God himself, and imposed upon the Israelites. Lev. 23.

And not only did they account themselves obliged to keep these days holy which were enjoined by the divine command, but those also which were appointed by human authority. Such were the feast of purim, to be kept two days successively, in remembrance of their deliverance from the malicious and bloody designs of Haman, Esther, 9 : 21; and the feast of the dedication of the temple, first observed at the rebuilding of their temple after their return from the Babylonish captivity, as you may read, Ezra, 6 : 16; and from that time perpetuated unto the days of our Savior Christ; who, though it were but of human and ecclesiastical institution, yet was pleased to honor that solemnity with his presence. John, 10 : 22. Besides, we frequently read of fasts, both personal and national, appointed upon some emergent occasions, to appease and divert the wrath of God; as the fast of the fifth and the seventh month for seventy years together. Zech. 7 : 5. And the like to these, without doubt, either our own private devotion or the public authority of the nation may, in the like circumstances, impose on us without violating this command of six days' labor.

But although this six days' labor was not so strictly required as not sometimes to admit the intervention of a holy rest, yet the seventh day's rest was so exactly to be observed as not to admit any bodily labor or secular employment. God would not have this holy rest disturbed by the tumultuous affairs and business of life; and we find this command strictly enforced by the double sanction both of a promise and threatening, Jer. 17, from verse 24 to the end: " If ye diligently hearken unto me, saith the Lord, to bring in no burden through the gates of this city on the Sabbath-day, but hallow the Sabbath-day, to do no work therein; then shall there enter into the gates of this city, kings and princes sitting upon the throne of David— and this city shall remain for ever. But if you will not hearken unto me to hallow the Sabbath-day—then will I kindle a fire in the gates thereof, and it shall devour the palaces of Jerusalem, and it shall not be quenched." Yea, God was so accurate about this, that he descends to a particular prohibition of several sorts of work which he would not have to be done on the Sabbath-day. On that day the Israelites were not to gather manna, Exod. 16 : 26; nor to gather in their harvest, Exod. 34 : 21; nor to buy or sell, Neh. 10 : 31; nor to tread the wine-press. Neh. 13 : 15; nor so much as to gather sticks, Numb. 15 : 32; nor to go from their places of abode to provide themselves food, Exod. 16 : 29; yea, so strictly were they tied to the observance of this Sabbath, that they might not so much as kindle a fire, Exod. 35 : 3, " Ye shall kindle no fire throughout your habitations on the Sabbath-day." Unto all these prohibitions from God the Jews added many superstitious and ridiculous ones of their own, not grave enough to be here mentioned; whereby they made that burden which was before heavy, to be altogether insupportable by their foolish and vain traditions.

Now the great question is, *How far these prohibitions concern us, and whether we are obliged to the punctual observance of them, as the Jews were.*

To this I answer in the *negative*, that we are *not*, for we are bound to *nothing by the law of Moses, but only what was of moral and natural right in that law.* As for other ordinances which were *positive*, we are *set free from them* by that liberty which Jesus Christ hath purchased for and conferred upon his church. We do not celebrate the Lord's day itself upon any obligation laid upon us by the letter of this fourth commandment, (for that expressly enjoins the seventh day from the creation, whereas ours is the eighth,) but only from the analogy and proportion of moral reason, which requires that a due and convenient portion of our time should be separated to the service and worship of God. But for the fixing of the very day, why it should be this rather than any other, we acknowledge it to proceed from the consecration of it by our Savior's resurrection, the institution of the apostles, and the consequent practice of the universal church of Christ in all ages, as I have already declared. And therefore should we as scrupulously and nicely observe it in all circumstances as the Jews did their Sabbath, possibly it would not be a sanctification of the Sabbath, but a fond and groundless superstition.

The Lord's day is therefore to be observed only in things that are in themselves *moral* and *rational*. Nor will this give any scope to the libertinism of those who would willingly indulge themselves either in worldly affairs or loose recreations on this day. For it is moral and rational that the whole of that day which is set apart for the worship of God should be employed in his worship. This likewise is moral and of spiritual obligation, that we do not our *own pleasure* nor speak our *own words* on his holy day, as the prophet expresseth it, Isaiah, 58 : 13.

This obligeth us christians as well as the Jews. For if a day be dedicated to God, certainly every part and parcel of it belongs to him, and we ought to rest from all our worldly employments that might steal away our thoughts and affections from God, or indispose us to his spiritual worship and service.

But yet this extends not to those small punctilios of gathering sticks, kindling a fire and preparing food for ourselves for these things doubtless may be done without being any moral impediments to our piety and devotion on this day. Yea, they may be moral helps and furtherances to it.

For notwithstanding this rest and cessation from labor which is required on the Lord's day, yet three sorts of works may and ought to be performed on that day, how great soever our bodily labor may be in doing them. And these are works of *piety*, works of *necessity*, and works of *charity*.

(1.) Works of *piety* are to be performed on the Lord's day; yea, on this day especially, as being the proper work of the day.

And such are not only those which consist in the internal operations of the soul, as heavenly meditations and spiritual affections; but such also as consist in the external actions of the body, as oral prayer, reading the Scriptures, and preaching the word. Yea, on this day are ministers chiefly employed in their bodily labor and spending of their spirits: yet it is far from being a profanation of the Lord's day; for holy works are most proper for holy days. And not only are such works to be performed on the Lord's day, but they were enjoined also on the Jewish Sabbath. Therefore saith our Savior, Mat. 12:5, "Have ye not read in the law, how that on the Sabbath-days the priests in the temple profane the Sabbath, and yet are blameless?" This word, therefore, of profaning the Sabbath, is not to be understood as if they did what was unlawful to be done on that day; but only of the hard labor they had in killing and flaying, and dividing and boiling and burning the sacrifices in the temple; which, had they not been instituted parts of God's worship, had been profanations of the Sabbath; but, being commanded by God, were so far from being profanations, that they were a sanctification of that day, and therefore the priests were blameless. On this account likewise were Sabbath-days' journeys permitted to the Jews: which though they were not actions of piety in themselves, yet were they actions tending towards piety, that those who were remote from the places of worship might assemble themselves together to hear the Scriptures read and expounded to them. This appears, 2 Kings, 4 : 23, where the husband of the Shunamitish woman expostulates with her : "Wherefore wilt thou go to the prophet to-day? It is neither new moon nor Sabbath." Whence it may be clearly collected, that they were permitted to travel a certain space to attend upon the worship and service of God. This Sabbath-day's journey some limit to a mile; others to two, the distance of the utmost part of the camp of Israel from the tabernacle of the congregation. But with very good reason it may be thought that the Sabbath-day's journey was *any distance from the place of their abode to the next synagogue;* which commonly not being above a mile or two, that distance was called a Sabbath-day's journey.

So that it appears that works of piety, or works immediately tending to piety, may lawfully be performed with the strictest observance of the Lord's day.

(2.) Not only works of piety, but works of *necessity* and of *great convenience* may also be done on the Lord's day.

And they are such without which we cannot subsist, or not well subsist; therefore we may quench a raging fire, prevent any great and notable damage that would happen either to our persons or estates, fight for our own defence or the defence of our country, without being guilty of the violation of this day: concerning the last of which history informs us that the Jews were so scrupulous as to suffer themselves to be assaulted and slain by their enemies, rather than they would on this day lift up a weapon to repel them, till Matthias persuaded them out of this superstition. 1 Maccabees, 2 : 40. And not only those works which are of absolute necessity, but those likewise which are of great conveniency may lawfully be done on the Lord's day, such as kindling a fire, preparing food, and many other particulars too numerous to be mentioned. We find our Savior defending his disciples against the exceptions of the pharisees for plucking the ears of corn, rubbing them in their hands, and eating them on the Sabbath-day. Mat. 12 : 1, &c. Only let us take this caution, that we *neglect not the doing of those things till the Lord's day, which might well be done before,* and then plead necessity or convenience for it; for if the necessity or convenience were such as might have been *foreseen,* our christian prudence and piety ought to have provided for it before this holy day; so that we might wholly attend on the immediate service of God in it with as few avocations and impediments as are possible.

(3.) Another sort of works that may and ought to be done on the Lord's day, are the works of *charity* and *mercy.*

For indeed this day is instituted for a memorial of God's great mercy towards us; therefore in it we are obliged to show charity and mercy : charity towards men, and mercy to the very beasts themselves. Hence, although the observance of the Sabbath was so strictly enjoined the Jews, yet was it to give place to the works of mercy whensoever a poor beast did but stand in need of it. So Mat. 12 : 11, " What man shall there be among you, that shall have one sheep, and if it fall into a pit on the Sabbath-day, will not lay hold on it and lift it out ?" And so again, Luke, 13 : 15, "Doth not each one of you on the Sabbath loose his ox or his ass from the stall and lead him away to watering?" Yea, and this the very heathens observed on their festivals; when other works were forbidden, yet works of mercy were expressly allowed, and by name the helping of an ox out of a pit.* Works of mercy therefore are to be done even to beasts themselves, whatsoever labor may be required to do them; and how much more then works of charity to men like ourselves! which charity is to be shown either to their souls or their bodies; for both many times are extremely miserable To their souls, in instructing, advising, exhorting, reproving, comforting and counselling, and praying for them; and if in any thing they have offended us, freely forgiving them: this indeed is a work of charity proper for the Lord's day, a work highly acceptable to God, and the best way that can be to sanctify it. Neither are we to forbear any work of charity to their bodies and outward man; hence our Savior severely rebukes the superstitious hypocrisy of the pharisees, who murmured against him as a Sabbath-breaker because he had healed some of their infirmities on the Sabbath-day. Luke, 13 : 14–16. "The ruler of the synagogue said unto the people with indignation, because that Jesus had healed on the Sabbath-day, there are six days in which men ought to work in them therefore come and be healed, and not on the Sabbath-day." See how our Lord takes him up. "Thou hypocrite! doth not each one of you, on the Sabbath,

---

* Macrob. Saturn. lib. 1. cap. 16.

loose his ox? &c. And ought not this woman, who is a daughter of Abraham, to be loosed from this bond on the Sabbath-day?" And so again, Mat. 12 : 10, Christ healeth *a man that had a withered hand*, and justifieth this work of charity to this man by their works of mercy to their beasts; and asserts, verse 12, "It is lawful to do well on the Sabbath-days." Yea, he appeals to their very consciences in this, whether a benefit done to a poor helpless creature could be counted a breach and violation of the Sabbath, Mark, 3 : 4, "Is it lawful to do good on the Sabbath-days, or to do evil? to save life, or to kill?" Certainly it is a right Sabbath-day's work to do good; and to put ourselves to any work and labor that may tend to the saving of life or easing of pain, or healing the diseases and sickness of our brother. And our Savior hath told us, Mark, 2 : 27, "That the Sabbath was made for man, and not man for the Sabbath." The strict and punctual observance of the Sabbath is to give place whensoever the exigence or good of our neighbor doth require it; for God prefers mercy before sacrifice.

Thus you see what *rest* is required from us on the Lord's day, and what *works* may be done on it without any violation of the law or profanation of the day. And this is the first thing in order to our sanctifying the Sabbath, to rest from the common and servile works of our ordinary callings and vocations. But,

2. Another thing in which the sanctification of the Sabbath doth especially consist, is *a diligent and conscientious attendance upon all the ordinances of God and the duties of his worship appointed to be performed on this day, and that whether in public, or in private, or in secret.*

(1.) Consider *what duties you are to be engaged in in the*

public and solemn worship of God on this day; for in them a great and principal part of the sanctification of it doth consist.

This I mention, in the first place, as of prime importance. For certainly as long as, through the mercy of God, we have the public and free dispensation of the Gospel, we ought not to slight or turn our backs upon this visible communion of the church; but to honor and own the freedom of the Gospel by our constant attendance on the dispensation of it; lest, despising the mercy of God in giving them to us so publicly, we provoke him, at length, most justly to necessitate us to those retirements which now so very many, out of sloth or faction, do so much affect. I pray God that this prove not the sad and direful consequence of the contempt that is cast upon public worship by some persons, whose only study and business it is to divide Christ, and make rents and schisms in his body the church.

The public duties which are necessary to the right sanctifying of the Lord's day are these:

Affectionate prayer, in joining with the minister, who is our mouth to God as well as God's mouth to us.

For as he is intrusted to deliver his sovereign will and commands, so likewise is he to present our requests to the throne of his grace. We ought heedfully to attend to every petition, to dart it up to heaven with our most earnest desires, and to close and seal it up with our affectionate *Amen,* so be it. For though it be the minister alone that speaks, yet it is not the minister alone that prays, but the whole congregation by him, and with him; and whatsoever petition is not accompanied with thy most sincere and cordial affections, it is as much mocking of

God as if thine own mouth had uttered it without the concurrence of thy heart, which is most gross hypocrisy. Consider what promises are made to particular christians when they pray singly and by themselves: "Whatsoever ye shall ask the Father in my name, he will grant it you." John, 15 : 16, and 16 : 23. What great prevalency then must the united prayers of the saints have, when they join interests, and put all the favor that each of them hath at the throne of grace into one common stock! When we come to public prayer, we are not to come as *auditors* but as *actors:* we have our part in it, and every petition that is spread before God ought to be breathed from our very hearts and souls; which if we affectionately perform, we may have good assurance that what is ratified by so many votes and suffrages here on earth shall likewise be confirmed in heaven. For our Savior hath told us, Matt. 18 : 19, that "if two shall agree together on earth as touching any thing that they shall ask, it shall be done for them by his Father which is in heaven."

Our *reverent and attentive hearing of the word of God,* either read or preached, is another public duty necessary to the sanctification of the Sabbath.

This was observed also in the times of the law, before Christ's coming into the world, Acts, 15 : 21, "Moses of old time hath in every city them that preach him, being read in the synagogues every Sabbath-day." Their synagogues were built for this very purpose; and as their temple was the great place of their legal and ceremonial worship, so these were for their moral and natural worship. In the temple they chiefly sacrificed; and in their synagogues they prayed, read, and heard. And every town, and almost every village, had one erected in it, as now our churches are, where the people on the Sabbath day assembled together, and had some portion of the law read and expounded to them. Much more ought we to give our attendance on this holy ordinance, now in the times of the Gospel, since a greater measure of spiritual knowledge is required from us, and the mysteries of salvation are more clearly declared to us. And shall not that tongue wither and that mouth be silenced which shall dare to utter any thing in contempt and vilifying of this holy ordinance! For such excellent things are spoken of the preaching of the Gospel, as "the power of God," 1 Cor. 1 : 18; the salvation of those who believe, v. 21; the sweet *savor of the knowledge* of God, 2 Cor. 2 : 14; that certainly whosoever disparageth it, rejects against himself the counsel of God, and neglects the only appointed means for the begetting of faith, and so for the obtaining of eternal salvation; for "faith cometh by hearing, and hearing by the word of God." Rom. 10 : 17.

Another public duty pertaining to the sanctifying of the Lord's day, is *singing of psalms*.

For this day being a festival unto God, a day of spiritual joy and gladness, how can we better testify our joy than by our melody? "Is any man merry?" saith St. James, chap. 5 : 13, "let him sing psalms." And therefore, let men object to this as they please, yet certainly it is a most heavenly and spiritual duty. The holy angels and the spirits of just men in heaven are said to sing eternal hallelujahs unto the great King; and if our Sabbath be typical of heaven, and the work of the Sabbath represents to us the everlasting work of these blessed spirits, how can it be better done than when we are singing forth the praises of Him that sits upon the throne, and of the Lamb our Redeemer? This is to join with the heavenly choir in their heavenly work; and to observe a Sabbath here, as like that eternal Sabbath there, as the imperfection of earth can resemble the glory and imperfection of heaven.

Another public duty belonging to the sanctifying of the Lord's day, is *the administration of the sacraments, especially that of the Lord's supper.*

And therefore it is mentioned, Acts, 20 : 7, "Upon the first day of the week, when the disciples came together to break bread," that is, to partake of the holy communion of the body and blood of Christ, "Paul preached unto them:" which intimates that the primary intent of their assemblies was to receive the Lord's supper; and that upon occasion of this the Apostle instructed them by preaching. It is most evident by all the records of the church, that it was the apostolic and primitive custom to partake of this most holy ordinance every Lord's day, and that their meetings were chiefly designed for this; to which were annexed prayer and preaching. I am afraid, sirs, that one of the great sins of our age is not only the neglect and contempt of this ordinance by some, but the seldom celebrating it by all. The apostle, where he speaks of this holy institution, intimates that it should be frequently dispensed and participated, 1 Cor. 11 : 26, "As often as ye eat this bread, and drink this cup." Let us consider, then, what dishonor they reflect on Christ, who, although this ordinance be too seldom administered, yet either totally withdraw themselves from it, or very rarely partake of it. I shall no longer insist on this, but leave it to God and your own consciences.

Thus much concerning the sanctification of the Lord's day in the public duties of his worship and service.

But what! hast thou no Sabbath-work to do after thou returnest from the congregation and public assemblies? Yes, certainly, the day is not done when the public assembly disperses: the whole of it is holy to the Lord. Therefore,

When you return every one to your families, there are *private and family duties* to be performed.

Walks and visits are not to be the evening-work of the Sabbath; but holy and spiritual conferences are then proper, either to bring to your remembrance the truths you before have heard, or to engage your own hearts, or the hearts of others, to admire and magnify God for all his great wonders of providence and redemption. Indeed, if a walk be thus improved, it may be a walk to heaven. So we find the two disciples, who on this day were walking to Emmaus, how they entertained themselves and shortened their way with spiritual and holy discourse. Luke, 24 : 13, 15. But they who have families to look after, will be best employed in seeing that those who are under their charge spend the vacant time of the Sabbath in holy exercises; either reading the Scripture, or giving an account of what truths they have been taught, or joining with them in praise and prayer to God; or, indeed, in all of these, in their several courses and order, till night calls for repose, and delivers them over, with sweet seasoning and blessing, to the labor and employments of the ensuing day and week. And,

If there be any spare time from these public and private duties, then sanctify it by entering into thy closet, and there unbosom thy soul before God in secret prayer, spread thy requests before him, lay open thy wants and desires. And though, perhaps, thou art not gifted to word a prayer, yet sigh and groan out a prayer; for thy God hears thee, and he understands the language of sighs, and knows the meaning of his Spirit in the inarticulate groans of his children. Here likewise in secret meditate on what thou hast heard; admire the glory of God in his works, the goodness of God in his providences, the infinite mercy of God in his promises. Certainly, meditation is one great duty of a Sabbath, without which, to hear the word of God only, is but to swallow our meat without chewing it. It is meditation that makes it fit for nourishment; this sucks the juice and sweetness out of it, incorporates it into us, and turns it into life and substance.

Thus if we endeavor to sanctify the Lord's day, the Lord will sanctify his day and his ordinances to us, and by them convey so much joy and comfort into our souls that they shall be a temporary heaven unto us, and fit us for that eternal Sabbath, where we shall continually give praise and glory unto Him that sitteth upon the **throne and to the Lamb for ever and ever.**

INTRODUCTION

TO

THE SECOND TABLE.

The whole sum of practical religion consists either in those duties which immediately concern the worship and service of God, or those which immediately concern our converse with and demeanor towards men. Both are compendiously prescribed in the Decalogue: the former in the first, the latter in the second table of the law.

I have already finished the exposition of the four precepts of the first table, and have discoursed both concerning the internal and also the external worship of God.

It remains now to consider the duties and precepts of the Second Table; all which concern *man* as their primary and immediate object.

But here, by the way, let us observe the distance that God puts between himself and us. We are, as it were, set at another table from him, as being infinitely inferior to his great and glorious majesty.

First, he prescribes what concerns himself; and then what concerns us: which teacheth us,

1. That *in all our actions, whether civil or sacred, God ought principally to be regarded*—his glory ought to be our

highest aim and end. This we are to seek in the first place; and, for the sake and interest of this, we are to promote as far as possible the good and benefit of men. This, therefore, condemns those who disturb and pervert the order of the law; and instead of serving men out of respect to God, serve God merely out of respect to men.

2. This teacheth us *to observe our due distance from God.* He challengeth all possible reverence from us, insomuch that he will not permit so great a disparagement to his honor as to have his concerns intermingled and blended with ours, no, not in the same table. And this checks the rashness of those who dare to rush in upon God with that insolence which is too common among some brainsick people, who think that communion with God consists in a familiar rudeness, and that they never draw near enough to him unless they run upon his very neck. But this only by the way.

In this Second Table are contained six precepts, all enjoining our duty towards man; who may be considered either as our superior, our equal, or our inferior. Our duty towards our superiors and inferiors is prescribed in the first of these six, and our duty towards our equals in the other five, all which respect our neighbor, either in his person or in the exterior gifts of wealth and credit.

His person is to be considered, either *naturally* or *mystically.* Naturally, as he is in himself and his own person; and so the sixth commandment provides for his security, *Thou shalt not kill.* Mystically, as he is in the state of marriage, which of two makes one flesh; and so care is taken for him in the seventh commandment, *Thou shalt not commit adultery.*

If we consider him in respect to his external gifts of wealth and good name, we shall find that the first is fenced about and secured by the eighth commandment, *Thou shalt not steal.* And his credit and good name is secured by the ninth, *Thou shalt not bear false witness against thy neighbor.*

And, because the violation of these laws by outward and flagitious acts proceeds from the latent wickedness and concupiscence of the heart, therefore God, who is a Spirit, and whose law and authority can reach even to the soul and spirit, hath not only prohibited the gross perpetration of these crimes, but hath strictly forbidden the inward and secret intention of them, charging us not to harbor so much as a thought or desire towards them; and this we have in the tenth commandment, *Thou shalt not covet.*

In the due performance of all these consists the observance of that second great command, Mat. 22 : 39, *Thou shalt love thy neighbor as thyself.*

THE FIFTH COMMANDMENT.

"Honor thy father and thy mother, that thy days may be long upon the land which the Lord thy God giveth thee."

This command respects *the mutual duties of superiors and inferiors:* and here we have a *precept* and a *promise.* The precept is, *Honor thy father and thy mother;* the promise, *That thy days may be long in the land which the Lord thy God giveth thee.*

Here we may, as formerly we have done, observe a ray of the infinite wisdom of God in the order and method of this commandment. For after he had prescribed laws for his own honor, his *next care is for the honor of our parents;* because they are, next under God, the authors and original of our life and being.

God, indeed, is properly and primarily our Father; and of him is the whole family in heaven and earth *named,* that is, of him they are and subsist: "In him we" all "live, and move, and have our being." Earthly parents do but convey to us that being which God had beforehand laid up in store for us.

Hence, when our Savior bids us "call no man father upon the earth; for one is our Father, which is in heaven," Mat. 23 : 9, this must not be understood as though we ought not to give the name and title of *father* to those who are our earthly parents, the "fathers of our flesh," as the apostle styles them, Heb. 12 : 9 ; but only that their paternity is not so original nor so absolute as God's, who is "the Father of our spirits:" who not only forms the mass of our bodies by his secret and wonderful power and skill, but creates our souls, and by his breath kindles in us such sparks of ethereal fire as shall never be quenched nor extinct to all eternity. And therefore, though we owe to the fathers of our flesh honor and reverence, as they are the instruments of our being; yet we owe much more, even unlimited and boundless respect and obedience to God, who is the prime cause and author of them.

But this word *father* hath also another sense in our Savior's speech. For the Jews were wont to call their doctors and instructors by the name of fathers; and gave up themselves, without hesitation or contradiction, to believe and follow their dictates.

When our Savior bids us call no man father on earth, his meaning is, that we must not so bind ourselves either to the commands or doctrines of any man, as to prejudice the authority which God, the great and universal Parent of all things, challengeth over us; but our obedience to their injunctions, and our belief of their instructions, ought to be cautioned with a subordination to the commands and notices of the Divine will: yet we may call and honor others as fathers, by yielding them a secondary respect, subservient to the honor and glory of God.

This command of honoring our parents is very large and comprehensive, and is not to be limited only to the grammatical signification of the word, but extends itself to all that are our superiors. And that appears, because honor belongs principally only to God; but, secondarily, and by way of derivation, to those also whom God, the great King, hath dignified, and made as it were nobles in his kingdom. For as the king is the fountain of honor within his dominions; so God, who is the universal monarch of all the world, is the true fountain of honor among mankind, ennobling some above others by titles and pre-eminence which he bestows upon them; and all such superiors whom he hath been pleased thus to raise, are to be honored by us as our *fathers*.

Hence our *governors and magistrates* are our *fathers*, and are so to be accounted and reverenced by us. Indeed, they are *patres patriæ*, "the fathers of their country;" for all government being at the first domestic and paternal, the father or chief of the family having power of life and death over his children, necessity at last taught them to devolve both the care and the authority of this charge on some selected persons, to whom they committed the government both of themselves and theirs: so that magistrates succeeding in the place and office of parents, are now the public fathers, having the same power devolved on them which formerly resided in the fathers of families. Hence we read that common and successive name of the kings of the Philistines, *Abimelech;* which signifies, *the king, my father.*

The master of a private family is likewise a father; and that not only with respect to his children, but to his very servants. Hence we find Naaman is called father by his servants: " My father, if the prophet had bid thee do some great thing." 2 Kings, 5 : 13.

A teacher in any art, science or invention, is also called a father. Thus, Gen. 4 : 20, 21, Jabal is said to be "the father of such as dwell in tents;" and Jubal to be ' the father of all such as handle the harp and organ."

So likewise a superior in wisdom and counsel is called

a father. So Joseph in his speech, Gen. 45 : 8, says, "God hath made me a father to Pharaoh."

Ministers of the Gospel have likewise the honorable title of fathers conferred upon them. And that both because indeed they are superior to the people in things appertaining to God, having the dispensation of the grace of the Gospel committed to them; and because, through the concurrence of the Spirit's operation with their ministry, they beget souls unto Jesus Christ. Thus Paul tells the church, 1 Cor. 4 : 15, that he was their father, having "begotten them through the Gospel." And therefore we have great reason to magnify our office, in the execution and performance of which we ought to demean ourselves as fathers, with all gravity and authority; and to let those know, whose affronts and scorn tend to the vilifying both of our persons and functions, that they despise not us only, but Jesus Christ who hath sent us, and the eternal Father who hath sent him. So he himself hath told us, Luke, 10 : 16, "He that despiseth you, despiseth me; and he that despiseth me, despiseth him that sent me."

Superiors in any gift of Divine Providence, whether of riches, or of age, or of knowledge, and the like, are to be reverenced and honored by us as fathers. So, 1 Tim. 5 : 1, 2, "The elders entreat as fathers, and the elder women as mothers."

Thus you see how large and copious this word *father* is, taking in many other relations and states of men besides those to whom it is now commonly applied.

Here then, in opening to you the sum of this commandment, I shall endeavor to show what are the mutual and reciprocal duties of these several relations which I have now stated.

1. Of natural parents and their children;

2. Of magistrates supreme and subordinate, and those subject to them;

3. Of husband and wife, for there likewise is a superiority resident in the one and obedience due from the other;

4. Of masters and servants;

5. Of ministers, and the people committed to their charge; and,

6. The duties of those who have a superiority, either in the gifts of God's grace or of his bounty, towards those that are inferior to them, and theirs reciprocally towards those that excel.

All these are here included, and honor is required to be given them accordingly by virtue of this command.

I know that, as there is nothing wherein the truth and power of godliness, and the very life of religion is more concerned than a conscientious performance of *relative duties;* so there is nothing that grates more upon the spirits of men than to be put in mind of and reproved about these duties which are of such common and daily occurrence in the whole course of our lives. Yet, I beseech you, lay your prejudices and affections under the authority of God's word, and be persuaded to believe these things to be exceeding weighty and momentous, how plain soever they may be, which not only the light and law of nature dictates to us, but the Spirit of God hath been pleased frequently to recommend in the Holy Scriptures, yea, more frequently and more expressly than any other duties whatsoever.

I begin with the *mutual duties of* PARENTS and CHILDREN.

And here I shall speak first of the *honor due to parents from their children;* and then of *what parents are obliged to do for their children.*

I. For the *former* of these the command saith, *Honor thy father and thy mother.* And this honor to parents consists in these four things, *reverence, obedience, retribution* and *imitation.*

1. Children are to *reverence* their parents.

Reverence is nothing but a love connected with awe; a fearfulness to offend, out of the respect we bear them. It is not such a fear as terrifies and drives us from the presence and company of those whom we dread, for that is slavish and tormenting; but a genuine, sweet and obliging fear; a fearful esteem and veneration; a fear that will engage us to attend on them, to observe and imitate them, and to abstain from doing any thing that might grieve or trouble them.

This reverence which we owe our parents is wont to express itself outwardly by two things, speech and gestures.

Our speech must be full of respect and honor to our parents; giving them the highest titles that their quality and condition will admit. Our language should likewise be humble and submissive. Talkativeness is an argument of disrespect; and by the answers of the lips the heart is tried and sounded. Therefore we find how mildly and reverently Jonathan speaks to his father Saul: although he were then pleading for his David, and managing the concern of his friend's life, which was far dearer to him than his own; yet see with what modesty he urgeth it, 1 Sam. 19 : 4, 5, "Let not the king sin against his servant, against David; for he did put his life in his hand, and slew the Philistine." And God blessed a speech so well tempered, and so full of soft and melting oratory, with success. Yea, we find an instance of a disobedient son in the parable of our Savior, Mat. 21, who, though he obeyed not the commands of his father, yet thought it too shameful a crime not to give him good words and reverend titles: verse 30, "I go, sir." And certainly it is but fit and meet that we should give *them* the best and the most obliging language who have taught us to speak, and please them with our words who have instructed us how to form them. Yea, that rude and boisterous language which many of the sons of Belial use towards their parents, is so odious and detestable to God that he hath in his law threatened to punish it with the same punishment as blasphemy against himself, Exod. 21 : 17, "He that curseth his father or his mother shall surely be put to death;" and, Prov. 20 : 20, "He that curseth his father or his mother, his lamp shall be put out in obscure darkness."

We must likewise show our parents reverence in our *gestures*, and deport ourselves with all lowliness and modesty before them, in bowing the body and showing all other external signs of respect. So we find, Gen. 48 : 12, that Joseph, as highly exalted as he was in the court of Pharaoh, when he brought out his sons to receive the blessing of Jacob his father, "he bowed himself with his face to the earth." And on the contrary, that an ill-conditioned look towards a parent is severely threatened: Prov. 30 : 17, "The eye that mocketh at his father, and despiseth to obey his mother, the ravens of the val-ney shall pick it out, and the young eagles shall eat it."

2. But as we must honor our parents with reverence, so we must especially with *obedience*, without which all external reverence is but mere formality, if not mere mockery. See that large charter which God has given to parents, Col. 3 : 20, " Children, obey your parents in all things, for this is well pleasing unto the Lord."

Our obedience to them may be considered either as *active* or *passive;* and we are obliged by God's command to yield them both: active obedience, in whatsoever is not contrary to the will and law of God; passive, in whatsoever they impose upon us that is so.

Hence we are to obey our parents in whatsoever honest calling and employment they will set us. David, though destined to a kingdom, is yet by his father Jesse appointed to keep the sheep. 1 Sam. 16 : 11. We ought not, till at last we are emancipated and set free by their consent, to enter into wedlock without their knowledge or against their consent; for we find that godly fathers have still taken the care of the disposal of their children in this affair, and the apostle, 1 Cor. 7 : 36, 37, declares that it is in the parents' power either to marry their children or to keep them in a single estate; but yet, no question, so as that children have still a negative vote, and ought not to be forced against their own will and consent. Yea, so far doth the authority of a parent extend, that it reacheth also to the very garb and apparel of their children, who ought to conform themselves therein according to their allowance and direction. Gen. 37 : 3.

But if parents shall abuse their authority, by commanding what is sinful, and what God hath contravened by his law and command; yet children are not hereby disobliged or freed from obedience, but only directed to choose the passive part of it, and to bear their wrath and choler, yea, and their punishments too, with all patience and submission. For, as the apostle speaks, Heb. 12 : 10, they oftentimes chasten us *after their own pleasure;* and yet we are to give them reverence. We ought to bear with their infirmities, whether they be natural or vicious, and endeavor to hide and cover them from others; and therefore we read what a curse was laid upon Ham for disclosing the nakedness of his father, Gen. 9 : 25; and indeed it is a cursed thing to expose the nakedness and weakness of our parents to the scorn and derision of others.

3. As we must honor our parents by reverence and obedience, so we must likewise by *remuneration and retribution*, requiting the benefits we have received from them, so far as we are able and they need. This the apostle expressly enjoins, 1 Tim. 5 : 4, "If any widow have children or nephews, let them learn first to show piety at home and to requite their parents:" that is, when they are fallen to poverty or decay, or otherwise require assistance from us, we are obliged liberally, according to our proportion, to afford it. And he affirms that this is good and acceptable before God.

And therefore we find our Savior sharply reprehending that unnatural doctrine among the Scribes and Pharisees which taught that children were freed from obligation to relieve their parents: "Ye say, whosoever shall say to his father or his mother, It is a gift, by whatsoever thou mayest be profited by me, and honor not his father or his mother, he shall be free." Mat. 15 : 5, 6. This place, as it is obscure and intricate, admits of divers **ex**positions.

Some say it was the doctrine of the scribes and pharisees, that although a man did not honor nor support his parents, yet he should be guiltless if he should tell them that he had offered in the temple a gift for his and their good, and that therefore they could require no more relief from him.

Others, that it was a solemn oath among the Jews, to swear by the gift or offering which was brought into the temple, and presented there as a sacrifice before God: which oath was obligatory in the highest degree, whatsoever the matter of it might be. Mat. 23 : 18. And the scribes taught, that if a man had sworn thus to his parents, "By the gift thou shalt have no profit by me," then he was for ever disobliged or freed from relieving them, were their necessities never so great and urgent. And according to this exposition the words should be thus translated: "But ye say, whosoever saith to his father or mother, by the gift if thou have any profit by me, (where must be understood some curse or imprecation upon themselves, which they did usually express, as, let me die, or the like) then he shall be free from the obligation of honoring, (that is, of relieving and maintaining) his father or mother."

Whichsoever interpretation be most consonant to the corrupt doctrine of the scribes, and the corrupt practice of the Jews, (as I suppose the latter is) our Savior condemns it for a most vile hypocrisy; making the commandments of God of none effect, through their traditions.

Certainly it is one of the most unnatural sins in the world, for children, who have ability and opportunity to relieve their necessitous parents, to suffer *them* to want a livelihood and comfortable subsistence who are the cause and authors of life and being unto their children.

4. But we must honor our parents by *hearkening* to their good instructions and *imitating* their godly practices

So, Prov. 6 : 20, "My son, keep thy father's commandment, and forsake not the law of thy mother." For although good instruction be, for the matter of it, always to be embraced from whomsoever it shall proceed, yet when it shall come from a parent it obligeth us not only because it is good, but because it is authoritative. Neither are we only to hearken to their counsel, but also to imitate the holy example of our parents; and therefore it is commended in Solomon, that he walked in the steps of his father David.

Suffer me only, in a word, to set home this upon the consciences of stubborn and disobedient children. Consider what your demeanor hath been toward your parents, to whom you owe yourselves, your lives, your education: benefits that can never be repaid them, although you should undergo all the hardships imaginable to make an acknowledgment of them. Can you imagine the cares, the parching thoughts, the perplexing fears which your tender parents are continually distracted with for your good? And will you so requite their love as to despise their persons, of whom you yourselves are a part, and make their very bowels rebel against them? Certainly, were there any ingenuousness of nature, or were not the principles of reason and equity quite spent and extinguished in you, the love and solicitude they have expressed for you would again return unto them, if not in equal measures, yet in the most ample and acceptable that is possible for you to render. And if there be any of you who, by your stubbornness and disobedience, have brought down the grey hairs of your parents with sorrow to the grave, consider seriously what an unnatural sin you have been guilty of: and because you cannot now beg pardon of them, beg pardon of God, the great and universal Father of all; beg that he would not revenge your disobedience to your parents, by the disobedience of your children towards you.—Thus you have seen what duties children owe to their parents.

II. Let us now see what are the reciprocal DUTIES OF PARENTS TOWARDS THEIR CHILDREN; for in all unequal relations the superiority rests only in one part, yet the duty is divided between both.

The duty, therefore, of parents respects either the *temporal* or *spiritual* good of their children, for both are given them in charge.

1. As for their *temporal* good, two duties are incumbent on them, *protection* and *provision*. And both of these are taught by the law of nature. Do we not see, even in brute creatures themselves, that a strong parental affection makes them dare unequal dangers, and expose their own lives to the greatest hazard, only to defend their young? We see with what indefatigable industry they either lead them to or bring in to them their food and nourishment, till they have taught them the art and method of providing for themselves, and living at their own finding. And if the instinct and impulse of nature be so powerful in irrational creatures, how much more should it prevail in us in whom reason should perfect nature; and we be the more careful, inasmuch as the charge committed to us is more noble: it is not a sparrow or a chicken that we are to look after, but a man, a king of the universe, designed for great employments and to great ends, an heir of the world; and, if we fail not in edu-

cating him, one who may be an heir of eternal glory!

Parents owe their children *protection*. This their weakness and helplessness often call for. How many diseases and dangers is their feeble infancy exposed to! and in their growing childhood, want of care and experience runs them daily into more. Now parents are to be their guards, and by their skill and strength fence off those wrongs and injuries that threaten them; and in so doing they perform not only a parental but an angelical work. "Take heed that ye despise not one of these little ones; for I say unto you, that in heaven their angels do always behold the face of my Father which is in heaven." Mat. 18: 10. And if God, the great Father of the whole family both in heaven and earth, hath out of his infinite tenderness and compassion appointed his holy angels to be the guardians of children—if it be so that they who attend the throne of his glorious Majesty should likewise attend the cradles, and beds, and wandering steps of little ones—it is not only inhuman for parents to neglect the care of their children, but devilish to do them hurt, or destroy them themselves: the too common practice of many wretches, who, to hide and cover their shame, either abandon or murder the fruit of their bowels.

But as parents owe their children protection from incident evils, so likewise they owe them *provision* of necessaries and conveniences, according to the rank and degree in which the Divine providence hath set them. This the Scripture often inculcates. Mat. 7 : 9, 10, "What man is there among you, whom, if his son ask bread, will he give him a stone? or, if he ask a fish, will he give him a scorpion?" intimating that we are bound to give our children what is fit for the sustenance of that life which they have received from us. And, indeed, they are our flesh and our bone; they are ourselves multiplied. Now nature teaches us to cherish and nourish our own flesh, as the apostle speaketh, Eph. 5 : 29. Nay, the apostle hath laid this charge exceeding high, 1 Tim. 5 : 8, "If any man provide not for his own, especially for those of his own house, he hath denied the faith, and is worse than an infidel:" and that because even infidels and heathens are taught by the light and law of nature to make provision for their own. And this provision is not only for the present, but our care is to extend farther, and according to our ability, bating the expenses of decency and charity, we are to take care for their future subsistence; and if we cannot leave them a patrimony, we are to leave them a trade and calling, whereby, through the blessing of God, they may procure their own livelihood. So the apostle, 2 Cor. 12 : 14, "The children ought not to lay up for the parents, but the parents for the children." And if we must place them out to a vocation, we must endeavor with all our prudence to fit it to their genius and inclination; for otherwise it will not be a vocation, but a vexation to them all their days : still remembering that if we piously design any to the work of the Lord, it should be those whom God hath endowed with the greatest gifts for so high a ministration. For it is a sin very like to that of Jeroboam who made Israel to sin, to consecrate priests unto the Lord of the refuse and vilest of the people, and to think those fit enough for the temple, who, through the deformity of their body or the defects of their minds, are not fit for a shop or for any other employment. So much for those duties of parents which concern the temporal good of their children.

2. But then they are obliged to others of a higher and nobler nature, which concern their *spiritual* good and have an influence on their eternal happiness.

(1.) A great duty which parents owe their children is to *instruct and admonish them, to educate them in the fear and knowledge of God.* This the apostle expressly enjoins, Eph. 6:4, Ye fathers, bring up your children "in the nurture and admonition of the Lord." And so, Deut. 4:9, Forget not "the things which thine eyes have seen—but teach them thy sons, and thy sons' sons." We find that God gives an honorable testimony concerning Abraham, and confides in him upon this account, Gen. 18:19, "I know Abraham, that he will command his children and his household after him, and they shall keep the way of the Lord, to do justice and judgment." And Solomon extols his father David for his care in instructing him, Prov. 4:3, 4, "I was my father's son—and he taught me also, and said unto me, let thy heart retain my words; keep my commandments and live."

This instruction must not be nice and critical, but familiar and obvious; teaching them such fundamental truths and principles of christian doctrine as are of absolute necessity to be known, and in such a manner as may be most suitable to their capacity and discretion.

And if parents would be but careful and conscientious in the performance of this duty, instilling into their minds, before they are filled with vanity, the knowledge of God, and of Christ, and of religion; and forming their wills, whilst they are flexible, to the love of piety and virtue, the next generation would not generally see so much debauchery in youth, nor so much obduracy in old age, as is now every where too apparent. By this means the minister's work would be half done to his hands. It would be needful only to feed his flock with strong meat, and to press them only to a vigorous and cheerful performance of those duties of holiness to which their pious education made them before inclined.

One method of this instruction is to read to them or cause them to read *the Holy Scriptures, and point out to them those things therein which are most agreeable to their age and apprehension.* Thus Timothy is said from a child to have known the Holy Scriptures. 2 Tim. 3 : 15. And doubtless he was trained up in that knowledge by the care of his mother and grandmother, whom the apostle honorably commends, chap. 1 : 5.

Another way is to *catechise and instruct them in the grounds and principal doctrines of religion.* Indeed a continued discourse is not so informing, nor doth it fasten and rivet instruction into young minds so well as where it is diversified by questions and answers. This makes them masters of their own ideas, and able to wield and manage them afterwards to their better advantage. And truly this I take to be the very reason why so many sit grossly ignorant under many years' preaching of the word to them, scarce able to give any tolerable account of the very first principles of the oracles of God, because they were never educated in this way of catechising: they were never tried nor searched, nor the strength of their memories and capacities exercised by questions. For running and continued discourses are like the falling of rain upon a smooth rock, where it trickles off as it descends; but questions and examinations are like digging it, and making it fit to retain what is poured upon it.

But whatsoever method you may judge most profitable,

yet certainly instruction in their tender years is absolutely necessary to season them betimes with the knowledge of the grounds of religion and a love and veneration of piety, which will afterwards have a mighty influence to keep them from being led away either with the errors or ungodly practices of unprincipled men. "Train up a child in the way he should go, and when he is old he will not depart from it." Prov. 22 : 6. For when the reluctance of corrupted nature is thus early mastered, and virtue habituated in them, as there must be strong conviction and almighty grace to break off the long-accustomed habits of sin, so there must be very powerful and prevalent temptations that shall induce such a one, whose knowledge of God and love of virtue have grown up with him from his childhood, to turn a recreant to his former profession and practice, and to forget that before which he can hardly remember any thing; or if, through the violence of temptation, he should be hurried into any extravagance and excess, his conscience hath a greater advantage to reduce him again than it hath upon others who are trained up ignorantly and barbarously. It will still pursue him and disturb him in his sins, and his early notions of piety and religion will imbitter the sweets which he fancied and others perhaps find in them; and his conscience will never leave crying, and clamoring, and threatening, till it bring him back, with tears in his eyes, and sorrow in his heart, and shame in his face, to his former regular and unblameable conversation.

3. Another duty parents owe their children, is *to give them good examples, to set before them the copies and pattern of those virtues which they teach.*

And this indeed is the most lively and the most effectual way to profit them. Thou who before thy child blasphemest the name of God by swearing or cursing, thou who abusest thyself and others by riot and intemperance, dost thou expect that ever he should reverence that holy and dreadful name which thou profanest; or love that sobriety and temperance which thou possibly mayest commend to him in words, but dost much more forbid him by thy deeds? For it is the glory and boast of children to be and to do like their parents. And although there be few so forlornly wicked and utterly abandoned to vice but that they would have their children love and practise virtue, and may perhaps sometimes exhort them thereunto; yet, alas, what effect can empty words have when they are contradicted and overborne by deeds? When the corrupt nature thou hast given them shall be improved by the ill examples thou daily givest them, what avail all thy exhortations and admonitions, unless it be to upbraid and reproach thyself, and increase both thine own condemnation and theirs too?

Even the heathen satirist (Juvenal) could say, " We ought to reverence and stand in awe of children;" that they see nothing vicious or dishonest in us, not so much for the shame of it as the example. For there is no pest so contagious as vice, the least converse will serve to rub it upon others, especially parents' vices upon their children, who, if they think it not obedience and a part of duty to imitate them, yet cannot but conclude themselves secure both from reproofs and corrections.

The practice of superiors hath certainly a mighty influence in forming the manners of those who are subject to them; for let them prescribe what rules and enact what laws they please, let their authority be as great as can be, yet their example will be far greater than their authority; and inferiors will be encouraged by it boldly to transgress when shame and consciousness of sin shall tie up the hands of those who should punish them. But now, when a godly parent shall not only, with the most tender and affectionate words that love can dictate, instruct his children in the ways of holiness, but walk before them in those ways; not only by admonitions show it to be most rational, but by constant practice show it to be most pleasant and delightful; certainly that nature must needs be most deplorably vicious which can in this case be refractory, and will not go whither both wind and tide lead him; whereas others possibly, who have only the breath of good instructions, are carried away headlong and drowned in perdition by the stronger current of evil examples.

4. If neither instructions nor good examples will prevail, then *correction and discipline is necessary*, and becomes a duty, though perhaps it may be as grievous to the parent to inflict it as it is to the child to suffer it.

I know there may be and often is excess in discipline, when choler and passion prescribe the measures of punishment. This is fierce and inhuman tyranny, and argues such parents to be devoid of natural affection. And this immoderate, ungoverned correction, is so far from profiting children, that it oftentimes exasperates them, and makes them the more stubborn and untractable; or else it only dispirits and stupifies them. And therefore the apostle hath twice cautioned parents against this provoking way of discipline. Eph. 6:4. "Ye fathers, provoke not your children to wrath." And again, Col. 3:21. "Fathers, provoke not your children to anger, lest they be discouraged."

Yet notwithstanding, where age and decency will allow it and prudence doth require it, it is sometimes necessary to use the severity of discipline.

And let not a foolish fondness here interpose, for certainly God loves his children with a much more parental affection than you can love yours; and yet he tells us, Rev. 3 : 19, "As many as I love I rebuke and chasten." And the apostle tells us, Heb. 12 : 6, " Whom the Lord loveth he chasteneth, and scourgeth every son whom he receiveth." If there be not a due exercise of discipline and correction, nothing else can be expected but that our children will wax wanton with us, and next rebellious against us.

This severity must be used betimes, before age and spirit have hardened them against the fear or smart of correction. The wise man hath told us, Prov. 13 : 24, " He that spareth his rod hateth his son, but he that loveth him chasteneth him betimes."

By faithful correction and discipline the parent may deliver the child *from greater sufferings and mischiefs* that else will follow. Better the rod than the tree. Thou mayst, for aught thou knowest, redeem his life by it; deliver him from the hand of justice and the eternal wrath of God; and mayst save his soul from everlasting smart and torment. So, Prov. 23 : 13, 14, " Withhold not correction from the child, for if thou beatest him with the rod he shall not die. Thou shalt beat him with the rod, and shalt deliver his soul from hell."

By this course too thou shalt *bring thyself much comfort;* most likely in his reformation; or if not in that, yet at least in the consciousness of having performed thy duty and done all that lay in thy power for his good. But what support and comfort can that parent have, who, when his children grow lewd and debauched, shall sadly reflect upon it that it was only his fondness and foolish pity which ruined them? Take this for certain, that as many deserved stripes as you spare from the child, you do but lay upon your own backs; and those whom you have refused to chastise, God will make severe scourges to afflict and chastise you.

5. There is another and a very principal duty which respects both the temporal and spiritual good of children, *fervent and earnest prayer to God for them;* without which all the rest will be ineffectual.

Whenever therefore thou comest to the throne of grace, bring these thy dear pledges on thy heart with thee. Earnestly implore of God that he would own them and provide for them as his own children; that he would adopt them into the family of heaven, make them heirs of glory and co-heirs with Jesus Christ; that he would give them a convenient portion of good things for this life, that they may serve him with the more cheerfulness and alacrity, and a large portion of spiritual blessings in heavenly things in Christ Jesus, and at length bring them to the heavenly inheritance. And know assuredly that the prayers of parents are very effectual, and have a kind of authority in them to imperate and obtain what they sue for.

This is the benediction or blessing which holy fathers in Scripture have bestowed on their children, and we find that their blessing was their destiny. Thus Jacob blessed his sons the patriarchs, and as it were divided among them the treasures of God's blessings; and God, the great Father, would not have the blessings of a father pronounced in vain, but ratified and fulfilled them in the success.

And as parents' blessings have great influence on their children, so likewise have their curses; therefore they should beware what they wish or pray against them. A rash and passionate curse is oftentimes direfully fulfilled, not only to the ruin of the children, but to the sorrow and repentance of the parents too late. We know how deep the curse of Noah stuck in Ham and all his posterity. For the words of a father are weighty and authoritative, even with God himself; and he will not lightly suffer them to fall to the ground when they are spoken either for or against those over whom he himself hath given them power and authority.

I shall close this topic with one word to those who are parents. Consider what a great charge God hath intrusted you with. In your hands are deposited the hope and blessing, or else the curse and plague of the next age. Your families are the nurseries both of church and state, and according to the care of them now, such will their fruits be hereafter. Consider, I beseech you, how you have managed this great trust. Are your *children like olive-branches round about your table*, each promising to bring forth good fruit in due season? Have you taken care, by your good instructions and good examples, to form the Lord Jesus in them? Have you taken care, by correction and discipline, to cut off all excrescences and *superfluities of naughtiness* from them? Or do they remain still sons of Belial; wild, rude, unnurtured, and disobedient? Certainly God will require an account of them at your hands; for they are his, and only left in your keeping and to your education. But alas, the lewd practices and the too ripe sins of youth do clearly convict parents rather of having encouraged wickedness in them than curbed it. And the wit and forwardness of their wickedness, beyond their years, make it evident that they have but borrowed it from your examples. Beware lest God punish you in them, and punish them for what they have learnt of you, and you in hell for not better instructing and admonishing them.

And if any of you have reason sadly to complain of the stubbornness and disobedience of your children, I beseech you seriously to reflect upon the cause of it, and consider whether it may not be justly imputed to thy want of care in their education, or to the bad examples thou hast given them; or possibly, by their rebellion and undutifulness towards thee, God justly punisheth thy rebellion and undutifulness towards thy father. I remember a story of a graceless and desperate young wretch, who, being thwarted by his aged father in some of his pranks, invaded his grey hairs, and dragged him by them along the ground, to the very threshold of his door. His poor old father suffered it silently till then; but then, looking pitifully upon him, he said, "Son, forbear now, and let me go; for I remember I dragged my father to this very place, and there left him: he acknowledged the righteous judgment of God in so just a requital. But whatsoever thy conscience shall suggest to thee to have been a provocation unto God thus to punish thee, (and certainly it is one of the greatest punishments that can befall a man in this world,) humbly crave pardon of him who is thy Father, and beg him that he would be pleased to turn the hearts of the children unto their fathers, and the hearts of all unto himself.

Thus we have considered the duties of parents towards their children, and the duties of children reciprocally towards their parents.

But I come now, secondly, to another class of fathers to whom we owe honor and reverence by the obligation of this command. And these are *Patres Patriæ*, "the fathers of their country," the MAGISTRATES and GOVERNORS that God hath set over us.

They are his deputies and vicegerents upon earth, and the authority with which they stand invested is originally in and derivatively from the supreme King of kings, and Lord of all lords. Their kingdoms are but the several provinces of his universal empire. He hath given them their patent to be his lieutenants and viceroys; for by him "kings reign and princes decree justice," Prov. 8 : 15, not by his permission only, but by his ordinance and appointment. And whereas a great and conspicuous part of the image of God consists in his sovereignty and dominion, he hath so expressly stamped this image of his upon them, that for their likeness to him in it he gives them the same glorious name by which himself is known, Ps. 82 : 6, "I have said, ye are gods;" and Exod. 22 : 28, "Thou shalt not revile the gods nor curse the ruler of thy people." And our Savior tells us, John, 10 : 35, that they are called gods, because the word of God came unto them : the word of God, that is the appointment and commission which they have received from God.

It is observable that as other inferior creatures revere the very countenance of a man and those few strictures of the defaced image of God which are still remaining there, and, although they far exceed in strength, yet they dare not, unless enraged, make use of it against their natural though weaker lords, so also God hath spread such an awe upon the face of authority, that a look or a word from lawful magistrates shall more daunt and terrify than the armed force of an enemy. There is some secret character that God hath imprinted on them which makes them venerable; and although their subjects as far exceed them in strength as they do in number, yet strength alone was never made to command, but rather to obey and execute; and power ought to be the servant of authority.

Nor hath God ordained magistracy only out of respect to some few whom he hath ennobled, that they might enjoy a privilege and prerogative above the common and vulgar sort of men; but he hath ordained it for the general good of mankind. Yea, and I have often and seriously thought that, next to the invaluable gift of Jesus Christ, the best and the greatest good that God ever gave to the world was this appointment of magistracy; for were it not for this, the whole world would be turned into a wilderness, and men into savage beasts, preying one upon another. Did not the fear of man restrain them when they have cast off the fear of God, did they not dread the infliction of temporal punishments when they slight the threatenings of eternal, we might be as safe among lions and tigers as among men, and find better refuge and better society in solitudes than in cities: within would be fears, without violence, and every where tumult, uproar, and destruction; our dwellings, our persons, our possessions, all exposed to the fury of bloody and merciless invaders; and, as the prophet speaks, Hosea, 4 : 2, " By swearing, and lying, and killing, and stealing, and committing adultery," they would break out until blood touched blood; and there would be no more peace nor agreement on earth than there is in hell. But the all-wise God, who hath subdued the beasts of the earth to man, hath likewise subdued man (who else would become more wild and brutish than they) unto man. So that those who stand not in any awe of the God of heaven, yet are awed by the gods of the earth; and those whom the thoughts of hell and eternal wrath cannot scare from wickedness, yet many times are driven from it by the thoughts of a prison or a gibbet.

Magistracy, then, being an institution of such great eminency and absolute necessity, let us see what are the duties of those who are invested with it, towards those under their authority; and then the duties of those for whose good they rule, reciprocally towards them.

I. Of THE DUTIES OF MAGISTRATES I shall speak but briefly, since we are chiefly concerned in the knowledge and practice of duties towards magistrates.

1. One duty of magistrates is to *appoint men of approved ability and integrity to be in authority under them.* For, since those high in authority cannot be omnipresent or omniscient, it is therefore necessary that they should hear with other men's ears, and see with other men's eyes, and act with other men's hands; and therefore they ought to make choice of such as are men of known fidelity and wisdom to commit so great a charge unto: for, be the fountain never so clear, yet the streams must needs be polluted if they run through filthy channels. Those high in authority therefore should do according to the counsel of Jethro, Exod. 18 : 21, "Provide out of all the people, able men, such as fear God, men of truth, hating covetousness; and place such as these over them." Where this course is not taken, but those are intrusted with command and authority who either neglect the government of the people or oppress them in

it, what doth the prince but give away the half or more of his kingdom? for what is not ruled is lost. Neither should these subordinate magistrates be too numerous; for the very multitude of them may possibly be more burdensome to the people than helpful to the ruler.

2. *Magistrates ought to distribute justice impartially, to maintain the cause of the poor oppressed, and to restrain the insolence of their proud oppressors.* This is a truly royal and princely virtue, which will prove not only an ornament to the crown but a safety to the throne. "For the throne is established by righteousness," saith the wise man, Prov. 16: 12.

3. *Princes and magistrates ought to be most exemplary for virtue and piety.* The eyes of all the people are upon them, and their actions have as great an influence on their subjects as their laws. "A good prince," said Paterculus, "teacheth his subjects to live well, by living well himself; and although he be greatest in command, is yet still greater in example." Therefore he is doubly bound to virtuous actions, both by his conscience and by his condition: the one as he respects his own personal good, the other as he regards the good of his people, who commonly take their measure from their superiors, and think imitation of their practices to be a more acceptable service than obedience to their laws.

But I cannot insist on every particular duty of magistrates, neither perhaps would it be here very proper.

In a word, therefore, they ought *to fear God above all;* to seek his honor and glory who hath raised them to honor; to be prudent in their designs, courageous in their performances, faithful in their promises, wise in their counsels, observant of their own laws, careful of the people's welfare, merciful to the oppressed, favorable to the good, terrible to the evil, and just towards all. Let them remember these two things: that they are gods, and therefore should rule and govern as they judge God himself would do were he visible here upon earth; and that they are men, and therefore must give an account unto the great God of all that trust which he hath reposed in them. And certainly if they be careful to perform every part of their duty, though we may look only at the splendor and glory of their state, yet the cares and troubles that attend it will be found so great and weighty that we shall find all reason in the world to make the burden of their crowns lighter by our ready and cheerful obedience. It was well observed by Lord Verulam, that princes are like the heavenly bodies, which cause good or evil times; and which have much veneration, but no rest. Essay of Empire.

It is the duty of all magistrates, of whatever grade, to see that the laws be executed according to their full intent, without respect of persons; neither fearing to punish the rich, nor sparing to punish the poor; making no difference between one person and another where the cause makes none. For whoever are thus partial want the courage and firmness that ought to be in a magistrate, and should make him as inflexible as the rule of justice itself; neither being frightened by the power or threats of those who are great, nor melted or softened with the cries of the mean; for the Scripture hath expressly forbidden them, Exod. 23 : 3, to " countenance a poor man in his cause;" and pity may sometimes as much bribe and corrupt judgment, as rewards. They ought to divest themselves of all passions, private interests and affections; to be impartial in the execution of justice upon the mightiest offender as well as the meanest; upon their dearest friends and relations as well as upon strangers or enemies. This will give strength and authority to the laws; which else are but cobwebs made to catch the smaller flies, while the great and strong ones break easily through. This is the way to conciliate reverence and veneration to the laws and government; and by this course "judgment shall run down our streets as water, and righteousness as a mighty stream."

In brief, because I would not too long insist upon this subject, though it be large and various, let magistrates, of what rank soever they be, seriously consider the weighty charge given them by God himself, 2 Sam. 23 : 3, "The God of Israel said, the Rock of Israel spake to me, he that ruleth over men must be just, ruling in the fear of God."

II. Let us consider *the* DUTIES WE OWE *towards magistrates and rulers*. These are in general three: *honor, obedience,* and *prayer to God for them.*

1. We must *honor and reverence* them. This is the apostle's command, 1 Pet. 2 : 17, "Fear God: Honor the king." We must give to them a threefold honor; in our *thoughts*, in our *words*, and with our *substance*.

We must honor and reverence them in our *thoughts*, looking upon them as the lively and visible images of God upon earth. Indeed the Divine perfections are the highest object of our reverence; and therefore as you would esteem and honor any for their wisdom or for their holiness, because these are some lineaments and draughts of the image of God; so you ought to reverence those to whom the Almighty God hath communicated authority; for this also is the image of God in them. Yea, and though it should so happen that they bear no other resemblance to God, neither in his wisdom, nor justice, nor holiness, but are wicked, cruel, tyrannical and unwise; yet that power and authority alone, with which they stand invested, challengeth our respect and reverence: for in this at least they are like unto God; and whosoever slighteth and despiseth them, slighteth and despiseth one of God's glorious attributes shining forth in them: we ought not to harbor any undervaluing or ill thoughts of them. But where a people are so happy as to be governed by those magistrates who have a whole constellation of Divine attributes shining in them; magistrates that are just and merciful, wise and holy; they ought to give them the greatest reverence that can belong to creatures, and to esteem and respect them next to God himself; and although all these should be wanting, yet that power and authority which God hath delegated to them is truly reverend and awful; and the wise man hath commanded us not to *curse the king, not in our thought*. Eccl. 10 : 2.

(2.) We ought to honor and reverence them in our *words*, speaking what good of them we know, and prudently concealing their vices or their infirmities. For to what else can it tend when we blaze abroad the faults of our rulers, but only to loosen the affections of the people from them? And how much more horrid a wickedness is it then falsely to calumniate them, and by little arts, and suspicious intimations, and half-sentences, to insinuate politic jealousies into the minds of the people, and to possess them with nothing but fears and sad apprehensions of what miseries and sufferings are coming upon them through the mal-administration of affairs, and either the design or neglect of their rulers! all which tends to nothing but to make the people either disdain or hate them. I beseech you, beware that you do not, by misinterpretations, traduce the actions of your lawful rulers, nor hearken to those who do; whose words and whose breath serve only to blow up the coals of civil dissension, which, if mercy prevent not, will break forth again into a raging and devouring war. Beware that you suffer none of those leeches to fasten upon you whose very mouths will draw blood. We have seen the sad experience of it already; and may justly fear, when we see them use the same methods, that they intend the same effects. The apostle gives such a black brand, 2 Pet. 2 : 10, "Presumptuous are they, self-willed, they are not afraid to speak evil of dignities."

(3.) We ought to honor them with our *substance* when the necessity of their affairs and public concerns calls for supply. And indeed this is but a debt we owe them; for we have somewhat of theirs in our hands, and it is no unjust demand for them to require their own. Tributes and public payments are theirs when made so by law; for the rest is ours no otherwise than by the same law; and therefore to withhold what is thus legally bestowed on them is no other than theft and an unjust detaining of what is none of our own. Hence our Savior commands us to "render unto Cæsar the things which are Cæsar's." Mat. 22 : 21. And the apostle, Rom. 13 : 7, "Render to all their dues : tribute, to whom tribute is due; custom, to whom custom; fear, to whom fear; honor, to whom honor." And although possibly sometimes the burden may fall heavy, yet we ought freely and cheerfully to contribute; partly considering that such is the privilege of our nation that nothing is imposed upon us by violence, but it is given by ourselves and is our own act; and partly that whatsoever we possess we owe the enjoyment of it to the blessing of government.

2. Another general duty we owe to magistrates is *obedience*. And for this we have as express and frequent commands as for any duty that belongs to christian conversation. Rom. 13 : 1, " Let every soul be subject unto the higher powers. For there is no power but of God; the powers that be are ordained of God." 1 Pet. 2 : 13–15, " Submit yourselves to every ordinance of man for the Lord's sake; whether it be to the king as supreme, or unto governors as sent by him, for so is the will of God." Neither is there any cause whatsoever that can supersede our obedience; for if their commands be lawful, we are to obey them by performing what they require; if they be never so wicked and unlawful, we are to obey them by suffering what they threaten. But I shall not now further prosecute this topic.

3. Another great duty towards our rulers is *fervent and earnest prayer for them*. So the apostle, 1 Tim. 2 : 1, " I exhort therefore, that, first of all, supplications, prayers, intercessions, and giving of thanks be made for all men; for kings and all that are in authority; that we may lead a quiet and peaceable life in all godliness and honesty." The charge laid on those in authority is greater, and the burdens pressing them are heavier than what lie on other men, and therefore they should be eased and helped by our prayers. The account they must render at the last day is greater; their temptations are more; and therefore they more need our prayers than other men. Let us therefore heartily perform this duty of praying for those whom God has placed over us; a duty not more benefi-

cial to them than to ourselves and the whole nation; for, if we can prevail for a blessing upon our rulers, we ourselves shall certainly share in it.

Having spoken of the mutual duties of parents and children, of magistrates and subjects, I shall now, *thirdly*, proceed to consider the duties of HUSBAND AND WIFE; for in this relation also, though it come nearer to an equality than the former, there is a superiority on the man's part, and subjection due to him from the woman.

And here whilst I am treating of this subject I beseech you give not way to any levity of mind or vanity of thoughts. Think it not a light, jocular thing, as too often the marriage-relation and the offices that appertain to it are accounted; for it is matter of duty that I am now propounding to you; and matter of duty is no less than matter of life and death eternal. And therefore I charge you that you attend to it; not to get advantages of sport and merriment one with another, and to object them to each other in a ludicrous and jesting way, as is every where too common a custom; but attend to it as a matter of as great seriousness and weight as any that belongs to the right ordering of your christian conversation: a matter that presseth your consciences to the due observance and practice of it; and if despised or neglected, will press your souls under guilt and sink them under wrath. And certainly they who are so vain as to think the duties of this relation to be of no great concern, must needs likewise be so impious as to impute trifling to the Holy Spirit of God, who hath so frequently and with so much earnestness and instance recommended them to us. There is scarce any one epistle wherein the apostles do not par ticularly insist on these things; and certainly what was worthy their care to write and teach, is worthy our care to learn and practise.

The duties therefore of married persons are either *special* or *common;* the *special* are those which are the duties only of one party to the other, either of the husband to the wife or of the wife to the husband; the *common* are those which belong to both, and are by both to be mutually performed.

I. I shall first consider the duties of A HUSBAND TOWARDS HIS WIFE. And they are,

1. *Conjugal love.* Indeed love is a beautiful ornament to all relations, but of this it is the foundation and first principle. It is love which ought at first to tie the marriage-knot; and it is love alone that can afterwards make it easy. No other respect whatsoever can keep it from wringing and galling us. And although want of love cannot dissolve the bond, yet it doth the joy and comfort of a married state. Now, of all the objects that are allowed us to love here on earth, a wife is the chiefest; yea, to be loved above parents, children, and friends, and the dearest of all other relations, Gen. 2 : 24, " Therefore shall a man leave his father and his mother, and shall cleave unto his wife." And if you would know the full measure of this love, the apostle hath prescribed it, Eph. 5 : 28, " So ought men to love their wives as their own bodies ;" and verse 33, " Let every one of you in particular so love his wife even as himself :" you must be as careful and tender of their good as of your own, and resent any injury done to them as much as if it were done to yourselves. And indeed there is great reason for it; for mar

riage makes of two, one mystical person; it doth but compensate our damage and restore the rib to our side again. And therefore by marriage two are said to be made one flesh, Mark, 10 : 8, " They twain shall be one flesh; so then they are no more twain, but one flesh." And therefore all violence and outrage against a wife, into which the rude and boisterous fury of some brutish men doth too often break, is as unnatural as if you should see a man beat, and wound, and gash himself. And certainly they are mad and distracted passions which take revenge on themselves. " No man ever yet hated his own flesh, (that is, no man acting rationally and as becomes a man,) but loveth and cherisheth it." Eph. 5 : 29. So that we are to love our wives with the same tenderness and naturalness of affection as our own beings, and they should be as dear to us as ourselves. And if you would have this high affection mounted a degree higher, see verse 25, " Husbands, love your wives, even as Christ also loved the church, and gave himself for it." If a natural affection will not suffice, behold here a supernatural one, and the greatest instance of love that ever was expressed or conceived brought to be the rule and pattern of ours. Christ loved the church, his spouse, although there were many spots, blemishes and imperfections in her; he loved her so as to leave his Father and cleave to his wife; he loved her better than himself and his own life, and shed his most precious blood for her; and rather than the wrath of God should fall upon his beloved spouse, he thrusts himself between and receives those heavy blows on his own person. So ought men also to love their wives; so infinitely, if it were possible; but, because it is not so, sincerely. Therefore,

(1.) *They must love them, though they often betray many weaknesses and imperfections:* these they ought meekly to bear with, though they must not countenance nor encourage them. Love will cover a multitude of faults; and so long as they are but faults and not crimes, we ought no more to divorce our affections than our persons from them. There is indeed a touchy love, which will cause great wrath for very small offences; but usually such kind of love turns into bitterness and exasperation; therefore offences of this nature should prudently be passed by only with a glancing reproof, or with a silence that shall be more instructive than noise and clamor. Here the apostle exhorts husbands, Col. 3 : 19, "Husbands, love your wives, and be not bitter against them."

(2.) *We should so love them as not to upbraid them with the necessities or incumbrances of a married life*, but be content to abridge ourselves of our former freedom, and to forego our former privileges, either of plenty or pleasure, which we enjoyed in a single condition, without reproaching them with it. Many fools there are who fancy nothing but joys and delights in a married life; but when they enter into it, and find many unexpected troubles and that they cannot live either at so much ease or with so much splendor as before, think to right themselves by perpetual brawls with their wives; imputing the cause to them, and charging on them all the burdens and inconveniences under which they both labor and of which commonly the woman hath the greater share. Now this is not to love as Christ loved the church; who, for her sake, stripped himself of his glory, and voluntarily humbled himself, first to the dust, and then to death, the cruel and cursed death of the cross.

(3.) *We ought so to love them as to interpose and step in between them and danger, and rather suffer it to fall on ourselves than on them;* for so Christ loved the church, and gave himself for it; redeeming it from the wrath of God by his own undergoing it, and delivering it from death by suffering death for it.

(4.) *We ought so to love them as to endeavor to promote the spiritual good of their souls;* and by good counsels and instructions insinuate into them the love of piety and holiness; that so, as Christ sanctifieth the church his spouse, we may also sanctify ours, and present them unto God without spot, or wrinkle, or any such thing.

Thus much of the first duty, which is love; on which I have insisted the longer, because it comprehends all other duties in it; for where there is this sincere and conjugal affection, although it may have different methods of expressing itself, according to the different tempers of men, yet it will certainly in this, as in all other cases, command the whole train and retinue of other affections to wait upon it, and see that nothing be wanting to the good of the object on which it is fixed. I shall therefore be the briefer in the rest.

2. Another duty of the husband is *provident care for his wife*. He ought, saith the apostle, "to nourish and cherish her, as Christ doth the church." He must therefore impart to her, according to his rank and ability, whatsoever may be for her necessity or comfort; and not waste that in riot and excess among his lewd and wicked companions, companions that the devil hath given him, which ought to be for the support of her whom God hath given him for his companion, and who in the meanwhile hath nothing to feed on but her sorrows, nothing to drink but her tears

See how deeply the apostle hath stigmatized such wretches, 1 Tim. 5:8, "If any man provide not for his own, and specially for those of his own house, he hath denied the faith, and is worse than an infidel."

3. Another duty husbands owe their wives is *protection from danger* when they are in jeopardy.

See how it was with David. When the Amalekites had burnt Ziklag, and with the rest of the prey had taken David's wives, he pursues them with no more than six hundred men, though they were a great host, and rescues his wives from their captivity. 1 Sam. 30:18. And indeed the weakness and feebleness of that sex, being more helpless in dangers than ours, and less able to relieve themselves, calls for this ready aid and succor from us; and he who is so churlish as not to afford it, is so unnatural also as to suffer a part of himself to perish. A wife is compared in Scripture to *a fruitful vine:* now a vine is a weak tender plant and requires support, and the husband should be as the house-side for her stay and support. So the woman was at first made of a rib taken from under the man's arm; the office of the arm is to repel and keep off injuries; which signifies to us that the husband ought to defend his wife from all wrongs and injuries to which she may be exposed.

4. Another duty is *instruction and direction.*

Therefore the husband is called her head, the seat and fountain of knowledge and wisdom, Eph. 5:23, "The husband is the head of the wife, even as Christ is the head of the church." And therefore as all direction and consolation is derived from Christ, so should the husband likewise communicate knowledge, and comfort, and guidance to the wife; hence he is called her *guide,*

Prov. 2 : 17. And St. Peter requires of husbands that they should dwell with their wives *according to knowledge*, and be able to advise and inform them in all emergent cases, especially concerning God and their souls. Whence St. Paul enjoins wives, 1 Cor. 14 : 35, that "if they will learn any thing, they ask their husbands at home;" and therefore much more is it required of the husband that he should have laid up a good stock of knowledge, and be able to teach them; lest such as creep into houses, and lead captive silly women, ensnare their wives. For such is the subtlety of deceivers, following therein the method of the Old Serpent, that they first begin with the woman, and then make use of her to seduce the man; for heresy, as all other sins, does first inveigle the affections, and then by them corrupts the reason. And therefore the husband should be well grounded and principled with knowledge, that he may keep his wife from being led away by the crafty subtlety of those who lie in wait to deceive; and who by good words and fair speeches, affected phrases and jingling expressions that have nothing in them but sound and error, pervert the hearts of the simple. But if, as it sometimes happens, God hath endowed the wife with a greater measure of prudence and solid and substantial knowledge than the husband, it is then his part to hearken to her advice, and to yield, not indeed to the authority of the counsellor as she is bound to do, but to the authority of the counsel; and this she ought to tender him with all respect and submission, not having power to enjoin what she knows to be best and fittest, but only with modesty propounding it, and with meekness persuading him to embrace it.

5. Another duty of the husband is *tenderness and mild-*

ness towards his wife; not causelessly grieving her eithei by speeches or actions.

That is a wretched family where those who are joined in the same yoke spurn and kick at one another. If the wife be careful in performing her duty, there belongs to her a kind and loving acceptation of it, and praise and commendation for it; or if she sometimes should fail, she ought not to be rebuked with bitterness, but with meekness, and in such a way that the reproof shall show more of sorrow than of anger. But perpetual brawlings and contentions, besides that they wholly embitter this state of life and eat out all the comfort of it, instead of preventing offences for the future, do usually provoke and exasperate to more, and are perhaps a greater fault in the husband than that which he exclaims at in his wife. Besides, it will certainly indispose them both to the performance of those duties which belong to them in their general and particular callings. It will hinder their prayers; for how can they lift up their *hands without wrath*, as the apostle commands, 1 Tim. 2 : 8, when they burn in choler one against the other? How can they pray to God for blessings upon each other, when they have been cursing and reviling each other? And as for the duties of their particular callings, do we not see that in those families where this baneful contention reigns they are commonly neglected, and all runs to wreck and ruin out of a kind of revenge that one party thinks to take upon the other: the husband out of discontent will not provide nor the wife manage, and so nothing is cared for but only how they may quarrel and rail at each other; a misery that many families fall into through the indiscreet heats and fierceness of the husband upon every trivial offence of the wife, though perhaps it was sometimes unthought of and sometimes unavoidable.

6. Another duty of the husband is to *give due respect and honor to his wife.*

Give "honor unto the wife, as unto the weaker vessel," 1 Pet. 3 : 7; for, being weak, she ought to be used with more respect and gentleness. Think honorably of her as the person whom God saw best and fittest for you in all the world; and be not tempted, so much as in a thought, to believe that any other could have been either so proper or so beneficial to you. Speak honorably of her, not divulging any of her failings and imperfections to her discredit, but giving her the due praise of those virtues and graces that are in her; for he that disgraceth his wife disparageth himself, and every one will censure him as guilty of folly either in choosing or in governing her. Treat her honorably; neither making thyself a servant to her humor, for that will dishonor thee, nor making her a slave to thine, for that is to dishonor her; but use her as thy bosom-friend, thy endeared companion, and, in every thing but authority, equal to thyself.

7. The last duty of a husband is the *prudent maintaining and managing of his authority.*

His authority over his wife is God's, who hath intrusted him with it; and our Savior illustrates his own authority over the church by the authority of a husband over his wife. Eph. 5. And therefore it is not basely to be betrayed, nor to be maintained with rigor and a tyrannical violence. But the right and most effectual way of keeping up this authority is by prudence and gravity, by soberness and piety, and a staid, exemplary, and strict life. This will cause a reverent esteem and veneration in the wife and in the whole family; whereas a humorsome lightness at one time, and as humorsome severity at another, will but expose us to contempt for the one and hatred for the other. It is a hard matter for him to be reverenced by others, who doth not first reverence himself; for he that will prostitute himself by foolish and ridiculous humors, or by vile and wicked actions, either injustice, or intemperance, or lying, &c. it is impossible but that he must fall under the scorn of his nearest relations. So Nabal's churlishness and drunkenness made even wise Abigail to call him fool: "Nabal is his name, and folly is with him." But where there is an excellent mixture of prudence and piety together, the one to be a guide and the other to be an example, these will make a man truly reverend, and induce the wife and the whole family to esteem and to imitate him.—Thus much for the duties of the husband towards the wife.

II. Let us next consider the DUTIES OF THE WIFE TOWARDS THE HUSBAND. These are,

1. *Subjection and obedience.* And this is required from them as absolutely and peremptorily as unto Christ himself, Eph. 5 : 22, "Wives, submit yourselves unto your own husbands, as unto the Lord." And again, ver. 24, "Therefore, as the church is subject unto Christ, so let the wives be to their own husbands in every thing."

And not only doth the apostle give authority and command for it, but he enforceth it by sundry reasons.

(1.) *The woman was made out of the man*, and therefore ought to be subject unto him. 1 Cor. 11 : 3, 8, "The head of the woman is the man. For the man is not of the woman, but the woman of the man." She is bone of his bone and flesh of his flesh, and therefore ought to pay him the homage of obedience and subjection for those materials of her being which she first received of him.

(2.) Because *the woman was made for the man*, and therefore ought to be subject to him. So, in the next verse, " Neither was the man created for the woman, but the woman for the man." She owes her being to the man's necessities and convenience; and the great end of her creation, next to the glory of God, was that she might be helpful and profitable to man. Gen. 2 : 18, " It is not good that man should be alone : I will make him a help meet for him :" therefore, having received their being for the sake of man, they ought to be subject unto him.

(3.) Another reason the apostle gives, is *the priority of the man's creation*, 1 Tim. 2 : 12, 13, " I suffer not a woman to usurp authority over the man. For Adam was first formed, then Eve :" therefore, in the same rank of creatures, it is but fit that he should be first in dignity who was first in nature. And,

(4.) Because by *the occasion of the woman sin entered into the world.* So verse 14, "Adam was not deceived; but the woman, being deceived, was in the transgression :" therefore it is but fit and just that she who made all mankind disobedient against God, should herself be made subject and obedient to man. And this sentence we find inflicted upon her as a punishment for her transgression, Gen. 3 : 16, " Thy desire shall be to thy husband, and he shall rule over thee." Not as though there would have been no subjection due from her to man if sin had not entered into the world by her means, for the reasons before alleged do manifestly prove the contrary; but that now her subjection is a **curse;** and whereas before it would have been easy and pleasing to her, now it is become burdensome and grievous: man being by sin made more humorsome and harder to be pleased, and she being made less able and willing to bear it, God justly and righteously punishing her by imposing on her a work which she herself hath made irksome and difficult. And let me add to these reasons of the apostle,

(5.) That *the man's titles imply superiority and authority over the wife*. Such as *lord*, 1 Pet. 3 : 6, "Sarah obeyed Abraham, calling him lord." He is likewise called the *head* and *guide* of his wife. 1 Cor. 11 : 3 ; Prov. 2 : 17.

(6.) The *husband represents Christ, the wife the church*, and that in this very particular of superiority and subjection; therefore, "as the church is subject unto Christ, so let the wife be to her own husband."

And here I shall consider what the apostle tells us, 1 Cor. 11 : 10, that *the woman was to have power over her head because of the angels;* which place, especially the latter clause of it, is diversely interpreted. But I think all agree in this, that this power which women were to have over their heads, was a veil or covering, which at other times, but most especially in the congregation, they ought to wear on their heads; and which, in the primitive times, covered not only their heads but all their face, as a guard to their modesty and a screen to keep off loose and wanton eyes. And this veil is called *power*, to signify that they were under the power and authority of their husbands. But the men were uncovered in their assemblies, as the apostle tells us, ver. 4, to signify that they had nothing over them, but were superior to all visible creatures, and subject only to God. This power, or veil, women were to wear *because of the angels;* not (as Tertullian did grossly conceive from that mistaken text, Gen. 6 : 2,) to hide their beauty from the sight and inspection of angels (for what veil could do that, or how can angels be affected with corporeal beauty?) but either by angels are meant the ministers of the church, before whom they are to show modesty and bashfulness, or else perhaps the celestial angels, who are always present and attending in the assemblies and congregations of the faithful; and therefore women should not do any thing unbecoming and unseemly before them; or lastly, because the angels themselves do reverence Christ who is their head, and in token of their subjection to him are said to veil and cover their faces, Isa. 6 : 2 ; and therefore women also, in token of their subjection to their husbands, who are their heads as Christ is of the church, should likewise cover their heads and faces with a veil. So we find, Gen. 24 : 65, that when Rebekah saw Isaac coming towards her " she took a veil and covered herself," as a sign of her subjection to him.

And this subjection is recommended to them by the example of holy women, to whose practice they ought to conform their own. So, 1 Pet. 3 : 5, " Holy women who trusted in God, being in subjection unto their own husbands." And St. Paul gives it in charge to Titus, to exhort wives that they " be discreet, chaste, keepers at home, good, obedient to their own husbands." Tit. 2 : 5. And himself exhorts them to the same duty, Col. 3 : 18, " Wives, submit yourselves unto your own husbands, as it is fit in the Lord."

These commands are so many and so express, that there is scarce any other duty which the Scripture doth urge with so much instance and earnestness, with such pressing reasons and enforcing motives, as this of the wives' obedience. The duty is frequently expressed, *submit yourselves;* and the manner of performing it, *be subject, as to the Lord: submit, in the Lord;* a phrase which carries in it three things: a *motive,* a *direction,* and a *limitation.*

The motive to obedience is, doing it *to the Lord.* And though, through the froward and peevish humors of the husband, they may have no other encouragement to observe and obey him; yet to the conscientious wife this will be encouragement enough, that the Lord will accept and reward her obedience: her heavenly husband, Jesus Christ, will account it as a service done to him. For marriage being a type of our mystical union to Christ, he especially is concerned that the duties of that relation be performed so as to bear some proportion to that spiritual mystery.

The *direction how to perform it* is, that it be done *as* to the Lord. She must obey her husband, not only with a design of pleasing him, but the Lord Christ. For were it not that God commands it from them as part of their duty and obedience to him, it might sometimes seem very fit that humorsome and self-willed men should be crossed; and that those who have no other reason but their will, should fail of that observance and obsequiousness which they tyrannically expect. But then consider, it is not the husband only that commands, but the Lord; and the wife must eye his sovereign authority through the authority of her husband; and then it will appear that though there be no necessity in what is required, yet there is a necessity she should perform what is required.

But the words import likewise a *limitation* of her obedience. The wife must submit and obey, but *in* the Lord, and *as* to the Lord: that is, only in lawful things, wherein, by her obedience to her husband, she may not offend against God.

Excepting this, in all other cases the wife is absolutely bound to obey the will and commands of her husband to the utmost of her power. It is true, he abuseth his authority if he command things unnecessary and unfit; but yet, neither her unwillingness to perform them, nor her judging them inconvenient to be done, can excuse her or exempt her from the obligation that lies upon her of a ready obedience: nothing can do this but the unlawfulness or impossibility of what is enjoined. In all other things, although they be never so contrary to her humor and inclination, she is bound by the law of God and nature to obey, and to submit, if not her judgment, yet at least her practice to the will of her husband, whether she think it fit or unfit to be done, so long as it is not unlawful: unless she can meekly persuade her husband to revoke his command, she is obliged to perform it. Otherwise, when the apostle commands wives to be subject to their husbands in every thing, it would signify no more than in every thing which they think fit; and this, certainly, is no greater a subjection than every husband would readily yield to his wife, and falls much short of the apostle's intent, who requires this subjection of the wife to the husband in every thing, as the church is subject unto Christ, which certainly is not in every thing she thinks fit, neither ought she to take upon her to judge or reject his laws, but to fulfil them.

2. Another duty of the wife towards her husband is *respect and reverence*. Eph. 5 : 33, Let " the wife see that she reverence her husband." Reverence consists in two things, *esteem* and *fear*.

(1.) She ought to cherish a high *esteem* of him, if not for his gifts and graces, yet at least for that relation in which he stands to her as her lord and her head, superior to her by God's appointment and ordinance. Yea, she must look upon him as that person whom God, out of all the numerous millions of mankind, hath particularly chosen and selected for her, and one whom he saw fittest and best to be her head and guide.

(2.) Another part of reverence is *fear;* not a servile, slavish fear, for that is inconsistent with love; but a respectful and loving fear, which will show itself in two things:

In her *care to please him;* endeavoring to conform her actions to his inclinations, so far forth as they are not repugnant to the supreme duty which she owes to God. 1 Cor. 7 : 34, "She that is married careth for the things of this world, how she may please her husband;" and therefore she will endeavor to comport herself in her speeches and in her gestures and in her whole demeanor, so as may render her most grateful and most amiable to him.

In her *joy in pleasing him* and *grief in offending him.* Indeed, a good wife should be like a mirror. A mirror, you know, hath no image of its own, but receives its stamp and image from the face that looks into it; so should a good wife endeavor to frame her outward deportment and her inward affections according to her husband; to rejoice when he rejoiceth, to be sad when he mourns, and to grieve when he is offended. This is that reverence which wives owe to their husbands; thinking highly and honorably of them for their place sake, and endeavoring to avoid and shun whatever may offend them; and therefore, those who are cross and vexatious, and either by clamors and contentious speeches, or by thwarting and peevish actions grieve and sadden the hearts of their husbands, let them know that they highly provoke the Lord, who hath commanded reverence and respect to be paid to the husband as his type, and as part of that reverence and respect which is due to himself.

3. Another duty of a wife is *helpfulness to her husband.* She ought, indeed, to be a help to him in every thing. To his *soul;* in furthering his graces and wisely and opportunely admonishing him to his duty at least by a holy and blameless conversation, so commending the Gospel of Christ to her husband that at length he may begin to esteem and reverence that piety which hath so adorned and qualified his wife; and "what knowest thou, O wife, whether," by such an exemplary life as this, thou mayest "save thy husband?" as the apostle speaks, 1 Cor. 7 : 16. To his *body;* by cherishing and being tender of it. To his *good name;* by endeavoring to augment and preserve it; reporting well of him, and silencing and convincing any scandalous rumours that may be spread abroad concerning him. To his *estate:* if she cannot bring in and get any thing to increase the stock, yet she ought prudently and frugally to manage what her husband intrusts her withal, and not to waste it vainly and profusely; for let her know that whatsoever is so spent or wasted is but stolen; and if she shall alienate any thing from her husband contrary to his consent, either expressly declared or else upon good grounds supposed to be tacitly granted and allowed, it is no better than theft; and therefore when we read that Abigail, without the consent of her husband, took a considerable present to bestow upon David to divert his ireful intentions, it may very well be supposed that if Nabal had known as well as she the dange

wherein he stood, he would have been as forward to encourage her to do it as she was ready and willing; and therefore, here were good grounds to suppose a tacit and implicit consent unto the action. The husband is the true and only proprietor of all, and though the wife hath a right to all, yet it is only a right of use and not of dominion: she ought not to dispose of his estate, or any part of it, contrary to his mind and consent. Her proper office is providently and faithfully to manage the affairs of the family that are committed to her oversight and care; and therefore, in the description of a good wife given us at large, Prov. 31, from verse 10 to the end, we find the whole of it taken up in showing her industry and care in ordering the affairs of the family.

4. Another duty of the wife is *modesty;* and that both *in apparel* and *behavior.*

(1.) In *apparel;* that it be according to her place and rank, not affecting gaudiness or strange fashions, nor yet affecting, on the contrary, a singularity of obsoleteness and outworn antiquity; for pride may be equally shown either way. The best temper is for them *not to wear garments to be taken notice of.* The apostle gives them this rule, 1 Pet. 3 : 3, 4, Let not the woman's "adorning be that outward adorning of plaiting the hair, and of wearing of gold, or of putting on of apparel; but let it be the hidden man of the heart, in that which is not corruptible, even the ornament of a meek and quiet spirit, which is in the sight of God of great price." And so St. Paul, 1 Tim. 2 : 9, 10, "I will that women adorn themselves with modest apparel, with shamefacedness and sobriety; not with broidered hair, or gold, or pearls, or costly array, but (which becometh women professing godliness) with good works." This indeed is the best ornament, that which makes them lovely in the sight of God, and that too which makes them esteemed by all sober and serious persons. Indeed, I do not think that costly array is in either of these places absolutely forbidden; doubtless gold and jewels may lawfully be worn if we keep ourselves within our rank and quality, and fashion ourselves to those who are most sober in that rank, rather than to those who are most light and vain. But the prohibition is to be interpreted either by the degree, that is, be not excessive nor vain in your apparel, which happens when the habit exceeds either the quality or the ability of those that wear it; or else it is to be interpreted by a comparison: let not the adorning be the outward adorning of wearing of gold or of putting on of apparel; that is, study not so much how to set off yourselves in your garments, as how to adorn yourselves with a meek and quiet spirit, with sobriety, modesty and good works, which is the richest and most beautiful robe you can wear.

(2.) As she must be modest in her apparel, so she must be in her *behavior and deportment.* Her countenance, gestures and speeches must be all fitted to show the inward calmness and serenity of her mind; and, therefore, imperious, clamorous and turbulent women are a torment and vexation to themselves, and more to their husbands. "The contentions of a wife," saith the wise man, "are a continual dropping." Prov. 19 : 13. And it is such a dropping as will at last eat and fret through his very heart, though it were made of stone.

III. There are likewise *common duties to be performed by both* THE HUSBAND AND WIFE MUTUALLY.

I shall only name them briefly. Such are fervent prayers to God, both severally and together, that he would be pleased to pour down his blessings and his graces on them, and give them wisdom to demean themselves towards each other aright; conjugal love; communion of themselves, of their estates, of their habitations; a mutual bearing of one another's weaknesses, with prudent and pious endeavors to heal and remove them; the nurture and education of children; the government of their family committed to their charge, for whom they are to provide not only what is requisite for their temporal good, but much more for their spiritual, inasmuch as their souls are much more worth than their bodies; and therefore they ought to observe constant family duties, and make choice of honest and religious domestics, and so far as in them lies keep out the infection of evil company from entering within their doors as carefully as they would the plague. And whilst they thus live and thus love, they have good reason to believe that, as they are joined in a near relation each to other, so they are both joined in a near relation to the Lord Jesus, who is the husband of his church and all the faithful in it; and when death shall dissolve their marriage-union and separate them one from the other, it is only to bring them to live for ever with that husband from whom they can never be separated nor divorced.—Thus much for the duties of husbands and wives.

Let us now, in the *fourth* place, proceed to consider the duties of another family relation, and that is between MASTERS and their SERVANTS.

For these also are comprehended under this commandment, *Honor thy father and thy mother*, since there is a confessed superiority of the one over the other; and on that account servants have honored their masters with the style and compellation of father. Thus, 2 Kings, 5 : 13, when those prudent servants sought to mitigate the rage of proud Naaman, who thought his greatness too much slighted by the prophet, in that he would only cure and not compliment him, they reverently call him *father;* his servants came near and spake unto him, and said, *My father,* &c.

And here not to discourse of dominion and servitude, whether the original and foundation of either be in nature and institution, nor of the difference of servants by war, purchase or compact; I shall only speak of what is more immediately pertinent to my subject, and what may be more instructive and profitable to you, viz. the *mutual and reciprocal duties of masters and servants.*

The duties that equally concern them both consist, in general, either in the right choosing or in the right using of one another.

I. I shall begin with THE SERVANT'S DUTY, and that,

1. As to the *choice of his master.* He ought, where his choice is left him free, to choose a faithful master, such a one as fears God and will be willing to promote the spiritual good and salvation of his soul; with such certainly he shall best serve, who do themselves serve God; where he shall have nothing but reasonable and lawful commands to obey and pious examples to imitate. Many poor ignorant souls have had cause for ever to bless God that his providence hath cast them into such families, where they have received the first knowledge and the first savor

of godliness. But if the servant be beforehand knowing and religious, what comfort can it be to him to live where there is a constant neglect of holy duties; nothing but excess and riot, and profaneness, and abusing of the name of God, and scoffing at his service and servants? Certainly necessity should hardly induce him, much less choice lead him to be a servant in a family where the devil is the master of it. The Psalmist sorely complains that he was forced to take up his abode among wicked and ungodly men, Psalm 120:5, "Wo is me that I sojourn in Mesech, that I dwell in the tents of Kedar!"

And as it cannot but be exceedingly burdensome and tedious to thee, and cut thy soul to the very quick, to be at the command of those who rebel against thy God, to hear his holy name blasphemed, his ways and worship and people derided, which are dearer to thee than thy very life, so is it very dangerous and full of hazard. It is hard to keep zeal and the sparks of grace and divine love alive when thou hast the greatest helps to it that can be administered; how wilt thou then preserve them alive when thou hast so many quench-coals about thee; when the floods of ungodliness shall compass thee about and surround thee? Either thou must dissemble thy piety, and that is the ready way to lose it, (for grace is like fire, stifle and keep it close and it will certainly die,) or else thou must put thyself upon the sore temptation of being mocked and scorned for it. Thou knowest not how far thou mayest forsake God and thy first ways for compliance sake. It is the hardest thing in the world to be religious alone, and to keep up zeal and affection for God when all that we converse with are wicked and ungodly. Vice is the most contagious plague, and it will be a very great wonder if those with whom thóu familiarly conversest, with whom thou eatest and drinkest and sleepest, do not at last infect thee. We see holy Joseph, by living long in the Egyptian court, had learned some of the court fashions, and could readily swear " by the life of Pharaoh."

Venture not thyself therefore into those families where the governors are either corrupt and erroneous in their principles, or lewd and dissolute in their conversation; for it will be hard for thee to swim against the stream both of example and authority; or if thou shouldst be able to bear up against both, it will cost thee more pains and struggling to do it than all the temporal advantages thou canst there reap will be worth to thee.

2. After thou hast made thy choice and art entertained, *consider how thou oughtest to demean thyself towards thy employer.*

And here if by what shall be said thy duty seem very hard to thee, yet it is no harder than it hath pleased God to make it; yea, and possibly not so hard as thy master's, for he is bound to give an account for thee to God, but so art not thou for him. Thy miscarriages shall be severely revenged on him if they have been through his default of needful instruction, or of care and discipline; but so shall not his upon thee. And therefore in this respect all inferiors have a mighty advantage to sweeten the lowness of their condition, that they shall not be punished for the sins of their superiors, but superiors may be for the sins of their inferiors, yea, and sometimes for their due obedience too, when they command them things though not unlawful yet unfit; for that may be a sin in a superior to command, which is a duty for an inferior to obey when commanded; and certainly in the end his task will be found easiest who is to obey, rather than his who commands. Here I remark,

(1.) *The chief and comprehensive duty of a servant is obedience to the commands of his master.* For this is absolutely enjoined them, Col. 3 : 22, " Servants, obey in all things your masters according to the flesh." And again, Eph. 6 : 5, " Servants, be obedient to them that are your masters according to the flesh." In all things that are not dishonest and contrary to the laws of God there obedience is required; yea, although in many things their commands should be impertinent or too imperious and tyrannical, yet servants in such cases are no more exempted from obedience than their masters shall be from punishment; for the unreasonableness of their commands they shall give an account to God their master; and thou, for withholding thy obedience, both to them and him.

(2.) Another duty is, a *patient suffering of reproofs and corrections.* Yea, and so patient are servants to be as not so much as to answer again, Tit. 2 : 9, " Exhort servants—to please their masters well in all things, not answering again." So strictly hath religion tied them up to obedience that they ought not to reply against a rebuke, nor to derogate so much from the authority of their masters as to murmur at it; and therefore to use violence against them is so high a degree of disobedience that it approacheth near to sacrilege.

Yea, and this quiet and silent submission is required also, not only where the servant hath given just cause for reproof and correction, but although he suffer from the groundless rage and passion of his master. See 1 Pet. 2 : 18–20, " Servants, be subject to your own masters, with all fear; not only to the good and gentle, but also to the froward. For this is thankworthy, if a man for conscience toward God endure grief, suffering wrongfully. For what glory is it if, when ye be buffeted for your faults, ye shall take it patiently? But if, when ye do well and suffer for it, ye take it patiently, this is acceptable with God." See here how urgently the apostle enjoins on them this duty. And indeed a duty so hard, so contrary to flesh and blood, had need to be pressed home upon your consciences. You ought to be patient, not only when you are justly reproved and corrected for your faults; but if the distempered rage of a master should break forth without any reason, or contrary to all reason; if he should reprove and buffet you, not for your faults but for your duty, you ought to take it patiently and not to strike again, no not so much as to answer again : that is, not to answer with taunts and invectives, but calmly and at fit and convenient seasons to present to him the justice of your actions and the reasons that moved you to them.

I must confess that of all things which belong to the duty of servants this is the most difficult; and there is nothing that can sweeten and facilitate it but only conscience of their duty and the acceptance and reward which they shall find with God for it; and therefore they had need to pray for a great measure of self-denial and mortification of those passions which will be apt to struggle in them on this occasion, and by an eye of faith look up to God to support them, esteeming it a chastisement inflicted on them by their heavenly Master; and that he, be their spirits never so high, will enable them to undergo it without any more murmuring than they would use against God himself, when he immediately afflicts them

(3.) Another duty of servants is *a reverential fear of their masters*. "A son honoreth his father, and a servant his master: if then I be a father, where is mine honor? and if I be a master, where is my fear?" Mal. 1 : 6. And the apostle hath commanded servants to "be obedient to their masters, with fear and trembling." Eph. 6 : 5. And again, 1 Pet. 2 : 18, "Servants, be subject to your masters with all fear." This fear is to be expressed by them in their speeches and actions.

In their *speeches*, by forbearing any clamors or irreverent muttering in their presence. Their words must be few and humble, giving them all those respectful titles that belong justly to their place and quality. Yea, and they must not only speak fair to them whilst they are present, but speak well of them when absent; begetting in others as good an opinion of them as they may; concealing their infirmities, and what they cannot speak truly of them to their credit, therein to be silent.

Likewise in their *actions* they ought to testify their reverence, conducting themselves with all the expressions of modesty and respect before them, and readily doing not only what their masters shall expressly command, but what they judge will be pleasing and acceptable to them; and therefore we have that expression, Psalm 123 : 2, "The eyes of servants look unto the hand of their masters, and the eyes of a maiden unto the hand of her mistress," intimating to us that good servants will not only readily obey when they have a verbal and oral command, but will be ready to take the least sign, the least beck from their masters, and strive not only to fulfil but even to prevent their commands by the readiness and respect of their obedience.

(4.) Another duty of a servant is *diligence in his master's affairs*. He ought to *set his mind* to them, and employ his time in them. For he is not faithful who is negligent; and he steals from his master who doth not use his strength and spend his time in his service. Every slothful servant is a thief; and so much advantage as he hinders his master of by his negligence and idleness, of so much he doth but rob him. And therefore in the Parable of the Talents, when the master takes an account of every man's improvements, he calls that servant who had not used his talent nor been industrious in his service, not only slothful, but wicked, " Thou wicked and slothful servant." Mat. 25 : 26.

(5.) Another duty is *fidelity and trust in what is committed to their charge;* not defrauding their masters, nor purloining from them the least value, but serving them with all faithfulness and integrity. So, Tit. 2 : 9, 10, " Exhort servants to be obedient unto their own masters—not purloining, but showing all good fidelity." And unto this appertains carefulness in preserving their master's estate; not wasting or consuming it either by riotous living or negligence. Doubtless many men have sunk and decayed under the unfaithfulness or carelessness of their servants, either stealing from them or prodigally wasting what was theirs. Let such know that every farthing stands upon account in God's debt-book: unless they make amends to their masters, if ever Providence shall enable them to do it, they must make a punctual payment to divine justice, which is infinitely the more dreadful creditor.

(6.) As trust in affairs, so likewise *truth in speech* is another duty of a servant. They ought to approve themselves such that their masters may repose themselves on their word. And as servants are the hands and the eyes of their masters, so they ought to make no other report to them than what is as certain as though they had touched it and seen it themselves. We read of Gehazi, that when he was returned from taking a bribe of Naaman, he stood very demurely before his master with a lie ready prepared in his mouth. " Whence comest thou, Gehazi?" "Thy servant," saith he, " went no whither." But this lie cost him a leprosy that stuck incurably to him and to all his posterity. I am loth to be uncharitable, but I much fear that if the same judgment were inflicted on every servant that comes to his master with a lying excuse, many families would be infected, and very few in this relation escape that loathsome contagion. Certainly it is only a cowardly, base, slavish fear that induceth one to this vile sin of lying. And, what! wilt thou be more afraid to offend thy master by confessing a fault, than to offend thy God by committing another to conceal it? What else is this but to heap up sin upon sin, and to make a single transgression become two thereby? A sin the most odious to God, who is truth itself; and usually most detestable to men, and with difficulty pardonable by them; for it imputes folly and ignorance to them, as being so weak that they cannot find out the matter. And therefore the Psalmist saith, " He that telleth lies shall not tarry in my sight." Psalm 101 : 7.

(7.) Another duty of servants, and it is the last I shall mention, is to serve their masters *with good will*, and in singleness of their hearts; not grudgingly, as of constraint, for that is slavish, but readily and cheerfully, as unto the Lord; "not as men-pleasers," only " with eye-service," being no longer diligent than their master's eye is upon them, but careless and negligent as soon as his back is turned; "but as the servants of Christ, doing the will of God from the heart;" as the apostle commands and directs them, Eph. 6 : 5–7.

Now to perform service to their masters as unto God and Christ, imports these two things:

A serious consideration *that God is concerned in every thing they do*, as the object of it. So, Col. 3 : 23, "Whatsoever ye do, do it heartily, as to the Lord." And therefore servants are commanded to have respect, not so much unto men as unto God. This is the way to ennoble thy service, be it never so mean; it is God whom thou servest in them, that God whom the greatest princes and potentates of the earth ought to serve. And be the employment what it will, yet the greatness and glory of that Master to whom thou doest it put an honor and dignity upon it.

To do service as unto the Lord, implies thy doing it on this very account, *because God hath commanded it*. Be the action what it will, yet if you can truly say that you do it not only because your master hath commanded it, but because God, his Master and yours, hath laid the authority of his command and injunction on you to obey him, this commends the service to God, and makes it an action done truly unto him.

And this may be a great encouragement to servants, (for indeed their condition generally wants encouragement) that though their employment may be the drudgeries of this life, and those possibly not very well accepted by their harsh and froward masters; yet, be their work never so painful and laborious, whilst they perform it out of conscience to God's command, it is accounted as done to him, and not to them; they are his servants more than theirs, and he will kindly accept and bountifully reward them.

II. Let us now proceed to those DUTIES WHICH MASTERS OWE RECIPROCALLY TO THEIR SERVANTS. And those consist, as before I noted, either in the *right choosing* or in the *right using* of them.

(1.) The master's first duty is a prudent care and circumspection in the *choice of his servants*. This is a matter of great moment, and that whereon the happiness and comfort, or else the misery and trouble of a family do very much depend.

Two qualifications in a servant ought chiefly to be regarded in the making choice of him. The one is *ability to fill his place* and manage those affairs which you commit to his care and trust. The other is *conscientiousness and piety in doing faithful service* not to thee only, but to God, the common Master of you both.

And indeed this latter is of more importance and of greater concern to thee than the former. For when thou entertainest a godly person, though possibly not so sufficient for thy employment as some others, it will be a commendation of thy charity that thou maintainest one of God's servants in thy family. But when thou entertainest a lewd profane wretch only because he is able to despatch his work, thou maintainest one of the devil's slaves, and takest into thy house a sworn servant to the deadliest enemy thou hast, which is justly reproachable both with folly and impiety.

Yet how little is this usually regarded! I know it is the custom of too many, that if they can light on those whom they think proper for their affairs, they never inquire what their principles or what their practices be as to religion, whether popish or factious, whether for the mass or the meeting; but choose them as they would beasts of burden, the most strong and able, and account it the only property of good servants to be able to perform their office and willing to drudge as much as they would have them.

But let them know that they make a very unwise and a very sinful choice. For such servants will assuredly make much more work than they despatch, and leave more filth in the house than they cleanse out. Though they be never so able and fit for their employments, yet think not such a one fit for thee who refuseth to serve that God whom thou thyself art bound to serve, and believe it to be a design of the devil to help thee to one who shall do thy work but undo thy family. One vile and wicked servant is enough to corrupt a whole household; for assure yourselves they come there to do the devil more service than you, and their examples and presumptions will seduce and draw others into the same excess with themselves.

For to this I impute the rise and growth of that general profaneness that is too reigning in most families, especially in those whose quality or estates require a numerous attendance. They are commonly too careless what ruffian and debauched servants they entertain; and their children, which else might be the ornament and glory of the nation, conversing with these, learn from them those first rudiments of vice which afterward their condition and wealth enable them to perfect into consummate villany. Here they learned the first taste of excess and intemperance; here they were taught the first syllables of oaths, and instructed how to lisp out curses and obscenity, and according to their proficiency were applauded by these impious wretches for their genteel docility and aptness. Such servants as these should be rooted out; not only are they the pests of particular families, but their influence reaches farther, even to corrupt those who may hereafter have an influence on the state and commonwealth; for they serve only to give youth the first relishes of sloth, and pleasure, and vice, which, by woful improvements, grow at last to be inveterate habits, and make them only a shame to their families and a curse to the state.

So it is proportionably in all humbler families: where the servants are wicked, the children ordinarily will be more ruled by their examples and flatteries than by their parents' authority and commands.

And therefore it highly concerns you to make a prudent choice at first, or, if therein you have been mistaken, as soon as you can to rid your houses of those vermin and caterpillars, which else will destroy the verdant and budding hopes of your children; and to bring in those who are sober, stayed and godly, who will make it their great care first to serve God and then you. Take the resolution of the royal Psalmist for your pattern and direction, "Mine eyes shall be upon the faithful of the land, that they may dwell with me; he that walketh in a perfect way, he shall serve me. He that worketh deceit shall not dwell within my house; he that telleth lies shall not tarry in my sight." Psalm 101: 6, 7. Certainly those will be the best servants to us who are faithful servants to God; or if they should be less fit for thy occasions, yet they will sufficiently earn their wages, though they only pray for thee.

It is said of Joseph, Gen. 39 : 5, when he was brought into Potiphar's house to be his servant, "that the Lord blessed the Egyptian's house for Joseph's sake; and the blessing of the Lord was upon all that he had, in the house and in the field." Godly servants bring a blessing along with them to the families where they reside: having such a servant thou hast a friend in court, one that can do thee kind offices in heaven through his interest at the throne of grace. And therefore, as it is thy duty, so it is thy wisdom and thy concern to make choice of such; these best know their duty; these will make most conscience of performing it; in their integrity and faithfulness thy heart may repose, and they will entitle thee and thy family to those blessings which attend them.

2. Another general duty of masters in relation to servants is, *rightly to use them when they are chosen*. And this consists likewise in two things, *government* and *provision*.

(1.) This *government* ought to be *prudent and discreet*, such as may maintain authority, and yet not be soured into *tyranny*. Therefore it should be a master's care to demean himself gravely before his servants; his very countenance and deportment should be enough to beget reverence in them. For when the master is vain and light, the servants will grow first familiar and then contemptuous.

Government consists in two things, *command* and *correction*. But that which doth most of all tend to make both effectual, is *good example*.

A master ought wisely to *command and enjoin* his servants what they should do. And herein is required much skill and prudence. For though servants ought not to inquire into the reasons of all that their masters bid them do, yet doubtless it is a very difficult matter for them to bring themselves to do that which is apparently vain and ridiculous; and by imposing such things upon them the master will much hazard the loss or diminution of his authority: therefore in laying his commands upon them he ought to have regard both to the *manner* and *matter* of them.

As to the *manner*, he ought not to command with rigor, with ill language and revilings, as is the custom of too many, who when they enjoin their servants any thing preface their commands with a reproach, which tends to nothing but to discourage them, to make them hate the employment and him that setteth them about it; and by this means we make our servants to become our enemies. The apostle therefore hath given this caution, Eph. 6 : 9, "Ye masters, do the same things to your servants, forbearing threatening." Nor yet should they prostitute their authority by any submiss entreaties, for it is an evil which the earth itself cannot bear, when a servant reigneth and bears sway over his master, as the wise man observes, Prov. 30 : 22; but there should be such an equal mixture of mildness with gravity, and love with authority, that the servant should not only be compelled but inclined by it unto obedience. Indeed there is required much evenness of temper in him that would make a good master; not to be hurried with violent and causeless passions, nor to be swayed by irrational humors; for nothing doth more detract from authority than humorsomeness, because servants not having any standing measure of what will please such a master, will at last grow careless of it, and despise the commands of him who is as much a servant as they are servants, yea, a very slave to his passions and humors, than which there cannot be a baser and a viler slavery; and therefore those who are servants to fickle and capricious masters, though they may seem very obsequious to them, yet cannot but secretly despise them; for power may indeed make their commands to be obeyed, but it is reason only and gravity that can make them venerable and reverend.

As to *matter* also, a master ought to *command nothing but what is lawful to be performed.* For both he and his servant have a supreme Lord and Master in the highest heaven, whom they both ought to fear and obey. And to every master let me say, thy servant's service is no farther due to thee than as it is consistent with the service of God; and when thou commandest any thing contrary thereunto, thou art not a master but a tempter. It is true, he is bound in conscience to obey thee, yet it is only in those things wherein the law of God hath left his conscience free; and therefore where the great and universal Lord hath laid a prohibition on him, his obedience is superseded, and thy commands do only bind thyself to guilt, not him to observance. He is bound to work for thee, but not to lie, nor to steal, nor to cheat for thee; and if thou art so wicked as to enjoin him any such thing, it is no uncivil answer to say to thee, as the apostle did, Acts, 5 : 29, " We ought to obey God rather than men." And further,

A master's commands must be not only *lawful* but *possible.* To command things impossible is the height of folly. And therefore when Abraham commanded his servant to procure a wife for his son, the servant prudently answers, What if she will not come ? upon which supposition his master acquits him from the oath of God that was betwixt them. "If the woman will not be willing to follow thee, then thou shalt be clear from this oath." Gen. 24 : 8. To command things impossible to be effected will but detract from the master's authority and lessen his esteem, and cause the servant to think his own discretion to be a better guide for his actions than his master's: yea, although the thing be not simply impossible in itself, but only to the servant, considering either his inability or employments; or if it be hugely inconvenient, or prejudicial, or unseasonable, the master ought not in conscience or prudence to exact it. For as to command things unlawful is impiety, and things impossible, folly; so to require things unreasonable and prejudicial is mere tyranny; and as such it is recorded of Pharaoh and his task-masters, who, to weary and wear out the Israelites, exacted the whole tale of bricks, but would not allow straw to make them.

Moreover, a master's commands ought not to be *vain and impertinent*, but he should have some swaying reason, though perhaps not always fit to be communicated to the servant, why he commands such things from him, a reason sufficient to satisfy his own judgment and his own conscience.

Again, it is the master's duty to *correct those servants that are stubborn and disobedient*. The wise man tells us, "There is a servant who will not be corrected by words, for although he understand he will not answer." Prov. 29 : 19. Yet here prudence must be the measure of what discipline is fit for them, according to their age, disposition and the nature of their offence. A reproof will work more effectually with some than stripes, and those who have ingenuous spirits will either be discouraged or exasperated by a too-rigorous usage. And God hath expressly interposed his will in this particular. "Thou shalt not rule over him with rigor, but shalt fear thy God." Lev. 25 : 43.

Indeed no correction is to be inflicted on them out of passion and revenge; but either for reformation and amendment, that they may be the more wary for the future; or for example's sake, to terrify others from the same or the like offences. Even a heathen could say, "*No wise man doth punish because the offence is already committed,*" for then it comes unseasonably and too late, "*but that it may not be committed again.*" Plato apud Lactant. de Ira Dei. c. 18.

But still be sure that the corrections be not immoderate and too severe: neither exceeding the proportion of the fault, for that is cruelty; nor unbeseeming thee to inflict, or the age and character of thy servant to suffer, for that will be reproachful to both. Generally reproof is the best discipline.

Now, to move you to mercy and lenity towards them, consider,

That *you yourselves have a Master, the great and glorious God.* This the apostle urges, Eph. 6 : 9, "Masters—forbear threatening, knowing that your Master also is in heaven." Think with yourselves how often you provoke him, and yet he bears with you although you are infinitely more inferior to him than any servant can be to you: this will calm your passions and cause you, if not altogether to wave, yet at least to allay and mitigate the rigor and severity of your chastisements.

Consider that *they are equal with you in respect to God.* It is true, they are your servants; but both you and they are fellow-servants to the great Lord and Master. And if thou in a rage shouldst take thy fellow-servant by the throat and imperiously abuse him, fear lest thy Lord may require it and vindicate his wrongs in the punishment of thy tyranny. "There is no respect of persons with him; but he that hath done wrong, shall receive for the wrong that he hath done." And what art thou, O vile worm, that thou shouldst domineer over thy fellow, who is moulded of as good earth and hath as precious and immortal a soul in him as thyself? For,

Consider that *thou art equal likewise in nature:* Divine providence only hath made the difference. Whence then such a supercilious disdain of servants, " as if," says Macrobius, "they did not consist of the same materials nor draw the same breath with thyself?" "They are servants, but yet they are men; they are servants, yea, rather, they are thy fellow-servants." And it is in the power of the same providence who hath subjected them to thee, to change the scene, to exalt them and bring thee into bondage. Why then shouldst thou despise them? whereas thou knowest not how soon thou mayest be brought under a more miserable servitude. They are servants out of necessity; when, perhaps, their masters are voluntary slaves. Some are slaves to their lusts, others to covetousness, others to ambition, and all to hope, all to fear. And there is no servitude so justly contemptible as that which is voluntary and wilful.

Consider again, that *he who is a servant to men may be the Lord's freeman;* whereas he that is free among men may be a slave to his lusts, and by them to the devil; and therefore we ought neither to think despicably of servants nor to use them severely, but to treat them with love, as our fellow-creatures, our fellow-servants, yea, and fellow-heirs of the same inheritance of life and glory.— Thus much concerning the master's duty in government.

(2.) The other particular, under the general duty of masters in relation to servants, is *provision;* and this ought to be both for their *temporal* and *spiritual* good, for the welfare both of their bodies and of their souls.

As for *temporal* provision, the master is bound to supply his servants with things necessary for them, according to the tenor of the agreement and compact made between him and them: "Masters, give unto your servants that which is just and equal." Col. 4:1. He ought to provide for them food and raiment; or else, in lieu of any of these, faithfully to pay them their agreed wages. "The wages of him that is hired shall not abide all night with thee until the morning." Lev. 19 : 13. And again, "Thou shalt not oppress a hired servant that is poor and needy—at his day thou shalt give him his hire: neither shall the sun go down upon it, lest he cry against thee unto the Lord, and it be sin unto thee." Deut. 24 : 14, 15. This oppression of servants, in withholding from them the covenanted reward of their labor, is a crying and provoking sin. So the apostle : "The hire of the laborers which have reaped down the fields, (so likewise of those who have done any other work and service for you,) which is of you kept back by fraud, crieth; and the cries of them that have reaped are entered into the ears of the Lord of sabbaoth." James, 5 : 4.

And as the master is to make temporal provision for their bodies, so much more is he to provide for their *spiritual* welfare and the good of their souls, inasmuch as their souls are incomparably to be preferred before their bodies.

Every master is to be both a *priest* and a *prophet* within his own family as well as a *king*. He is to instruct them in the will and laws of God; to inform their ignorance, resolve their doubts, excite and quicken them to the service of God; to rectify their errors and mistakes, to pray with them and for them, to direct them in the way that leads to heaven and happiness; and, above all, to walk before them in it by his holy and pious example.

But how few masters are there who conscientiously perform this duty! Do not the most think it enough if they provide necessaries and conveniences for the body, the dull, outward and earthly part of man? and, indeed, it were enough, if they had only beasts to look after.

But remember, thy servants and those who belong to thy charge have precious and immortal souls, capable of eternal glory and happiness, but liable to eternal misery and torments; and God hath intrusted thee with these souls of theirs, and will require them at thy hands. What a heavy and tremendous doom will pass upon thee when God shall demand at thy hands the souls of thy servants, or of thy children, which have perished through thy default! Will it be enough then to plead, " Lord, I fed and clothed them, and was careful of their health and welfare?" Yea, indeed, if their bodies only were committed to thy care, this were enough; but see, there they stand condemned and ready for eternal flames for the ignorance which thou oughtest to have informed, for the profaneness which thou oughtest to have chastised and hindered, for those neglects of holy duties in which thou oughtest to have gone before them; and therefore, though they shall die and perish in their sins, yet their blood will God require at thy hands, whose carelessness or evil example hath hardened them in wickedness and led them on securely to destruction.

Let me therefore warn you who are masters and heads of families, that as you regard the welfare of the souls of those under your charge, yea, of your own souls, which are deeply engaged and concerned in theirs, you will use all diligence and industry in promoting their spiritual good, that you may at the last day present them with joy before the tribunal of God: "Lo, here I am, and the children and servants that thou hast given me." That you may with joy and triumph present them before the throne of justice then, be frequent in presenting them before the throne of grace now. Let not a day pass without its stated hours of prayer in your family. Instruct those that are ignorant; reduce those that are erroneous; admonish and rebuke with all authority those that are faulty; discard those that are contumacious and incorrigible; let not a scoffing Ishmael, a scorner and derider of piety and holiness remain within your doors; and especially be careful that both you and your family do strictly observe and sanctify the Lord's day, for therein consists a great part of the life and strength of religion, and this day usually gives a seasoning to all the days of the week. Prepare your families by private duties for public; let none of them stay at home from the ordinances but upon great and urgent necessity; suffer them not to wander, some to one pastor and some to another, but where the ordinances of God are duly dispensed; and whither thou thyself art called, thither do thou lead thine, that as they receive their bodily food in thy house, so they may receive their spiritual food in the house of God; take an account of their profiting by what they hear; be as careful to see thy family well employed in the service of God upon the Lord's day, as to see them employed in thine own service and affairs the other days of the week; and therefore be not long nor unnecessarily from them; for God hath made thee his overseer, and if his work go not forward in private family duties, especially on the Lord's day, thou canst never expect a blessing upon what they do for thee.—Thus much concerning the mutual duties of masters and servants.

The *fifth* class of relative duties that I shall treat of, is that of PASTORS AND THEIR FLOCKS, MINISTERS AND THEIR PEOPLE. For between them also is such a relation of superiority and inferiority as brings them under the direction of this commandment.

We do not arrogate too much to ourselves nor take too much upon us when we affirm that we are superior to the people, and have an authority over them in things spiritual and appertaining unto God. And although, through the vices and defects of some who are dignified with this high honor, and partly through the meanness of their outward state and condition, not only their persons but their office be sunk into scorn and contempt; yet I cannot but, with the apostle, magnify mine office, which is truly excellent and venerable; and it is the great sin of the people to despise this calling, although the follies and indiscretions of ministers themselves may not only occasion but invite them to do it.

Here I shall plainly set down the reciprocal duties which they ought mutually to perform to each other.

I. The DUTIES OF MINISTERS either respect their *call*

to that office, or their *management and discharge* of it.

1. The great duty that respects their *call*, is to look to it that they be rightly called; that they do not rashly thrust themselves into so sacred a function unless they be duly set apart thereto.

For, as the priests under the law were "taken from among men, and ordained for men in things pertaining to God, to offer gifts and sacrifices," as the apostle speaks, Heb. 5 : 1, so likewise the ministers of the Gospel are to be duly sanctified and set apart for this high employment, to stand before the Lord, and to minister in things that appertain to his worship; and it is an intolerable presumption for any to intrude themselves into this lot without being selected thereunto or duly authorized by that order which God himself hath appointed and left unto his church. "For no man taketh this honor unto himself but he that is called of God," as the apostle subjoins, verse 4. And therefore God complains of those prophets whom he had "not sent," and "yet they ran;" and to whom he had "not spoken," and "yet they prophesied." Jer. 23 : 21 Audacious-undertaking men it seems they were : like some of late days, who thought their forwardness alone a sufficient consecration, and the seal of whose commission bears only the stamp of their own impudence.

Now to the *due constitution* of a minister there is requisite a *twofold call*.

(1.) He must have an *inward call;* which consists both in the gifts of the Holy Spirit, and also in the inclination of his will to use them for God's glory in this holy ministration.

He must be endowed with a competent knowledge of the truths of the Gospel; without which the great end of the ministry cannot be attained, which is to teach and instruct the people. It is indeed the duty of the ministry to strive after eminency in this knowledge; for they are the lights of the world, and should be able to diffuse abroad their beams, that they may enlighten those that are ignorant and sit in darkness. But yet there is no stated measure nor standard for their knowledge; for we find that our Lord Jesus Christ, the great minister and teacher of the world, sent forth his disciples to preach when yet they were very ignorant of many important truths of the Gospel. Eminent knowledge is therefore necessary for their duty, but competent knowledge is necessary for their office.

Sanctifying grace and a holy life and conversation are also indispensable in the ministry. They may indeed sustain the office without this; for we find a Judas sent forth with the same authority and commission as the rest of the disciples. Yea, and the apostles who had Christ himself for their master and instructor, yet are by him sent to attend on the ministry of the scribes and pharisees; who, though they were very wicked and ungodly hypocrites, yet because they sat in Moses' seat, that is, because they had a rightful authority to teach the people, therefore he commands his own scholars to hear and obey them: "Whatsoever they bid you observe, that observe and do." Mat. 23:2, 3. God may feed his people as he did Elijah by a raven, and make a cold breath kindle the sparks of grace in the hearts of others and blow it up into a flame. But yet it is profitable to the people to sit under a minister who shall go before them in example as well as in doctrine; who not only prescribes them rules of holiness, but is himself an example of those rules. Such a one, who speaks from the heart, is likely to speak to the heart; and having himself experienced the ways of holiness, can more savorily recommend them to the acceptance of his flock. And certainly he will be more likely to speed in his errand, when he shall persuade them to nothing but what he hath found the goodness and sweetness of in himself. All others are but like those Mercurial statues which in old times were set up in cross ways with their hands extended to point out the right road to passengers, but themselves never walked in them. These indeed may be serviceable. But a minister should not only be a director, but a leader; he should not only point out the way, but walk before his flock in it. And it is commonly observed that it is the labors of such that God most usually owns and crowns with success.

(2.) As he must have an inward call in the gifts of the Spirit of God, so likewise he must have an *outward call* by a solemn separation to this work, through imposition of hands. This gives him the ministerial power, and invests him with authority to dispense the ordinances of Jesus Christ as an officer and minister of the Gospel. And this authority St. Paul calls a gift, "Neglect not the gift that is in thee, which was given thee by prophecy, with the laying on of the hands of the presbytery." 1 Tim. 4 : 14. This gift here spoken of I take to be the ministerial office conferred upon him by ordination, according to those predictions and prophecies which were before given of him by some divinely inspired men, who foretold that he was by God designed for the work of the ministry, and should glorify God by a careful discharge of it; of which we read chap. 1, verse 18.

2. When we are assured that our call is right and according to the will of God, there are then many other

duties incumbent on us in the due exercise of our calling.

(1.) We ought to be *good examples* to the flock. This St. Paul most expressly enjoins Timothy, "Be thou an example to the believers, in word, in conversation, in charity, in spirit, in faith, in purity." 1 Tim. 4 : 12.

Indeed it is very sad to consider how the unsuitable conversation of ministers doth quite enervate all the force and strength of their doctrine and exhortations. For, let them speak with the tongues of angels and preach as holily and powerfully as if the Holy Ghost did immediately inspire them, yet, if their lives be loose and their conversation contradictory to their doctrine, the people will be ready to conclude that so much strictness is not necessary, that they only urge it as a matter of high and nice perfection in religion, and that certainly they know a nearer way to heaven than through so many severities which they press upon the people, and therefore they will take the same course and run the same venture that their ministers do.

And how is it likely that such a ministry should be effectual to bring others to holiness, when the minister himself declares to all the world, by his actions, that he looks upon it as unnecessary? What hold can his admonitions and reproofs take upon the consciences of men? certainly his own guilt must rise up in his throat and choke his reproofs. For consciousness of the same miscarriages will retort, whatever we can say against others, more strongly upon ourselves, and suggest to us that it is but base hypocrisy to blame that which we ourselves practise. With what face canst thou press others to repent and reform? what arguments canst thou use to prevail with them, who, by continuing in the same sin, dost thyself judge those arguments to be of no force?

Indeed, it were a temper to be wished and prayed for, that we could only respect how righteous the reproof is, and not how righteous the person who gives it, and be content to have our motes plucked out though it be by such as have beams in their own eyes; that we could learn that hard lesson which our Savior gives his disciples, to do as they say, but not to do after their works; for, indeed, there is no more reason to reject sound admonition because it comes from an unsound heart, than there is to stop our ears against good counsel because it is delivered perhaps by one who has an offensive breath. But yet so it usually fares, that when ministers of defiled and loose lives shall yet preach up holiness and strictness to their people and, as they ought, reprove them sharply for their sins, they will be apt to think, "What! is he in earnest? and doth he not see that he himself is as bad or worse? With what face can he thunder out wo, and wrath, and hell against my sins, which yet are no more mine than his own? Doth he think to fright me with denouncing threats and curses, when he himself, who stands as fair a mark for them as I, slights and contemns them? Or doth he envy me my sins and would engross them all to himself?" And thus, with such carnal reasonings, drawn from the evil examples and wicked lives of ministers, they sit hardened under their preaching, and account all they say but as a lesson they must repeat and a tale they must tell to get their living by. Certainly, such shall perish in their iniquities, but the blood of their souls God will require at your hands.

But when a minister walks conscientiously and exemplarily before his flock, his doctrine gains a mighty advantage to work upon them by his life. This is building up the church of Christ with both hands; showing them both the equity and the easiness of that holiness which he persuades them to by his own practice. When he reproves, his reproofs break in upon the consciences of his hearers with conviction and authority, and if they do not reform, yet at least they daunt and terrify them, and make them self-accused and self-condemned. " Here is one that reproves me for sin, who believes it to be as evil as he represents it by his own eschewing it. Here is one that denounces wrath if I repent not, who doubtless believes it to be as terrible as he declares it by his own carefulness to escape it." Certainly, preaching never comes with such power and energy into the conscience as when the minister preacheth as well by his works as by his word, and, to induce the people to it, is first obedient himself to the truths which he teacheth them. Men are easier led by examples than by precepts, for, though precepts are the more exact, yet examples are the more easy way of teaching, and he is a perfect workman who joineth both together, neither teaching what he will not do, nor doing what he dares not teach: and therefore it is observed of our Lord Jesus Christ, the great teacher of his church, that he *began both to do and teach*. Acts, 1: 1.

Now ministers must be exemplary both in *themselves* and in their *families*.

In *themselves* they "must be blameless, as the stewards of God; not self-willed, not soon angry, not given to wine, no strikers, not given to filthy lucre: lovers of hospitality, lovers of good men, sober, just, holy, temperate," as the Apostle sums up their duties, Tit. 1 : 7, 8 These are the things which will give them a good report among those which are without, and will recommend the doctrines and truths which they teach, to the acceptation and love of their very enemies and the enemies of their holy profession.

They must likewise be exemplary in their *families:* a minister must rule "well his own house, having his children in subjection, with all gravity." 1 Tim. 3 : 4. And because there are so many who are ready maliciously to asperse us, we must, by a serious and circumspect conversation, cut off all occasion from slanderous tongues; that they who watch for our halting may be ashamed when they can find nothing to reproach us with save in the matter of our God.

But if any such there be, who speak like angels but live like devils; who, when they are in the pulpit, it is pity they should ever come out, and when they are out, it is a great pity they should ever come into it again; who are heavenly lights in it, but hellish fire-brands out of it; would to God they would consider how they destroy the very end of their calling, and, instead of converting souls, do but harden them in their sins; making men abhor the offerings and ordinances of the Lord; putting arguments in their mouths to justify their continuance in their wickedness, or else prejudices in their hearts; causing them to depart and separate from holy institutions, because dispensed by profane and scandalous ministers. Let them pretend never so highly to uniformity and obedience; yet, certainly, these are the men who have made all our separatists that now sadly rend our church in pieces; for when the sheep see a wolf set over them instead of a shepherd, no wonder if they run from him and scatter into other pastures. It is in vain for them to tell people that they ought to be obedient to the laws of the church, when those that tell them so are not obedient to the laws of God their Father.

And oh, that they would but consider not only the damage which they do to the church, of which too many of them seem zealous propugners, but the heavy wo and wrath which they bring upon their own souls. Every sermon they study they do but draw up a bill of indictment against themselves, and every time they preach they do but pronounce the sentence of their own damnation. We unto such pastors, when they whom Christ hath set over his sheep shall themselves be found at the last day standing among the goats!

(2.) Another great duty of ministers is a *diligent and conscientious employment of their gifts and talents.*

They must be both able and willing to teach. They themselves must be well grounded in the knowledge and doctrine of Christ: "the priest's lips" should preserve " knowledge, and men should seek the law at his mouth; for he is the messenger of the Lord of hosts." Mal. 2 : 7. And therefore the apostle rejects a novice, a raw, ignorant and unexperienced person; for "if the blind lead the blind, both will" be in danger of falling together "into the ditch." And God himself tells such ignorant and foolish teachers, "Because thou hast rejected knowledge, I also will reject thee, that thou shalt be no priest to me : seeing thou hast forgotten the law of thy God, I will also forget thy children." Hosea, 4 : 6.

And as they must be able to teach, so they must be *diligent* in teaching. A "necessity is laid upon them, and wo unto them if they preach not the Gospel," as the apostle speaks, 1 Cor. 9 : 16. They ought to be instant in season and out of season, 2 Tim. 4:2, "Preach the word; be instant in season and out of season: reprove, rebuke, exhort with all long-suffering and doctrine." Not as if ministers must be continually in the exercise of preaching, but they ought to preach *in season*, that is, in the ordinary and stated times for it, and *out of season*, that is, on extraordinary occasions, when the necessity or usefulness of the church shall require it.

Their doctrine also ought to be *sound* such as cannot be condemned: "Speak thou the things which become sound doctrine." Tit. 2:1. It must have its authority either from the express words of Scripture, or the analogy of faith rationally deduced from Scripture; for he that preacheth false doctrine inconsistent with these, doth but mingle poison with his people's meat.

It must likewise be *profitable*, not setting before them alien and unintelligible notions, or such thin airy speculations as can scarce consist with sense, much less with divinity, for this is to give them wind instead of food. "Charge them before the Lord, that they strive not about words to no profit, but to the subverting of the hearers." 2 Tim. 2:14. And, Tit. 3:8, "These things I will that thou affirm constantly; that they which have believed in God might be careful to maintain good works. These things are good and profitable unto men."

Their preaching, moreover, must be *plain and suited to the capacity of their hearers*, as much as can be without disgusting any; for he that shall only disgorge and tumble out a heap of bombastic theatrical words, at which the people only stare, and gape, and wonder, preacheth to them in an unknown tongue, although he speak English: and this is but to give them stones instead of bread.

Again, their preaching must be *grave and solid, not slovenly and too much neglected,* for that will but beget a nauseating in the hearers; nor yet too nicely and sprucely drest, for that will be apt to divert the attention from the matter to the phrase. Their sermons ought to have a comely and matron-like, not a gayish and meretricious attire. The truths they preach must be delivered in such words as may adorn but not hide nor bury them, such as may rather recommend the doctrine to the consciences, than the art and rhetoric of the preacher to the errors and fancies of the hearers.

And, finally, they ought to preach *powerfully and with authority:* " These things command and teach." 1 Tim. 4 : 11. We come to the people in the name of God, and are his ambassadors, and therefore ought to deliver his message boldly, being sent to the people by the King of kings and Lord of lords; and those who mince his errand, as if they were afraid to speak that which God hath given them in commission, shall at their return unto him receive the reward of treacherous and unfaithful messengers.

There are very many other duties which cannot without too much length be particularly insisted on. As *hospitality,* according to the measure of their estates. They must be " given to hospitality." 1 Tim. 3 : 2. They must be " lovers of hospitality." Tit. 1 : 8. And therefore they ought to be liberally and plentifully endowed, that they may make their table a snare in a good sense, and may get some to follow and observe them though it be but for the loaves; and here it will be a good point of their wisdom if they can handsomely make use of such opportunities (as we find our Savior did after he had miraculously fed the multitude) to break unto them the bread of life, and with their bodily nourishment to feed their souls.

Then *gravity*, in their discourse and in all their converse. A minister should neither speak nor do any thing that is unseemly. Intemperate mirth, clamorous talk, scurrilous jestings, but especially the least syllable of an oath, although it be never so much varied and disguised, in a minister's mouth, as it is wicked, so it is utterly misbecoming the dignity of his profession, and renders him mean and contemptible.

Again, a pious and assiduous care in *visiting the sick*, who may receive good advice and counsel then, although perhaps they have all their lifetime before despised and refused it. You may possibly do more good by the sick-bed than in the pulpit, for death is a terrible and thundering preacher; and he must be a most forlorn and obdurate wretch who will not listen to your admonitions when the hopes of a long life, which made him formerly reject them, have forsaken him.

And once more, *diligence in catechising and instructing the younger in the principles of faith and religion*. Root them well at first, and they will continue stable ever after. This will save yourselves and your successors much labor; for if once you can insinuate into their minds piety and verity, they will grow up to farther degrees of perfection in the ordinary course of your ministry, and be your comfort and rejoicing here, and your crown and glory hereafter.

There are many other duties necessary to the right discharge of the ministerial function, but those already mentioned may suffice. And all others may be reduced to some of these.

I shall therefore conclude this part of the subject with

my earnest request that you would ever seriously meditate upon that charge which God gives the prophet, and in him all ministers: "Son of man, I have made thee a watchman unto the house of Israel; therefore hear the word at my mouth and give them warning from me. When I say unto the wicked, thou shalt surely die; and thou givest him not warning, nor speakest to warn the wicked of his evil way, to save his life; the same wicked man shall die in his iniquity; but his blood will I require at thine hand. Yet if thou warn the wicked, and he turn not from his wickedness, he shall die in his iniquity, but thou hast delivered thy soul." Ezek. 3 : 17–19.

II. Having considered the duties of ministers to their people, we come now to the PEOPLE'S DUTY TOWARDS THEIR MINISTER, which is especially *twofold*, that of obedience and honor.

1. *Obedience*, in being persuaded by his good advice and admonitions.

We have this most expressly commanded, Heb. 13 : 17, "Obey them that have the rule over you;" that is, not only civil magistrates and your rulers in state affairs, but ministers also; for so it is added, "for they watch for your souls as they that must give an account; that they may do it with joy, and not with grief." And they are called "the elders that rule well." 1 Tim. 5 : 17.

I know that this obedience to ministers is a duty so utterly forgotten in the practice of most men, that I doubt if there may not be some prejudice in them against these places of Scripture by which it is so plainly enjoined. Alas, that ever Christ and his apostle should invest us with such authority, which when we assume we are looked upon by the people as almost as ridiculous for it as if we had only a reed in our hands and a crown of shame rather than of dignity put upon our heads, and are accounted of rather as insolent usurpers upon their liberty than as officers empowered by God himself! Sirs, we take to ourselves no power over you but what God hath by his patent and charter given us; and when we propound to you the will of God revealed in his word, or in cases not so clearly determined therein do give our judgment as those who have found mercy to be accounted faithful, we do and may challenge your obedience to it in the name of our Lord Jesus Christ. For we find that in those particular cases wherein the apostle had no express revelation from Christ, yet he prescribes to the Corinthians what he judges fit for them to do, and by that direction obliged their practice; not indeed simply and absolutely, yet so that, in such circumstances as the apostle supposeth, they had sinned if they had done otherwise than he directed them. We desire not to lord it over God's inheritance by any burdensome imposition of things, either unlawful or in themselves unfit. But when we require from you those things which God himself hath commanded, or if not expressly commanded, yet which are, in the judgment of those to whom you owe obedience, thought convenient and lawful to be done, I know not how you can excuse yourselves from disobedience against God if in these cases you be not obedient unto us. And if you call this usurpation, and a taking too much upon us, you do but speak the language of Korah and his accomplices, Num. 16 : 3, and shake not so much ours as God's title and authority over you, who hath given us this power and commission.

2. Another duty of the people is to *honor* their ministers as their spiritual fathers.

Yea, the apostle speaks of a *double honor* due to them, 1 Tim. 5 : 17, " Let the elders that rule well be accounted worthy of double honor." All must have that honor given them which is due to their function; but those who rule the flock well, καλως, that is, not barely commendably but excellently, must have this honor doubled to them; and those who not only thus rule but excel others in teaching them likewise, must have this double honor doubled upon them, especially they that labor in the word and doctrine.

We owe them the honor of *reverence*. We ought to honor and esteem them for their office and their work's sake. So, expressly, 1˙ Thess. 5 : 12, 13, " We beseech you, brethren, to know them which labor among you, and esteem them very highly in love for their work's sake." And again, Phil. 2 : 29, " Receive him therefore in the Lord with all gladness; and hold such in reputation." And certainly they who cast any contempt on ministers, either by injurious actions or reviling speeches, do not so much despise them as Christ who sent them. " He that despiseth you, despiseth me," saith our Savior, Luke, 10 : 16. And God will not leave this sin unpunished, yea, he speaks of it as an almost unpardonable crime : " They mocked the messengers of God, and despised his words, and misused his prophets, until the wrath of God was against his people, and there was no remedy." 2 Chron. 36 : 16.

Again, we owe them the honor of *maintenance*. So, Gal. 6 : 6, " Let him that is taught in the word, communicate unto him that teacheth in all good things." And there is good reason for it; for, "if we have sown unto you spiritual things, is it a great thing if we shall reap your carnal things?" saith the apostle, 1 Cor. 9 : 11. What you give them is not a matter of bounty and mere voluntary benevolence; and the minister who so accounts or receives it, undervalues his authority and wrongs his right; but it is your duty and his due. He must have a competent and liberal maintenance, not stinted to bare necessity; but it should be liberal, such as may enable him to relieve the necessities of others, to provide comfortably for his own family, and to use hospitality in his house. This is his due, and he owes you no more thanks for tendering it than you do him for receiving it. Not here to dispute the divine right of the tenth part, (which yet was not all that was due to the ministers under the law, for they had a considerable accession by offerings and sacrifices,) I think it certain that the encouragement of ministers under the Gospel should equal if not exceed theirs, inasmuch as our labor is far greater and our ministry more excellent than theirs. But they who think it fit to keep ministers poor and dependent, may well be suspected to do it in favor of their own vices; for how shall he dare to reprove them, who is afraid of losing part of his stipend? But whilst the gentleman in black must sit below the salt, and after dinner converse with the better sort of serving men, there is no danger that he should be so audacious as to find fault; or if he should, no great heed will be taken to what so despicable a thing as he can say.

It remains only to notice, in the *sixth* place, the mutual duties between SUPERIORS AND INFERIORS, or those who differ in the gifts of *Divine bounty.*

These may be considered either as the gifts of *special grace* or of *common providence.* Of which briefly.

I. THE GIFTS OF SPECIAL GRACE. God endows some with an excellent measure of *sanctifying grace ;* and is pleased to show the world, by a few rare and choice instances, how wonderfully he can sublime our corrupted nature, and how near he can exalt human frailty to an angelical perfection. This indeed is the most excellent of all his gifts, and that which we ought most earnestly to covet and desire; for although other gifts, as knowledge, wisdom, power, &c. do in some imperfect manner assimilate us to God, yet sanctification and holiness far transcend all these, both because it stamps on us the resemblance of the Divine nature in that attribute which is its greatest glory, (whence God assumes it to himself that he is *glorious in holiness,*) and likewise because God hath highly honored it, and given it the dignity and prerogative to be the only means of bringing us to the complete and eternal fruition of our felicity.

1. Those whom God hath thus blessed with an eminent degree of this his best gift ought,

(1.) *To beware that they do not secretly despise their weaker brethren in their hearts; nor with a censorious austerity reject those whom God hath received.*

It is often seen that fellow-servants are more inexorable towards each other than their common Lord and Master ; and that those errors and infirmities which are rather the slips of thoughtlessness than the products of a resolved will, can hardly obtain pardon among men, though God hath forgiven and forgotten them. This ariseth from a spiritual pride, which makes us envious towards those who excel us, and scornful towards those who fall short; for when men grow conceited of their own excellencies and attainments they will be ready to condemn other men's duties as formal hypocrisy, and their sins as total apostasy; they will mistake the smoking flax for a reeking dunghill, and be forward imperiously to cast them out of God's family though themselves were but lately received into it out of mere charity.

Certainly this is a spirit, (though it too much prevails in this broken and shattered age, wherein every one thinks so much the better of himself by how much the worse he thinks of others,) yet this I say is a spirit utterly misbecoming the sweetness and mildness of the Gospel, which teacheth us to be meek and gentle, forbearing one another and forgiving one another. It would better become thee, O christian, not to observe other men's falls, but to look to thine own standing: "Thou standest by faith, be not high-minded, but fear." Rom. 11 : 20. It is the worst way that so excellent a thing as divine grace can be perverted, when it makes thee proud and censorious.

For my part I should much more confide in the security of an humble soul that creeps along to heaven, though with a slow yet an even pace, than in the ecstatic zeal and fervor of those who perhaps far outstrip others, but also contemn them. For the one is still pressing forward, and regards with admiration those who excel; but the other is often looking back with disdain upon those who are slower than himself; and whilst he minds not so much his way as the advances he hath made, offers many advantages to the devil to trip him up and give him many a sore and shameful fall.

And therefore, O christian, the more eminent thy

graces are, the more need hast thou to pray and strive for humility. The tallest cedars had need have the deepest roots, otherwise the storms and winds will easily overturn them : so truly the higher any grow, the more they spread and flourish like the cedars of God, beautiful in their leaves and plentiful in their sap, the more need have they to be deeply rooted in humility; or else, believe it, the wind and tempest of temptations, to which they stand more exposed than others, will not only sorely shake them but utterly overturn them, when those whom they shall despise as mean shrubs shall stand secure, and with a tender pity weep over their fall.

(2.) Another duty of such as are eminent in grace is, *to improve the grace they have to the benefit and advantage of others.*

God hath given thee a large portion, that thou shouldst be helpful to thy brethren. The stock of grace which he hath offered thee, is not only that thou thyself shouldst live well upon it, but it was intended for the relief and comfort of the whole family.

Hath God endowed thee with *a clear and distinct knowledge of the mysteries of the Gospel?* Know that this lamp was lighted up in thee that thou shouldst give light unto others, that thou shouldst diffuse and scatter abroad its rays round about thee; to inform the ignorant, guide the doubting, confirm the wavering, resolve the scrupulous, reduce the erroneous and convince the malicious opposers of the truth. This is not the minister's duty only, though more eminently and especially his; but it is the duty of every private christian whom God hath blessed with a large measure of true knowledge more than others, still keeping within due bounds and limits.

Or, hath the Holy Spirit kindled in thy breast *a flame of Divine affection?* And is it not to this end, that thou shouldst breathe warmth into the languishing desires of others, and by holy conference and spiritual discourse, illustrating the beauty of holiness, the excellency of true piety in itself and the rewards which it brings after it, apply thy heavenly fire unto their chill and freezing hearts until thou hast enkindled them too and set them on a flame, that so both together might burn with vigorous love towards God and his Christ?

Or, hath God exercised thee with *grievous trials and violent temptations?* Wherefore is it, but that thou shouldst the better know how to succor those that are tempted, and by thine own experiences counsel and comfort those who are ready to sink under their load, which not only the weight but the unusualness makes the more intolerable? For the greatest accent and emphasis that such do usually put upon their miseries is, that never any before were so severely afflicted, never any before were so violently assaulted. Let them know that no temptation hath befallen them but what is common unto men, and that thou thyself hast come triumphantly from under the like. Expound to them the depths and methods of Satan, unravel his wiles and subtleties, stretch out the entangled folds of that old and crooked serpent; for therefore hath God comforted you in all your tribulations, that you might be able to comfort them who are troubled, with the same comforts by which yourselves have been comforted of God; as the apostle speaks, 2 Cor. 1 : 4.

Or, if thou art not so fit either for instruction or counsel, yet at least let thy graces be beneficial to others, *by a holy and exemplary conversation.* If thy graces cannot shine through thy gifts, yet at least let them shine through thy life, that others seeing thy good works, may give glory to thy heavenly Father. And therefore never complain that thou canst not honor God in so noble a way as others, that thou canst not speak nor plead for him as others do. If thou livest to him thou pleadest for him; for certainly a holy life is a much better commendation of holiness than all the elaborate encomiums of art and rhetoric.—These are the duties of those that excel in grace.

2. As for others whose graces are less, one duty of theirs is,

Highly to love and esteem those whose graces are more eminent and conspicuous. God is the comprehensive and ultimate object of our love and veneration, and therefore the nearer any creature approacheth to the similitude of God, the more ought we to esteem and prize it. Now God is not more strikingly represented in any thing than in the holiness of his saints. This is the most perfect portraiture and image of him who hath styled himself " the holy One of Israel." They are begotten of God, made partakers of the Divine nature, and conformed to his image; therefore, as we would adore this glorious attribute of God in its infinite original, so we ought to esteem and venerate it in those happy souls to whom God hath communicated some rays of it. " Every one that loveth him that begat, loveth him also that is begotten of him," saith the Apostle, 1 John, 5 : 1, because of the likeness he bears to his heavenly Father; and the more express this resemblance is, the more intense and the more endearing should our affections be. We ought to associate with them; to make them our bosom-friends, our confidants, and our companions; our delight should be in the saints, and in the excellent ones of the earth, as David professeth his to have been, Psalm 16 : 3.

Another duty of the less eminent in grace towards those who are the more eminent, is *imitation of their holy examples; following them wherein they follow the Lord Christ.*

If thou seest others far outstrip thee, mend thy pace, endeavor to overtake them, tread in the same steps, and do thy very utmost to keep even with them: envy not their graces, but be sure to emulate them.

Indeed, some there are who, that they might not seem to be behind the best, prove hinderances and pull-backs to them, lest the forwardness of their zeal and piety should be a reproach to their own sloth: like truants at school, who, lest their fellows should get too much before them, do what they can to entice them from their books. But this is a most wicked envy, and the root of it is pride and laziness.

But a holy emulation never repines at nor hinders the proficiency of others: it rather would by all means promote it, but it will put us upon endeavors to be as forward as any. It will not be a curb to them, but a spur to us. And such an emulation as this every true christian should highly cherish. For the shame of being outstript is as great an incentive as any that can be given to virtue. Christians are like a company of men running in a race: every one should strive and strain every nerve and sinew to be first at the goal—the first that should lay hold on the prize and reward.

And here *be sure you set your pattern right.* Take not the most noisy and airy christians, who glory in talk and censures. Take not one who hath an affectation of being religious after a new mode and fashion. Take not one who seeks to raise a fame for piety only by decrying or condemning this or that form of profession, and who, if there were no differences among us, would lose very much of his reputation for sanctity; for these are only torrents that run with a violent stream, but they are shallow, and we know not how soon they may grow dry and deceive the hopes of those who come to refresh themselves at them. But propound those to yourselves for examples who are of fixed principles and sober practice; who are grave and solid; who, in all the duties that belong to a christian conversation, labor to do them substantially rather than ostentatiously; who live within God and themselves; who have deep thoughts and solid expressions of duty; and whose actions are suitable and correspondent to both. Such a one is the Christian in deed; and such, for some such there are, I recommend to you for your imitation. And yet there is no man that walks so uprightly but that sometimes he steps awry. And therefore be not led by a blind and implicit adherence to any man, but continually eye the rule; and wherein soever any forsake that, be they apostles, yea, or if it were possible, even angels themselves, therein forsake them.—Thus much for the mutual duties of superiors and inferiors in respect of grace.

II. Let us next consider them in respect to the gifts of God's COMMON BOUNTY, which he promiscuously distributes both to the good and to the bad. I shall but briefly mention them.

God's gifts of providence may respect either our *per-*

sons or else our *outward estate.* Those which respect the person, are either gifts of the *mind* or of the *body.*

(1.) Those *who excel in gifts of the mind*, in knowledge, and wisdom, and parts, a profound judgment, or a winning elocution, *ought to improve these to the good and advantage of others:* not as Ahithophel did his politic counsel, or Tertullus his flattering oratory, to oppress right and equity; but to guide and advise, for the benefit of mankind and the glory of God.

For these gifts, though they are not sanctifying, yet may be very serviceable to the church. Hiram, though a stranger to the commonwealth of Israel, yet provided many excellent materials for the building of the temple. So God doth many times embellish those who are strangers to him with many admirable ornaments of understanding and learning, and makes use of the materials, which they have prepared and laid in, for the edification of his church. And as Noah employed many to build his ark, who were themselves overwhelmed in the deluge; so God many times employs such as these to build his ark, the church, who yet may at last be swept away with the deluge of his wrath, and drowned in perdition.

These, though they should possess such gifts without any sanctifying and saving grace, yet are very useful men, and our duty is to esteem aud reverence them, to love their excellencies and to encourage their labors, to praise God for them, and pray for an increase of their gifts. How much more then, when their natural and acquired endowments are conjoined with sanctifying grace, and the love of the truth as much possesses their hearts as the knowledge of it does their heads! It is a sordid baseness to detract from any man's worth or extenuate his abilities by some slanderous *buts* and *exceptions*. This is the disingenuous practice of many, who think all that added to their own praise which they thus nibble away from another man's.

(2.) Another superiority which God grants some over others, is that of *old age*, which is of itself reverend and entitled to respect; and we ought to give that due respect to it which both nature and the law of God requires: " Thou shalt rise up before the hoary head, and honor the face of the old man, and fear thy God." Lev. 19 : 32. God hath put a signal honor upon it by styling himself the *Ancient of days*, Dan. 7 : 9; and he threatens it as a great judgment upon a people, Isa. 3 : 5, that the children shall behave themselves proudly against the ancients. We read how severely a scorn cast upon an aged prophet was revenged on those children which mocked his baldness. A reverend awe before the aged is not only a point of manners, but part of a moral and express duty; and therefore it is said of Elihu, Job, 32 : 4, that he " waited till Job had spoken, because they were elder than he ;" and verse 6, he saith, " I am young, and ye are very old; wherefore I was afraid, and durst not show you mine opinion."

And if such respect and reverence be due to them from others, they ought chiefly to reverence themselves, and by grave, and prudent, and holy actions, to put a crown of glory on their own gray head. They ought not to be vain and light in their converse, nor children of a hundred years old, nor by the folly and wickedness of their lives expose themselves to that contempt which will certainly be cast on them where age is not accompanied with gravity and prudence. And therefore we find, Prov. 16 : 31, " The hoary head is a crown of glory, if it be found in the way of righteousness :" otherwise, instead of being a glory, it is but a double shame and reproach.

(3.) There is another sort of the gifts of common providence wherein some excel others, and that is *riches and honor*. Those who are distinguished by these the Scripture calls fathers. Nabal, though he were a fool and a churl, yet David in his message to him doth implicitly call him father, 1 Sam. 25 : 8, " Give, I pray thee, whatsoever cometh to thine hand unto thy servants, and to thy son David."

Their duty is to be humble towards their inferiors, knowing that it is only external goods, and those the least considerable of all the stores of God's blessings, that make them to differ from others, and to communicate to the relief of others' necessities, that they may be rich in good works, and make themselves friends of the mammon of unrighteousness, that when they fail they may be received into everlasting habitations; for he that is rich only in hoarding and keeping up his store, is no better to be accounted of than the base earth which locks up more treasures in its bowels than they can in their chests.

And the duty of their inferiors is to pay them all due respect according to what God hath bestowed upon them; to acknowledge the riches of God in making them rich, and to endeavor to promote, so far as in them lies, the spiritual good of their souls, that they may not be rich here and undone eternally. For a rich man may be more universally instrumental either of good or evil than others can, and therefore to win such a one to the faith, or to preserve him stable in it, is a most charitable work, not only to his soul in particular, but to the church of Christ, the affairs of which may be much advanced by such a man's wealth and interest.

Thus I have at last gone through the mutual duties of many relations involved here in this fifth commandment; some *natural,* some *civil,* some *ecclesiastical,* and some *economical:* I know not with what acceptation or success.

Possibly some may think these things too mean and trivial to be so long insisted on. But let me tell such, that *relative duties,* as they are the most difficult of all to perform, so they are the best trials of true christianity and the power of godliness. He that endeavors not to walk closely with God in these, let his notions and profession be never so lofty and sublime, it will be no uncharitableness at all to judge that all his pomp is but a mere form of godliness and a hypocritical ostentation.

Let me exhort you, therefore, in the fear of God, that ye be much in pondering these things. There needs no great labor to understand them, nor to find out mysteries and concealed depths in them. It is true, they are plain, but they are of daily use, and it is but reasonable that we should not be long understanding what we are continually to practise.

Let me subjoin but one *general rule* and I have done. It is this: *in all these mutual duties it is no excuse for the one party to fail of the most conscientious and careful performance of what belongs to him because the other doth so.* For certainly another man's sin cannot excuse mine; and God hath bound us in duty not only one to another, but all of us to himself. Therefore though others may break their obligations and covenants with us, yet that doth not take off our obligation to them. Should the father be careless of and cruel to his child, yet this doth not at all exempt the child from paying duty and obedience to his father. Should a master be tyrannical over his servant, yet the servant's duty remains still stated and unaltered, to reverence, fear and obey his master. Should a minister be careless of the flock committed to his charge, yet his people are still bound to give him respect and honor in regard to his office. Should a magistrate tyrannize over his subjects, yet still they are to own him and obey his commands in all lawful things. For mal-administration of any office or any authority by superiors cannot countenance and excuse want of duty in inferiors. Still we are as carefully to perform what God hath required as if our superiors were the best parents or magistrates or masters in the world; and if there be any wrong done, or defect on their part, we must leave it to Him to reward our conscientious obedience, and to punish their wilful offences. And so likewise it is incumbent on superiors to perform their duties faithfully and conscientiously toward their inferiors, be they never so perverse, ungrateful or rebellious, for their faults cannot excuse our neglects.

Having spoken thus much of the *precept* in this large and comprehensive command, *Honor thy father and thy mother*, I come now to the PROMISE added as a motive and encouragement to obedience, *that thy days may be long in the land which the Lord thy God giveth thee.* This promise God's faithfulness stands engaged to fulfil to all that are dutiful and obedient.

And here we may observe, that whereas the free and genuine administration of the Gospel promises eternal life and the joys and glories of heaven to believers, the old law runs generally upon earthly and temporal blessings; and among them insists frequently upon length of days and a happy and prosperous life, as the chiefest blessing and highest expectation of human nature; yet this must not be understood as if the promises of the law were only for these beggarly and earthly concerns, but because this procedure was more suitable to the whole system of that early instruction wherein God thought fit to discipline them by types, and to lead them to the sun by shadows. Therefore, as he allayed his own spiritual worship with the mixture of very many external rites and pompous observances, so he propounded to them likewise their eternal rewards by temporal and earthly promises; and, by both, attempered their religion to their state of infancy, bringing it down, as much as possible, to the verdict of sense; reserving the manly and heroic duties of believing his word without a pawn to the more grown ages of the church.

But however, though these promises made to the Jews were thus typical, yet these figures were not altogether so figurative as not to be properly understood and fulfilled. Though heaven were typified by Canaan, yet God's veracity would have suffered if he had brought them to heaven, the true land of promise, and not given them their inheritance in the earthly Canaan. So likewise, that God might be true to his promise, it is not enough that he rewards the obedient with eternal life; but his faithfulness stands obliged to prolong their temporal life to such a duration as may be fit at least to make a type of the everlasting rest.

Neither doth the more spiritual dispensation of the Gospel look upon this blessing of long life as a thing below its cognizance, but propounds it as a promise of moment, though it be now divested of its typical use and stands for no more than itself signifies. And therefore we find that the apostle puts a value upon this fifth commandment on this very reason, that it is "the first with promise." Eph. 6 : 2, 3. And St. Peter at large transcribes that passage of Psalm 34, "What man is he that desireth" to live, "and loveth many days? Let him depart from evil, and do good." And St. Paul tells us that "godliness is profitable unto all things, having promise of the life that now is, and of that which is to come." And what is there that can concern this life more than life itself? God's faithfulness is, therefore, obliged by promise to lengthen out a holy and obedient life.

Nor will it be very hard to vindicate his faithfulness in the performance of this promise. God does indeed suffer many to grow old in their sins, whose youth began their course of wickedness with rebellion against their parents, and who continue, to their decrepid days, their impieties and rebellions against God; and early towardliness and piety I know are often looked upon as mortal symptoms—God seems to shorten their days to whom he here promiseth a long life—but since this present life is nothing else but a tendency and preparative to eternity, neither it nor any thing in it can be called good but only as it relates to our eternal state. And therefore all promises of earthly blessings must necessarily imply this condition, that they shall be literally fulfilled to us *if they may promote our eternal happiness:* otherwise they would not be promises, but threatenings, and that which we apprehend to be a blessing would indeed prove no other to us than a snare and curse. We may boldly challenge long life when all the circumstances of it will tend to our everlasting welfare. But God, who knows how frail and yielding the best of us are, and in the series of his divine providence sees to what prevailing temptations we shall be exposed, oftentimes in mercy abridges this promise, and takes us from the world, lest the world should take us from him; and deals with us as princes deal with duellists, they make them prisoners that they may preserve them: so God, that he might preserve his people from their great enemy, commits them to the safe custody of the grave. And if this be to be unfaithful, certainly his faithfulness would be nothing else but an art to circumvent and undo us, should he, only to keep that inviolate, perform those promises which would be to our hurt and detriment. Nor, indeed, can any man, whom God hath blessed with a right judgment and due esteem of things, be willing to compound for the continuance of this present life at the hazard or diminution of his future happiness.

THE SIXTH COMMANDMENT.

Thou shalt not kill.

The Commandments of the Second Table all immediately respect our duty to our fellow-men, whom we may consider either as under some peculiar differences, or in their common nature.

We have already spoken of the duties that belong to them under the first acceptation, as they are differenced into superiors and inferiors. There are other duties which appertain universally to all, under what difference soever they may be considered, whether they be superiors or inferiors, or equals among themselves; and these are contained in the five following precepts, all which concern our neighbor either in his *person* or in his *exterior gifts of wealth or good name*.

His *person* is to be considered either naturally or mystically. *Naturally*, as he is this individual man; and so the sixth commandment provides for his security, *Thou shalt not kill*. *Mystically*, as he is in the state of marriage, which of two makes up one mystical person; and so care is taken for him in the seventh, *Thou shalt not commit adultery*.

If we consider him in his *external gifts*, his *estate and substance* is safeguarded by the eighth commandment, *Thou shalt not steal*. His *reputation and good name* by the ninth, *Thou shalt not bear false witness against thy neighbor*.

And as a strong fence set about him, and also about the

other laws, that neither of them be violated, God hath not only prohibited the *outward acts of gross and flagitious crimes*, but the *inward lurking motions to evil in our thoughts and affections ;* and this in the tenth commandment, *Thou shalt not covet.*

I shall begin with the first of these, which takes care for the security and indemnity of our persons, THOU SHALT NOT KILL.

I. This command forbids, *first*, that barbarous and inhuman sin of MURDER, that first-born of the devil, who was *a murderer from the beginning ;* the first branded crime that we read of, wherein natural corruption contracted by the fall vented its rancor and virulence; the sin of Cain, that great instance of perdition, "who slew his brother" Abel, "because his brother's works were righteous and his own evil."

Neither doth this precept confine itself only to forbid the actual sin of murder, but all degrees and all causes of it; as hatred and rash anger, revenge, and slanders, and false accusations, and whatsoever may prejudice the safety of our neighbor, or tempt us to see him perish when it is in our power to rescue and relieve him.

Some have extended the sense of this prohibition, *Thou shalt not kill,* even to brute creatures, holding it unlawful to slay any of them for the use and service of our life. Possibly indeed unmercifulness even towards them, and a cruel tormenting of them, not to satisfy our occasions and necessities, but our unreasonable passions, may be reducible as a sin against this commandment, for all acts of cruelty are so; but simply to kill them for our necessity cannot. God, the universal Lord both of them and us, hath granted us this prerogative in our charter, to have the power of life and death over them. "Every moving thing that liveth shall be meat for you." Gen. 9 : 3. And doubtless we may put them to any kind of death that the necessity either of our food or physic will require. This killing, therefore, forbidden in the text, refers only to men like ourselves; and therefore it is very properly rendered by others, *Thou shalt do no murder.*

2. Yet, *neither is every killing of a man murder;* for there are several cases wherein although one kill another yet he is no murderer; as,

(1.) In *the execution of justice.*

Magistrates and such as have lawful power and authority may and ought to put capital offenders to death; and if they do not, God will charge it on them as their sin. It is an ancient law upon record, Gen. 9 : 6, "Whoso sheddeth man's blood, by man shall his blood be shed;" as if there were no other way for expiation, no other method to wash away the stain and guilt of blood, but only by his who unjustly spilt it. And again, Deut. 19 : 21, "Thine eye shall not pity, but life shall go for life." And indeed if we rightly consider it, this is not to butcher up mankind, but to preserve them. God hath commanded magistrates to kill, that he might prevent murder; for our nature is so extremely corrupt that there is no other effectual way to hinder us from killing but by enjoining the magistrates to do it. And therefore as physicians, in cases of violent and immoderate bleeding, do often open a vein in another part of the body as the best method to stop it by revulsion; so, when the body politic bleeds by private rage and revenge gushing out into murders, the way to stop this blood is to shed blood.

Neither doth our Savior's command not to *resist evil*, Mat. 5 : 39, gainsay this legal and punitive way of bloodshedding. For those words do only forbid private revenge, not public. We must not be judges in our own causes, nor, when we apprehend ourselves wronged, carve out to ourselves what measures of revenge our wrath and fury shall dictate. We, who have no authority nor commission, ought not to take life for life, nor eye for eye, nor tooth for tooth, much less life for an injurious word or an idle quarrel. We must not repay with the least revenge those who have done us the greatest wrongs, in which sense we must not resist evil; but, if we have in any thing suffered wrong, we ought to bring all our causes and complaints to the magistrate; for into his hands hath God put *the sword* of justice. Rom. 13 : 4.

Revenge is so sacred a thing that none ought to intermeddle with it but those whom God hath appointed; for he hath solemnly ascribed it to himself, Heb. 10 : 30, " Vengeance belongeth unto me : I will recompense, saith the Lord." And he hath constituted the magistrate as his deputy in this work and office, and therefore he only ought to revenge by punishment proportionable to the nature of the crimes committed.

So that, to speak properly, it is only God, and not man, that sheds the blood of wicked persons. The magistrate receives his commission from God, and doth it as his minister and servant; yea, and in doing it, is so far from doing a cruel and unjust act, an act that will either pollute his hands or stain his conscience, that it makes him the more holy and pure. And therefore when Moses called the Levites to slay those idolaters that had worshipped the golden calf, he speaks of it as a holy function : " Con secrate yourselves to-day to the Lord; even every man upon his son, and upon his brother; that he may bestow upon you a blessing this day." Exod. 32 : 29.

(2.) There may be bloodshed *in a just and lawful war*, without the charge or crime of murder.

Indeed we are commanded *to follow peace with all men;* and *as much as lies in us,* and *if possible,* to have peace *with all men.* Rom. 12 : 18. But sometimes, through the ambition and turbulent spirits of others, through their politic designs of picking unjust quarrels, it may be no longer possible to maintain peace; and in this case, where we have right and equity on our side, it is lawful to wage war. I speak not now of private differences between person and person; but of public, between nation and nation : in which case the supreme magistrate hath the power of making war and proclaiming peace.

There are some who decry this assertion, and think it contrary to the temper of a christian, who is a son of peace, to be a man of war. I confess there is nothing that can justify war against another nation, but either

Necessary defence against an unjust invasion. Or,

Recovery of what is unjustly taken away; as David pursued the Amalekites, who had carried his wives away captives. Or,

The punishing of some great injury and wrong; as David likewise warred against the Ammonites for the contumelious usage of his ambassadors.

But, where the cause is just, the manner in which we prosecute it warrantable, the authority which engageth us in it being rightly constituted over us, I see nothing but that it is very fit when it is very necessary to take up arms, and in a public war to right ourselves upon injurious enemies. For as there may be many wrongs done by one party against another, who must be judged by the law common to them both; so there may be many wrongs done by one nation against another, which if they will not consent to redress, there being no common magistrate nor common law over them both, (except the law and right of nations, of which the more powerful usually make little account,) in this case, certainly, the injured may very justly have recourse to war; for, what law is to persons of the same nation, that war is to persons of a different nation.

We read that among those many penitents that came to John the Baptist for instruction, when soldiers also came he did not bid them lay down their arms or their commission. He preached not to them, fight no more, kill no man; but gave them directions how they should demean themselves in their calling: which he would not have done if he had thought their calling itself unlawful. He bids them "Do no violence, accuse no man falsely, but be content with your wages." Luke, 3 : 14.

Neither did our Savior when he so highly commended the centurion for his faith, rebuke him for his profession, but extolled him for taking the ground and argument of his faith from his military calling, Luke, 7 : 8, "I am a man under authority, having under me soldiers; and I say unto one, go, and he goeth; and to another, come, and he cometh; and to my servant, do this, and he doeth it." This very calling of his he urgeth Christ with, and makes it an argument to strengthen his faith, that certainly Christ was able to cure his sick servant, because if he who was but a captain had such authority over his soldiers as to command them to come and to go at his word, how much more absolute power had Jesus, as **Lord** both of life and death, over all bodily diseases, to command them to come and go at his pleasure! This I take to be the force and reason of his words, upon which Christ gives him this large testimonial and encomium, verse 9, " When Jesus heard these things, he marvelled at him, and turned him about and said unto the people, I have not found so great faith, no, not in Israel" But enough of this.

(3.) A man may shed blood *in the necessary defence of his person* without being guilty of murder, when he is suddenly assaulted by those who attempt to take away his life and he hath no other means left him to secure it. In this case, there being no possibility of having recourse to a magistrate for protection, every man is a magistrate to himself.

But here, because all cases of blood are tender, let me caution you that it is not enough that the danger be impending, but it must be instant and present; such wherein a man's life is in all probability lost if he doth not stand upon his defence. For in dangers that are only threatened and approaching, we ought to trust Providence, and to use our best diligence to work our escape from them. But if the assault be sudden and no way of escape visible, we may lawfully take away the life of him who unjustly seeks to take ours; for this is not a design to *kill him*, but to *preserve ourselves*.

Yea, we find, Exod. 22:2, that God allows the killing of a thief, if he break into a man's house by night, but not so if he attempt it by day. And possibly the reason of this law might be because, when any cometh upon another in the night, it might be presumed that he takes the advantage of the darkness not only to steal his goods but to harm his person; and therefore God allows it as lawful to kill such a one as a part of necessary defence: from which I think we may safely conclude that it is lawful also to kill those who attempt upon our goods, when we have reason to fear they may likewise design upon our persons.

(4.) There is yet one case more, and that is *accidental bloodshedding*, which is not chargeable with murder when blood is shed without any intention or purpose of doing it.

Such a case we find mentioned in Scripture, as when in hewing of wood from a tree the axe should slip and kill a man's neighbor. Deut. 19: 5. And therefore for such innocent manslayers God himself appointed cities of refuge, that they might fly to them and be safe from the avenger of blood.

But here we must look to it that we be employed about lawful things; otherwise, if we be doing that which is unjustifiable, which accidentally proves to be the death of another, this cannot be excused from murder: and 1 am sure God exacts the same punishment for it. Therefore it is said, Exod. 21: 22, that if men strive among themselves and hurt a woman that she die, though it was not intended by them, yet life shall go for life: because their strife and contention between themselves is an unlawful action.

There ought also to be a due care taken to avoid any mischief that may happen upon doing a lawful action, by giving notice to those who come in the way of danger, and forbearing to do it whilst they are there.

But in all cases where the death of another is *intended*,

let it be upon never so violent and sudden a passion, although there were no prepensed and rancoring malice borne towards him before, and howsoever our laws may be too favorable to it and call it manslaughter, yet doubtless it is in conscience and in the sight of God wilful murder. For the manslayer, whom the Scripture mentions distinct from the murderer, is only he who slays his neighbor accidentally; not designing nor intending him any harm. This is the only manslaughter which our law is pleased to call chance-medley; and whatsoever is not this is murder, and ought as such to be punished.

2. Murder may be either *of a man's self or of another*. Both of them are most black and heinous crimes.

(1.) As for *self-murder*, many of the ancient heathens thought this the most heroic and gallant way of dying, and would have recourse to it on very slight occasions, accounting it a universal remedy that nature had put into their hands to rid themselves of any trouble which they were loth to bear.

Yet some even among the heathen have very sharply as well as justly taxed this wicked custom, among whom that saying of Aristotle in his Ethics is very considerable: "For a man to die only that he may avoid poverty or crosses, is not gallantry, but mere cowardice, and declares that he wants courage to encounter them." In this particular this heathen had a better illumination than the author of the book of Maccabees, who very unworthily commends one Razis, a Jew, for choosing rather to destroy himself than yield to his enemy—a passage in this book, besides divers others, which evidently proves those books not to belong to the canon of Scripture, but to deserve to be called as they are, Apocryphal.

And truly self-murder, next to the unpardonable sin against the Holy Ghost, is, I think, the most dangerous and most desperate that can be committed; and as it leaves so little room for repentance, it leaves but very little for hope and charity. Those wretched creatures whom God hath so far abandoned as to permit them to fall into this horrid crime, had they but the least care of their eternal salvation, would certainly tremble when they are offering violence to themselves, considering that they must instantly appear before God, and lift up those hands at his great tribunal which they but a minute before imbrued in their own blood. It is a sin which, when the devil tempts men to, he cannot make use of his most prevailing wile and stratagem, for when he tempts to other sins he still drills on the sinner with hopes of living to repent and reform, and promises him mercy and forgiveness; but this of self-murder precludes all such hopes and expectations, for they die in their sins, yea, their death is their sin: and what a forlorn estate are they in who resolve that their last act shall be a damnable sin! These are self-murderers to purpose, and destroy not only their bodies but their souls too.

Consider again that it is a sin committed against the very standard and rule of our love to others; for God hath commanded us to love others as ourselves, and therefore as we may not murder another, so much less may we murder ourselves. And those who are hurried to this impious act, as they do actually destroy themselves, so they do virtually and interpretatively murder and destroy the whole world; and are as guilty before God as if, together with themselves, they had murdered their parents, their children, their nearest relations, and all mankind besides; and that, because they destroy that fundamental law which should regulate their love to their neighbors, and which is the stated rule according to which they should endeavor after their welfare and preservation.

Therefore if ever the devil work upon thy melancholy and discontented pride to tempt thee to this damnable and almost unpardonable sin, be sure to collect all thy strength unto thee, and with infinite abhorrence of it command him to depart. Let not any shame, or poverty, or horrors of conscience fasten this hellish temptation upon thee, for know assuredly that if thou hearkenest unto them and puttest them in execution, there is no probability but that thou must pass from temporal sufferings to eternal torments; which, be thy condition in this life never so deplorable and wretched, thou hast no reason to hasten, but wilt in hell think that they came too soon upon thee.

(2.) The *murdering of another* is a most heinous and black sin, a sin that God doth usually by some wonderful method of his providence detect and bring to punishment; and which dogs the consciences of those who are guilty of it with horrid affrights and terrors, and hath sometimes extorted from them a confession of it when there hath been no other proof nor evidence.

The two greatest sinners that the Scripture hath set the blackest brand upon were both murderers, Cain and Judas: the one the murderer of his brother, the other first of his Lord and Master, and then of himself.

And God so infinitely hates and detests murder, that although the altar were a refuge for other offenders, yet he would not have a murderer sheltered there, but he was to be dragged from that inviolable sanctuary to ex ecution, according to that law, Exod. 21 : 14, " If a man come presumptuously upon his neighbor and slay him with guile, thou shalt take him from mine altar, that he may die." And accordingly we read, 1 Kings, 2 : 30, 31, that when Joab had fled and taken hold on the horns of the altar, so that the messengers who were sent to put him to death durst not violate that holy place by shedding his blood, Solomon gives command to have him slain even there, as if the blood of a wilful murderer were a very acceptable sacrifice offered up unto God.

And indeed, in the first prohibition of murder that we have, God subjoins a very weighty reason why it should be so odious to him, Gen. 9 : 6, " Whoso sheddeth man's blood, by man shall his blood be shed; for in the image of God made he man." So that *homicidium est Deicidium*, " to slaughter a man, it is to.stab God in effigy;" for though the image of God's holiness and purity be totally defaced in us since the fall, yet still every man, even the most wicked and impious that lives, bears some marks of the image of God in his intellect, the freedom of his will, and his dominion over the creatures; and God will have every part of his image so revered by us, that he who assaults man is esteemed by him as one who attempts to assassinate God himself.

Murder is a crying sin. Blood is loud and clamorous. The first that ever was shed was heard as far as from earth to heaven : " The voice of thy brother's blood crieth unto me from the ground." Gen. 4 : 10. And God will certainly hear its cry and avenge it.

(3.) But not only he whose hands are imbrued in the blood of others, but *those also who are accessory are guilty of murder*. As,

Those who command or counsel it to be done. Thus David became guilty of the murder of innocent Uriah; and God in drawing up his charge, accuseth him with it, 2 Sam. 12 : 9, " Thou hast slain him with the sword of the children of Ammon."

Again, *those who consent to murder are guilty of it.* Thus Pilate, for yielding to the clamorous outcries of the Jews, " Crucify him, crucify him," though he washed his hands and disavowed the fact, yet was as much guilty as those who nailed him to the cross.

He also who *concealeth a murder is guilty of it.* And therefore we read, Deut. 21 : 6, 7, that in case a man were found slain and the murderer unknown, the elders of that city were to assemble and wash their hands and protest that they had not shed this blood, neither had their eyes seen it; intimating that if they had seen and concealed it, they had thereby become guilty of the murder.

Those also who are in authority and do not punish a murder when committed and known, are themselves guilty of it. Thus when, by the wicked artifice of Jezebel, Naboth was condemned to die, although Ahab knew nothing of the contrivance till after the execution; yet, because he did not vindicate that innocent blood when he came to the knowledge of it, the prophet chargeth it upon him, 1 Kings, 21 : 19, " Hast thou killed, and also taken possession ?" The guilt lay upon him, and the punishment due to it overtook him, although we do not read that he was any otherwise guilty of it than in not punishing those who had committed it.

And those magistrates who, upon any pretext whatever, suffer a murderer to escape unpunished, are said to pollute the land with blood, Num. 35 : 31–33, " Ye shall take no satisfaction for the life of a murderer; but he shall be surely put to death. So shall ye not pollute the land wherein ye are; for blood it defileth the land: and the land cannot be cleansed of the blood that is shed therein, but by the blood of him that shed it."

II. But in this commandment not only the perpetration of murder, and the actual embruing our hands in the blood of our brother is prohibited; but likewise all CAUSES and OCCASIONS leading to it. As,

First, *Envy*, which is the rust of a cankered soul, a foul, meagre vice, that turns the happiness and welfare of others into our misery and torment. Thus Cain first enviously repined at the success and acceptance of his brother's sacrifice, and this quickly prompted him to murder.

Secondly. *Unjust and immoderate anger*, which, if it be suffered to lie festering in the heart, will turn into the venom of a perfect hatred. This is not only a cause but a degree of murder, and as such it is accounted by our Savior, who is the best expositor of the law, Mat. 5 : 21, 22, " Ye have heard that it was said by them of old time, Thou shalt not kill—But I say unto you, That whosoever is angry with his brother without a cause, is in danger of the judgment; and whosoever shall say to his brother, Raca, shall be in danger of the council; but whosoever shall say, Thou Fool, shall be in danger of hell-fire." Which passage I have already explained. But,

1. *Anger is not*, as envy, *simply and in itself unlawful;* for,

(1.) There may be *a virtuous anger* as well as *vicious:* an anger that merits praise and commendation; and is so far from being a sin, that it is a noble and generous grace. To be moved with indignation for the cause of God when his glory is eclipsed, his name dishonored, his ordinances profaned, his sanctuary polluted, his people vilified, this is a holy anger, and may well lose the common and vulgar appellation of anger, and pass under the name of zeal. Such was our Savior's against those that defiled the temple, when with a miraculous authority he whipped them out and vindicated the house of God unto the worship of God, from the usurpation of the god of this world, mammon. And therefore we find that passage, Psalm 69 : 9, applied to this action of Christ: " The zeal of thine house hath eaten me up." So likewise when, by their hypocritical silence, they seemed to discountenance and disallow the curing of a man on the Sabbath day, it is said " He looked round about upon them with anger, being grieved for the hardness of their hearts." Mark, 3 : 5.

(2.) There is also *an innocent and allowable anger*, when we have just provocation to it; for religion doth not utterly root out and destroy the natural passions, but only moderate and regulate them. We may be angry, but we must not sin in our anger, Eph. 4 : 26, " Be angry," but " sin not." And,

(3.) There is *a vicious and sinful anger*, which is a rash and foolish passion, a short phrenzy, that puts a man for the present quite beside himself, and so agitates the spirits that the blood boils about the heart and sends up such sooty fumes as darken the understanding and deprive him of the use and benefit of his reason.

The two ingredients that make up anger are grief for some injury conceived to be done unto us, and desire of revenge, to discharge our gall and choler upon those that have wronged us, as if we gave ourselves ease by laying a load upon others.

2. *Two things especially make anger to be evil and sinful.* When it is *without cause,* and when it is *without bounds.*

(1.) *Causeless anger* is a kind of murder, when men will fret and rage, although there be no provocation at all given them. Some men's gall overflows so much that upon every trivial occasion, or perhaps when there is none but only their own umbrage and suspicion, they fly out into intemperate speeches and revengeful acts, and are presently all in a flame and combustion when there is nothing to irritate them but their own choleric fancies: like clouds that break out in thunder and lightning when all the fire and sulphur is bred only in their own bowels.

See this testy spirit in Jonah, who, though he were a holy, yet it seems by his history he was a very passionate man. First he is angry that God would spare Nineveh after he had prophesied ruin and destruction to it: he grows into a pet even with the mercy of God, as if he circumvented him and designed to make him accounted a false prophet: " It displeased Jonah exceedingly, and he was very angry." chap. 4 : 1. Jonah is angry because God is appeased: he thinks the Almighty too easy, and can hardly forgive that mercy which so readily forgave the Ninevites. And again, when God had caused a worm to destroy the gourd which he had prepared to shade this hot and angry head, Jonah falls into another fit of bitter passion for the loss of so poor a thing as his gourd; and when God meekly expostulates the cause with him, " Doest thou well to be angry for the gourd?" his passion so far transports him that he dares to return this malapert answer even to the great God, Yea, " I do well to be angry," to the very *death*. See here how his gall overflows and taints both his reason and his religion: he hurls his fury about against God and men. And as he sits in his booth, looking and praying daily that fire and brimstone might come down from heaven to consume that great city, when he saw his expectation frustrated and the date of his prophecy expired without the accomplishment of it, he quarrels with God, storms against every thing, is weary of his life, and it would seem could almost have fired the city himself rather than it should have escaped.

(2.) As causeless anger, so *immoderate anger* is a great sin and a committing of murder in our hearts.

Anger may be immoderate either in *degree* or in *continuance*.

It is immoderate in *degree*, when it is vehement and excessive, transporting us beyond our due bounds and temper.

I know no law that forbids a christian to resent an injury. Our Savior Christ himself, when he was buffeted was sensible of and reproves that insolence, John, 18: 23, " If I have spoken evil, bear witness of the evil; but, if well, why smitest thou me?" Christianity doth not make men stocks, but keeps them from being furies; it doth not root up, but only prune our anger and cut off all superfluities of naughtiness from it. It may, when just cause is given, warm but not fire our spirits; but when it breaks forth into reviling speeches, or into revengeful actions, be sure it hath catched fire then, and is enkindled of hell.

And yet the just anger of superiors as magistrates, or

masters, or parents, may lawfully break forth upon inferiors in inflicting due punishments. Nor will this fall under the guilt of a sinful revenge, but a just reward, whilst they are careful that the punishment exceed not the fault and crime committed.

But for those who have no authority over others to seek revenge upon them, either by railing or defaming speeches, or by the paying injury for injury, is a transgression of this commandment, the effect of immoderate anger and a kind of murder in them.

Anger may also be immoderate in *continuance*. For age will sour it into hatred, and turn what was wine into vinegar. Therefore the apostle counsels us, "Be angry, and sin not." But how may that be done? "Let not the sun," saith he, "go down upon your wrath." Eph. 4 : 26. And indeed he that goes to bed and sleeps with anger boiling in his breast, will find the scum of malice upon it the next morning.

This is a passion which, if it be long cherished, will drive away the Spirit. For how canst thou think that the dove-like Spirit of God will reside where the heart remains full of gall; or that the celestial flame of divine love should burn bright and clear where there are so many thick fumes and vapors continually rising up to damp and choke it? How darest thou betake thyself to rest without first invoking the great God and locking up thyself by prayer into his custody and safe tuition? And how darest thou pray whilst wrath burns and rankles in thy breast? Canst thou in faith pray for forgiveness, who dost not thyself forgive? Our Savior hath expressly told us, that if we "forgive not men their trespasses, neither will our Father which is in heaven forgive us our trespasses;" and therefore as long as anger and desire of wreaking our revenge upon those that have wronged us are entertained by us, so long we invalidate our own prayers by not performing that condition, without which God will never hear nor accept them. And therefore be sure you be no longer angry than you may lawfully abstain from prayer. For we are commanded to "lift up holy hands without wrath." 1 Tim. 2:8. Certainly dissension and animosity with men is no fit temper to prepare us to hold communion with God. And therefore though thy gift be ready to be laid upon the altar, remember thyself, look inward and see whether all be quiet and calm there, if there be no grudge, no anger against thy brother. If thou findest any, either go first and actually reconcile thyself unto him, or if opportunity will not suffice for that, purge out the leaven of wrath and malice, and reconcile thyself unto him in thine own heart; for under the law no offering of the Lord was to be mingled with leaven, and now under the Gospel God will accept of no oblations that are offered up unto him with the ferment of wrath and passion. Although it may surprise us, yet let it not possess us. See what the wise man counsels us, Eccles. 7:9, "Be not hasty in thy spirit to be angry:" or if through haste and thoughtlessness it may seize upon you, yet let it not dwell there; for he adds, "anger dwelleth in the bosom of fools." And certainly the calm and peaceable Spirit of God will not dwell in that house where there are perpetual tumults and discords, and where our unruly passions make such a noise and uproar that his secret whispers and suggestions cannot be heard.

Thus you see what kind of anger is sinful—that which is causeless, and that which is immoderate either in de

gree or in duration. And likewise what anger is lawful—
that which is zealous for God's glory, and that which is
rightly tempered for our own and our neighbor's good.

3. Let us consider *whence sinful and unwarrantable
anger usually proceeds*. You shall find this bitter fruit to
have likewise its root of bitterness. The causes of it are
commonly these:

(1.) *Pride*, and an overweening conceit of ourselves.

Pride is the fruitful mother of many vices; but it nurseth none with more care and tenderness than this of anger; and therefore the wise man tells us, Prov. 13 : 10, that only from " pride cometh contention;" and indeed, as the philosopher observes, anger usually ariseth from an opinion that we are despised and contemned. Now the proud man thinks every one contemns him that doth not value him as highly as he values himself—that is, beyond all reason; and if he cannot meet with such fools, he grows angry and discontented with all the world. Arist Rhet. 50, 2, c. 2. Plut. de Irâ Cohib. cap. 12.

Proud flesh about a sore is always tender and cannot bear the least touch; and so proud persons, if they be never so little touched, presently grow enraged and think they have a great injury done them if others do not as much admire and respect them as they do themselves.

Whoever is much a self-lover cannot fail of frequent occasions to make him angry. Now the proud man is the greatest self-lover in the world; and the misery is that he usually loves himself without a rival; and if all do not yield to him, to say what he shall dictate, and to think what he shall determine, and to do what he shall prescribe, he takes it for a high affront; and as he hath given himself an authority over others, he looks that they should submit to it and acknowledge it. And others, perhaps having no less pride, or possibly more reason, refusing to gratify his vain and arrogant humor, quarrels and dissensions arise, and endless jars and discords.

(2.) Another cause of this passion is *the weakness and feebleness of nature.* And therefore it is truly observed by Plutarch, that those who are of the most infirm natures and weakest constitutions are most harassed with it; as children more than men; old age more than the staid part of life; and sick persons more than those that are in health. For anger is a great weakness, and therefore lodgeth most in the weakest; ants and pismires, and such little creatures, are most busy with their stings; whereas strong and generous creatures must be much provoked before they will be injurious.

There are many other causes of the violent stirring of this exorbitant passion: as over-much love of vain trifles, which if they come to any mischance, as usually they do, we are apt to be disturbed at it; easiness to believe at the first recommendation, and engaging our affections in things before we have had trial and experience of them, which afterwards proving quite contrary to our expectations, the disappointment will excite our choler, &c. But I shall not insist on these.

III. Let us therefore proceed to lay down some RULES FOR THE RESTRAINING AND MODERATING OF ANGER; and that in others and in ourselves.

1. In *others.* It is a hellish sport for us to irritate and stir up anger in others, only for us to laugh at or to make our advantage by it: scarce a less sin than to make others drunk that we may abuse them, for prevailing passion is

for the time a kind of drunkenness, and both are a degree of frenzy and madness. Thou oughtest not, therefore, unnecessarily to exasperate thy brother, whom thou knowest prone to this great weakness; otherwise be assured that all his intemperate speeches and rash actions shall be imputed to thee, and are thy sins as well as his; and whatever revilings he dischargeth against thee shall at last also be charged upon thee, and what a foolish thing it is for thee to bear the sting of them here and the punishment of them hereafter! The wise man hath told us, Prov. 14 : 9, that they are "fools" who "make a mock at sin." And if thou, for thy recreation, provokest any to an indecent and unbecoming passion, know that such laughter is deadly to thyself, and thou art like those poisoned persons who laugh themselves to death.

To prevent and suppress anger in *thyself*, (for there it doth most hurt, since another man's anger is none of my guilt, if I have neither been faulty in stirring it up nor too easy to catch the flame from him,) take these following *rules and directions*.

(1.) *Labor and pray for a meek and humble spirit.* Think lowly of thyself, and then certainly thou wilt not be angry if others conspire with thee in thinking and speaking of thee as thou dost of thyself. Most commonly anger, as I have said, proceeds from an opinion of being despised: now do thou first of all despise thyself, and then all reproaches and injuries will signify no more to thee than that other men approve thy judgment, and that certainly can be no cause of anger. Thou wilt not be angry for want of a ceremony or demonstration of respect which others impose or exact, nor wilt thou quarrel with any for not relying on thy judgment or contradicting thy sentiments, when thou shalt reflect upon thine own ignorance and frequent mistakes. They are the high hills whose heads are wrapped about with clouds and tempests, when the humble valleys are calm and serene; so humble souls that lie low in their own esteem remain undisturbed, when lofty persons are still molested with the tempests of their own passions.

(2.) *Consider how often thou givest God occasion to be angry with thee,* which if he should take, thou wert for ever undone. He bears many affronts and indignities at thy hands. And who art thou? a poor vile worm. And who is he? even the great Almighty God, the universal King of heaven and earth, that he should put up with such wrongs at thy hands! And shall God daily take injuries from such a wretched nothing as thou art, God who is thy Lord and Master; and wilt not thou bear them patiently from thy fellow-servant, who it may be is in every respect equal to thee, but only inferior to thee in this, that he provokes thee unjustly? Certainly, were we as tender towards our brethren as we all desire God should be towards us, could we forbear others as we ourselves would be forborne, there would never be any quarrel commenced, or if it were, it would be soon compounded. What saith the Psalmist? "He will not always chide; neither will he keep his anger for ever. He hath not dealt with us after our sins, nor rewarded us according to our iniquities." Psalm 103:10. Let this great example be ours, not to be soon moved to anger, and quickly to free ourselves from it. Indeed many there are that are slow to anger, and in that they imitate God; but then they are tenacious and retentive of wrath, and hardly placable again: their anger is like an impression upon some hard metal, very difficultly made, and as difficult to be effaced. Let such consider what would become of them if God should be as slow to be reconciled to them as they are to their brethren. Nay, he is infinitely more wronged by you than you can be by them; and yet he so far condescends as first to seek reconciliation. And, although he be infinitely able by the least expression of his wrath and power for ever to destroy you; yet "herein God commendeth his love unto you, that when ye were enemies, ye were reconciled unto him by the death of his Son." Certainly whoever doth but seriously reflect upon the infinite patience and forbearance of God, if he hath any sweetness diffused into his soul by that consideration, if he hath any conscience of imitating his heavenly Father in that which is his most adorable attribute, if he hath any care to ascertain unto himself the pardon and remission of his own offences, he will therein find a powerful influence to sway him to the like acts of mercy and forgiveness.

(3.) *Beware of prejudice against thy brother.* For prejudice is a very ill interpreter of actions, and will be sure to expound them in the worst sense. Be not easy to believe that those who offend thee do it with design, or that they despise and undervalue thee. Rather think it any thing else than contempt of thee. Believe that his offences proceed rather from his folly and indiscretion, or that he is forced and necessitated to do it, that others have put him upon it. If they be thy friends that wrong thee, suppose it to be only a fault of their too great familiarity and a misgoverned intimacy. If they be such as are subject to thee, believe that since they know thou hast power to chastise them, they would not do it purposely to provoke thee. If they be vile and sordid persons, trouble not thyself with their affronts, for thy reputation is above them Thus, I say, incline to believe it any thing rather than a designed abuse. For though a strict jealousy over our reputation and aptness to think ourselves wronged seem to proceed from generousness and a sense of honor, yet indeed they proceed only from baseness and weakness of mind. Whoever accounts himself despised by another, is in a sense less than he, and confesseth himself his inferior. He is the noble and heroic-spirited person who is unshaken with the petty affronts and injuries of others, and hath so much stable confidence in the integrity of his actions that he cannot believe any can traduce him or them: whereas to be angry at them doth but in a sort justify slanders, and will beget a belief that that is not altogether groundless whereat he shows himself so much concerned. It is an old maxim of prudence, "If you be angry at railings, you seem to acknowledge them; if you contemn them, they vanish."

(4.) *Be not familiar with any angry person.* For as one fire will kindle another, so it is likely that his choler will kindle thine, till both flame into an inordinate and extravagant passion. See the direction expressly given us, Prov. 22 : 24, 25, "Make no friendship with an angry man; and with a furious man thou shalt not go, lest thou learn his ways, and get a snare to thy soul." Indeed there is no such fuel to wrath as wrath, and it is a very hard matter to refrain from being angry with him who will causelessly be angry with us. And as thou must shun the company and acquaintance of choleric persons, so likewise of scoffers; for a scoff and a jeer is many times more provoking than a blow, and nothing will sooner kindle the coals of contention than a biting taunt: therefore Solomon adviseth us, Prov. 22 : 10, "Cast out the scorner, and contention shall go out; yea, strife and reproach shall cease."

(5.) It is very good counsel, *if thou feelest any motions of this unruly passion begin to stir in thy heart*, that thou *arrest it for some time before thou either speak or act*. Let this mud have some time to settle again, that reason may in the meanwhile recover her throne and direct thee how to govern thyself like a wise man and a christian. Speak not whilst thou art in the impetuous hurries of thy passion; for it was well said by Plutarch, that " it is good in a fever, but much better in anger, to have a tongue kept clean and smooth." Plut. de Irâ Cohib. Put an interval of time between thy anger and thy action; for those who act in the violence and paroxysms of their anger, do either they know not what, or else what they may have reason to repent of; and therefore Solomon tells us that " the discretion of a man deferreth his anger," Prov. 19 : 11; and "the beginning of strife is as when one letteth out water." Prov. 17 : 14. At first when a man cutteth the bank of a river, the passage is but little and the stream may be easily stopped, but by continual running it will wear away the earth and widen the gap, and whole floods and currents will pour out where but some few drops were intended.

(6.) *Contemplate the ugliness and deformity of this sin in others;* how it makes men brutish in their souls and deformed likewise in their countenances. It inflames the face, fires the eyes, and makes a man look like a fury, deafens the ears, froths the mouth, makes the heart beat and pant, the tongue stammer, the voice harsh and rough, the speech precipitate and oftentimes ridiculous: briefly, it puts the whole man into a preternatural fever, and transforms the body into a monster and the man into a devil.

And what! shall I give way to passion, so uncomely a passion that will make me scorned when I would seem most terrible? Certainly, were there no other thing whereof to accuse this immoderate anger, it were enough to render it odious; but when it not only destroys what I was, but seeks the ruin and destruction of others, it concerns me to stop it in its first rise and ebullitions, lest the boilings of my blood proceed so far as to attempt the shedding of the blood of others.

THE SEVENTH COMMANDMENT.

Thou shalt not commit Adultery.

In considering the former commandment we have seen what care God takes for the security and indemnity of every man's person. This command extendeth farther, and provideth for his security as he is considered mystically in marriage-union, which of twain maketh one flesh. The one defends him from the violence of bloody rage and revenge, the other from the violations of impure lusts.

I judge it not convenient to be too circumstantial in showing you what is prohibited under this precept. I know that some, especially the popish casuists in their treatises of moral divinity, such as Sanches, Diana, &c. have spoken of these things so minutely, and with such a filthy accurateness, that they violate the very eyes and fancies of their readers; rather *teach* vice than *condemn* it; and instruct the ignorant to sin skilfully rather than convince the guilty to bring them to repentance. Some wickednesses there are which it is far better not to reprove than to name; it is more expedient to leave those who are guilty of them to be lashed by their natural light and conscience, than, by agitating such crimes, teach others not so much to abhor as to practise them. And let this be my apology if I pass over this subject with more than my accustomed brevity.

1. I shall speak of the sin which is here literally and expressly *forbidden*, and this is,

1. The detestable and loathsome sin of *adultery*. This sin, properly taken, is a sin committed between two persons, the one or both of them married to another. In any view it is a most heinous sin, but on the married person's side most inexcusable and intolerable. In Gen. 39 : 9, it is called a " great wickedness against God," even on the unmarried man's part. And in Lev. 20 : 10, and Deut. 22 : 22, the temporal punishment assigned to it is no less than death, the same punishment that belonged to murder.

And if human laws were as severe in the punishment of the sin as divine, the fear of it might possibly be of greater influence to deter men from such filthiness than either shame or the denunciation of eternal punishment. Yea, we read in history, Speed's Chron. p. 289, that our progenitors, the English Saxons, even while they remained pagans and idolaters, so hated this sin, that they made it, yea, and simple fornication also, punishable with death, which they severely inflicted on those that were found guilty; and this custom continued among them after they were converted to Christianity, until the year of Christ 750, when the antichristian see of Rome, the mother of whoredoms, abrogated this law as too rigorous for christians. Job calleth it " a heinous crime ; yea, an iniquity to be punished by the judges ; a fire that consumeth to destruction." Job, 31 : 11, 12.

But though they who are guilty of this sin may escape the judgment of men, either through the secrecy of their wickedness or the too gentle censures of the law, yet they shall not escape the righteous judgment of God, nor those everlasting punishments that he hath prepared for them in hell, Heb. 13 : 4, " Whoremongers and adulterers God will judge."

SEVENTH COMMANDMENT. 361

Two things in this sin of adultery make it so exceeding heinous, namely, the *licentiousness and incontinency* of it, in letting loose the reins to a brutish concupiscence, and in yielding up the body to pollution and the soul to damnation; and the *injustice* of it, it being a deceit of the highest and most injurious nature that can be. Consider,

(1.) *It is the violation of a most solemn vow and covenant;* and so adds perjury to unfaithfulness; alienating that person to another, who, by the most sacred and the strictest obligations, is bound only to that partner and yoke-fellow to whom God and their own consent, and the legal rights of the church and state have addicted them.

(2.) *It is also the source and cause of a spurious and supposititious birth;* bringing in a strange blood into the inheritance of lawful children, whereby this unfaithfulness becomes theft as well as perjury.

But though this sin of adultery be alone mentioned in the command, yet, according to the rules laid down in the beginning of this work, *all other kinds of uncleanness* are also forbidden under the name of this one gross crime. For the law of God is perfect; and as all manner of chastity, both in our thoughts, speeches and actions, is there enjoined us, so likewise whatever is in the least contrary and prejudicial to a spotless chastity and an inviolate modesty, is hereby forbidden. And therefore,

2. This commandment forbids the uncleanness of *fornication*, a sin which properly is the sin committed betwixt two single persons, and which, though it hath not some aggravations that belong to the other, yet is an abominable sin in the sight of God.

I know how it is extenuated by the impure Romanists,* as a small stain that may easily be washed off by the sprinkling of a little holy water. But it is no wonder if they who have drank deep of the cup of fornications of the great whore, and are guilty of spiritual fornication, should speak lightly of corporal fornication also.

But let us hear how God, who is infinite purity, hath sentenced this sin, when he threatens that he himself will judge whoremongers; and tells us, 1 Cor. 6 : 9, 10, that " neither fornicators, nor idolaters, nor adulterers, shall inherit the kingdom of God." No, the New Jerusalem which is above, is a holy city, and no unclean thing shall ever enter into it. " Without are dogs, and sorcerers, and whoremongers, and murderers, and idolaters." Rev. 22 : 15. And it were well with them if all their punishment were only to be left without; but there is a lake of fire prepared for them, into which they shall be cast and plunged—the fire of hell, to punish the flames of lust. Rev. 21 : 8, " The fearful, and unbelieving, and the abominable, and murderers, and whoremongers (you see how, in both places, they are joined with the vilest and most infamous sinners,)—shall have their portion in the lake which burneth with fire and brimstone, which is the second death." The apostle reckons this as one of the works of the flesh, Gal. 5 · 19, " The works of the flesh are manifest, which are these, adultery, fornication, uncleanness, lasciviousness," &c. and he exhorts us to a careful mortification of it, Col. 3 : 5, " Mortify, therefore, your members, which are upon the earth, fornication, uncleanness, inordinate affection," &c.

---

* Mazarin. in Psal. li. Durand. Sent. l. iv. dist. 33. 92. **Emman. Sa.** Art. 20. Tit. Episcopus.

SEVENTH COMMANDMENT. 363

3. Here likewise are forbidden all *incestuous mixtures*, or uncleanness between those who are related to each other within the degrees of kindred specified, Lev. 18, from the 6th to the 18th verse; whether the kindred be by affinity or consanguinity, that is, whether by former marriage or by blood and descent. And the nearer any persons are so related to us the greater is the abomination if we approach unto them, whether it be with pretence of marriage, which in this case is null and void, or without any such pretence.

4. Here is likewise forbidden *polygamy*, or a taking *a wife to her sister;* that is, to another. Lev. 18 : 18. God indeed seemed to connive at this in the holy men of old, yet it never was otherwise than a sin from the foundation of the world. And therefore the prophet Malachi refers us to the primitive institution of marriage, to show the obliquity of this practice, Mal. 2 : 15, " Did not he make one ?" that is, Did not he create one woman for one man ? " Yet had he the residue of the Spirit," that is, the same Spirit and power, whereby he created all things in the world, resided still in God, and therefore he could easily have formed more women as well as one had he not purposed to oblige them one to the other solely, and to teach them, by their being paired at first, not to seek a multiplication of wives afterwards. Therefore polygamy was unlawful in the beginning, even then when the necessity of increasing the world might seem to plead for it; and how much more unlawful now when that necessity is ceased! Besides this, the apostle hath commanded, 1 Cor. 7 : 2, " Let every man have his own wife, and every woman her own husband."

5. Moreover, here are forbidden all those monsters of

unnatural lust, and those prodigies of villany and filthiness which are not fit to be named among men, but are punished upon beasts themselves, as you may read, Lev. 20 : 15, 16, and Lev. 18 : 22, 23.

6. All those things that may be *incentives* to lust, and which add fuel to this fire, are likewise forbidden in this command; as all impurities of the eyes, of contact, of lewd and obscene speech; all immodest spectacles, wanton actions, uncivil and garish attire; or whatever else may kindle, either in ourselves or others, any unchaste affections; for all these things do but lay in provision for the flesh, to fulfil it in the lusts thereof.

7. Because this law is spiritual, therefore it not only forbids the gross outward acts of filthiness, but the *inward uncleanness of the heart;* all lustful contemplations and ideas, and evil concupiscences.

For it is not enough to refrain unchaste desires from breaking forth into act, but we must also refrain our hearts from entertaining any such desires. These flames pent up in the heart will soot and consume it; and though its ruin be more invisible, yet it will be sad and fatal. As there is a heart-murder, so there is a heart-adultery; and he that commits speculative uncleanness and prostitutes his thoughts and imaginations to the impure embraces of filthy lust, is, according to our Savior's interpretation, guilty of the transgression of this command; so, Mat. 5 : 27, 28, "Ye have heard that it was said to them of old time, thou shalt not commit adultery: but I say unto you, that whosoever looketh on a woman to lust after her, hath committed adultery with her already in his heart." Thus you see what is prohibited.

II. I shall next speak of the exceeding HEINOUSNESS of this sin, and why it is so justly odious to God, and ought to be to us.

1. It is a sin which *murders two souls at once*, and therefore the most uncharitable sin in the world.

Other sinners can perish singly. The swearer damns none by his oaths but himself, and although he curse others to the pit of hell, yet he shall descend thither alone The drunkard with his intemperance drowns but his own soul in perdition. The bloody murderer may say with Lamech, Gen. 4:23, " I have slain a man to my wounding, and a young man to my own hurt." And indeed all other sinners, though their wickedness prompt them to draw in associates and partakers with them, yet the nature of their sin doth not require a partnership in their guilt, but they may be solitarily wicked and perish alone: only this sin of adultery necessarily requires partnership, and involves another in the same condemnation. And is it nothing to thee that another's damnation shall be set upon thy score, and the blood of their souls charged upon thine for ever? Think with yourselves what horrid greetings these unclean wretches will give each other in hell, when they who have here wallowed together in beastly sensuality shall there wallow together in unquenchable flames, and with ineffable anguish exclaim against and curse both themselves and one another—the one for enticing, the other for consenting, and both for fulfilling their impure desires.

Or, suppose that God should vouchsafe thee repentance unto life; yet, art thou sure that his justice and severity will not harden the other in this sin to which thou hast been the author and persuader? How know est thou but they may persist, and perish in their wickedness? Divine vengeance may snatch them away without affording them space or grace to repent. And is it nothing to thee that thou hast damned a soul as well as defiled a body, and, for the satisfying of thy brutish lust, hast brought upon them everlasting woes and torments? If God hath granted thee mercy, how anxiously solicitous oughtest thou to be to deliver those out of the snares of the devil whom thou hast entangled therein, and by all holy counsels and remonstrances recover them to God by repentance! Or, if a speedy execution of Divine justice should cut them off before, what a sad consideration will it be to thee that thou hast eternally ruined a poor soul! This, if thou hast any sense of sin, or of the wrath of the great God due unto it, will make thee go mourning all thy days, and bring down thy gray hairs with sorrow to the grave.

2. It is *the most degrading of all sins.*

It debaseth a man from the excellency of his nature, and resembles him to the condition of brute beasts. The perfection of a man is, to govern himself according to law and reason; to bound and circumscribe his actions by the rules of what is fit and honest: whereas beasts show the inferiority of their natures by the scope and range of their unguided appetites. Hence the prophet compares adulterers to "fed horses—every one neighing after his neighbor's wife." Jer. 5 : 8. And God joins such impure persons with the vilest and most detestable of brute beasts, Deut. 23 : 18, " Thou shalt not bring the hire of a whore, nor the price of a dog into the house of the Lord thy God for any vow; for even both these are an abomination to the Lord thy God."

3. It is a sin which *most of all obscures and extinguishes the light of a man's natural reason and understanding.*

Nothing so much darkens the understanding as the fumes of lust, Hos. 4 : 11, "Whoredom, and wine, and new wine take away the heart." And to this the apostle gives testimony, Eph. 4 : 18, 19, "Having the understanding darkened, being alienated from the life of God through the ignorance that is in them because of the blindness of their heart; who being past feeling, have given themselves over to work all uncleanness with greediness." So far doth this beastly sin besot the mind and befool men, that, according to the chaste and modest phrase of Scripture language, it is frequently called *committing of folly;* as if there were no folly like to this, and it alone deserved to carry away the name and title from all other sins: and indeed it is a most notorious and egregious folly, for a short pang and epilepsy of sensual delight to betray the soul to a gloomy dulness, bitter remembrance, guilt, and eternal shame and death.

4. It is a sin justly the *most infamous and scandalous amongst men.*

A sin that brands them with the greatest shame and reproach, a reproach that can never be wiped away. And certainly if such a one doth ever seriously consider his own sin, he cannot but be ashamed of himself; for although there be a shame consequent upon the act of every sin, yet the credit and reputation of a man is never so deeply blemished nor so foully stained by any sin as that of adultery, Prov. 6 : 32, 33, "Whoso committeth adultery with a woman lacketh understanding: he that doeth it, destroyeth his own soul. A wound and dishonor shall he get and his reproach shall not be wiped away." Yea, the dishonor of adulterous parents is so foul, that, like a black blot, it diffuseth and spreadeth itself even upon their children. Deut. 23 : 2. A bastard was not to enter into the congregation of the Lord unto the tenth generation.

5. Consider that this sin of uncleanness is *a kind of sacrilege*, a converting of that which is sacred and dedicated, unto a profane use.

What saith the apostle, 1 Cor. 6 : 19 ? "Know ye not that your body is the temple of the Holy Ghost?" And if it were a sacrilegious impiety to turn the temple of God, which consisted only of vile materials, wood and stone, to vile and inferior uses; if our Savior's zeal burned within him when he saw the sanctuary turned into a market, and the house of God made a den of thieves; how much more heinous wickedness is it to convert the living temples of the ever-living God, even our bodies, which were redeemed and consecrated to God by the precious blood of Jesus Christ, unto impure and unclean uses, and to turn his sanctuary into a stew! "The body is not for fornication; but for the Lord. And your bodies are the members of Christ." Will ye "then take the members of Christ and make them the members of a harlot ? God forbid." And the apostle thinks this sacrilegiousness of uncleanness so high an aggravation of the sinfulness of it, that he insists on it again, 1 Cor. 3 : 16, 17, "Know ye not that ye are the temple of God, and that the Spirit of God dwelleth in you ? If any man defile the temple of God, him shall God destroy : for the temple of God is holy, which temple are ye."

6. Consider if all these things will not prevail, the *dreadful punishment* that God threatens to inflict upon all who are guilty of this sin.

Yea, he speaks of it as a sin that he can hardly be persuaded to pardon; a sin that puzzles infinite mercy to forgive, Jer. 5 : 7–9, " How shall I pardon thee for this ? When I had filled thy children to the full, they then committed adultery, and assembled themselves by troops in the harlots' houses. They were as fed horses in the morning: every one neighing after his neighbor's wife. Shall I not visit for these things ? saith the Lord, and shall not my soul be avenged on such a nation as this ?" And, indeed, God doth often in this life visit this sin : sometimes by filling their loins with strange and loathsome diseases, Prov. 6 : 26 ; sometimes by reducing them to extreme beggary; for this sin, as Job speaks, is " a fire that consumeth to destruction, and would root out all his increase." Yea, this very sin is so great a punishment for itself, that the wise man tells us, Prov. 22 : 14, that those whom God hates shall fall into it. Yea, and to express the exceeding sinfulness of this sin of uncleanness, the apostle tells us that God made it the punishment of several other sins as black and horrid as can be well conceived. When he had spoken, Rom. 1 : 23, of the gross idolatry of the heathen in worshipping images and falling down before stocks and stones, he subjoins, verse 24, that for this cause " God also gave them up to uncleanness :" as if uncleanness were bad enough to punish idolatry, and those were sufficiently plagued for their spiritual uncleanness who were abandoned over unto corporal pollutions. But, though this sin may sometimes escape infamy through concealment, and other temporal judgments of God through his patience and forbearance, yet it will certainly find them out at the last; and then those who have burned together in lust, shall burn together in unquenchable flames. "They shall have their portion in the lake that burneth with fire and brimstone."—These are the demonstrations of the *heinousness* of this sin.

III. Let me now give you some CAUTIONARY RULES AND DIRECTIONS, by observing which you may be preserved from the commission of this sin. And,

1. Be sure that you *keep a narrow watch over your senses.* For these are the sluices which, instead of letting in pleasant streams to refresh, do commonly let in nothing but mud to pollute the soul. There is no actual filthiness in the heart of any but came in by these inlets. Through these the devil casts in abundance of filth—he stirs up indwelling lust, and by the sinful objects which the senses convey to the soul, he dungs that ground which of itself was too fruitful before. Thus the devil makes use of an adulterous eye to range abroad and fetch in provision for uncleanness, and by it, as by a burning-glass, he sets the heart on fire, and then blows up the flames through the ears by hearing lascivious discourses. Therefore make a covenant with thine eyes, and carefully divert them from all loose glances and all alluring and enticing objects; stop thine ears against all filthy communication; and if any begin such obscene talk as is the common raillery of our days and almost of every company, blush not thou to reprove them, but by thy reproofs make them blush at their own shame and wickedness.

2. *Addict thyself to sobriety and temperance*, and by

these beat down thy body and keep it in subjection to thy reason and religion. Certainly the excesses of those who indulge themselves in gluttony or drunkenness will froth and foam over into lust. And therefore it is said Jer. 5 : 7, that when the Israelites were "fed to the full, they then committed adultery."

3. *Continually exercise thyself in some honest and lawful employment.* Lust grows active when we grow idle. Therefore as *fulness of bread,* so likewise *idleness* is reckoned as one of the sins of impure Sodom. Ezek. 16 : 49. David, when he walks idly upon the roof of his house, lies open to the snares and is inveigled by the beauty of Bathsheba: had he then been at his harp and his psalms, he might have driven the evil spirit from himself, as formerly he did from his master Saul. Running streams preserve themselves clear and pure, whereas standing pools soon corrupt and breed noisome and venomous creatures. While our mind is employed there will be no time left for lust to dally with our fancy nor to dandle an unclean affection in our thoughts, and therefore it may be remarked as a considerable circumstance in Joseph's rejecting the enticements of his lewd mistress that the text saith, " He went into the house to dispatch his business," Gen. 39 : 11, noting to us that the honest care of our affairs is an excellent preservative to keep us from this sin of wantonness and uncleanness.

4. But, above all, *be earnest and frequent in prayer*, and if thou sometimes joinest *fasting* with thy prayers, they will be shot up to heaven with a fuller strength. For this sin of uncleanness is one of those devils that " goes not out but by fasting and prayer." God is a God of purity. Instantly beg of him, that he would send

down his pure and chaste Spirit into thy heart to cleanse thy thoughts and thy affections from all unclean desires. Beg that the Holy Ghost would but once touch thy heart with the dear sense of his eternal love, that he would diffuse such a celestial flame through thy soul as may ravish it with a heavenly zeal and ardor, and make it scorn to stoop to the ignoble love of poor inferior objects. Represent to him that thy body is his temple, and thy heart his altar in it, and desire of him that no strange unhallowed fire may flame on his altar.

Whilst thou diligently and conscientiously makest use of these means, thou mayest comfortably expect to be kept pure and immaculate—innocent in thy soul and clean in thy body; and as thou hast kept thyself undefiled here, so hereafter to be found worthy to walk with the *Lamb in white.*

THE EIGHTH COMMANDMENT.

Thou shalt not Steal.

The foregoing commandment, as you have seen, requires chastity in our persons. This requires honesty and uprightness in our dealings; a virtue immediately founded upon that first practical principle of all human converse, which our Savior lays down, Mat. 7 : 12, " Whatsoever ye would that men should do unto you, do ye even so to them;" and which he recommends to us as the brief sum and epitome of all the Scriptures; " for this is the law and the prophets."

The principle of this command carries such innate light and clear evidence in itself, that the very heathens do frequently inculcate it in their writings as the primary dictate of that morality which they taught. It is a maxim which we all assent to, not by any elaborate instructions, or dint of arguments, or any long train of consequences; but because it strongly masters our understandings by its native evidence, and springs up in us an unpremeditated resolve of reason. Both God and nature have set it up as a standard in our consciences; and usually there needs no other judge of our actions towards others, than our own conscience comparing them with what, in the like cases, we would think just and fit to be done towards ourselves.

It may be we are all partial to ourselves in our present concerns; and whilst we look only that way, we may possibly seek all advantages to promote them, though to another's detriment; but both reason and religion teach us to put ourselves in their stead, and then to manage all our transactions with them as we ourselves would judge just and reasonable, were their condition ours.

Therefore when thou dealest with another thou shouldst first be both parties to thyself. As for instance, a servant should sit down and consider with himself what respect he would require were he in the same circumstances with his master, and had servants under him. Children should consider what duty and obedience they would expect were they parents of children; subjects, what honor and submission they might reasonably demand were they magistrates; and so in any other relation. And when they have thus seriously pondered it in their own thoughts, let them then perform the same duties to others in their real condition which they judged to belong to them in their personated condition; for it is a never-failing rule for the direction of our practice, *that what thou judgest due to thyself, wert thou in another man's condition, is certainly as due to him in his own;* and if thou actest not accordingly, thou betrayest a great deal of selfishness and sinful partiality.

This is a rule applicable to all affairs; and there is scarce any one occurrence of a man's life but he may regulate himself in it according to this direction. And indeed there is scarce need of any other. Whatsoever thou hast to transact with thy brother, though perhaps thou mayest spy advantages upon him, and such as, if thou shouldst take, possibly he might never know or never be able to redress; yet then take thy conscience aside and seriously ask whether thou couldst be content and think it honest and just to be so dealt with thyself; if not, whatsoever the temptation be, or how much soever thou mightest gain by hearkening unto it, reject it with scorn, as that which would induce thee to violate the first principle of common honesty among men, and contradicts all the laws both of nature and Scripture.

Were this rule but more generally observed among men the world would not have such cause to cry out of rapine, extortion, oppression, fraud and injustice, as now it hath. The rich would not grind the faces of the poor, nor the poor causelessly clamor against the rich; superiors would not tyrannize over inferiors, nor inferiors murmur or rebel against superiors; but an equal peace and uniform justice would overspread the face of the whole earth, and righteousness would " run down our streets as a mighty stream."

Let me therefore once again recommend it to you (for indeed I cannot press it too often) that you would frequently set *this golden rule* before your eyes, to do nothing to any other person, which, were you in his capacity, you would think unjust to be done unto yourselves; and whatsoever you would expect from others as your due were you in their place and they in yours, to perform the very same to them; for otherwise you cannot but condemn yourselves in your actions whilst you do that which upon this supposition you cannot but be convinced is unjust, and withhold that which you know to be due, and which yourselves would expect should be yielded to you by others. This is a dictate of nature and right reason, this is the sum of the law and the prophets; and all those various precepts which are given us in the Scriptures for the conduct of our lives are but as so many lines that meet all in this centre; and if we apply it to each particular command of the second table, we shall find them all founded upon this, and to be interpreted by it. We are required to honor superiors; to abstain from murder, from adultery, from theft, from false accusations, from coveting what rightfully belongs to another; and all this according to the same measures by which we would have others perform these very duties to us. So that self, which is now the great tempter to wrong and injure others, were it governed according to this universal maxim, would be the greatest patron and defender of other men's rights and dues.

I have the longer insisted on this principle, both because it is of such general influence to the right ordering of our conversation, and also because the most visible and apparent violation of this natural law is by the sin of theft forbidden in this commandment.

I. THEFT, IN GENERAL, is an unjust taking or keeping to ourselves what is lawfully another man's. He is a thief who withholds what ought to be in his neighbor's possession, as well as he who takes from him what he hath formerly possessed.

All theft presupposes a right and propriety; for where nothing of right appertains to me, nothing can be unjustly taken or detained from me.

1. Certain it is, that *God is the great Lord and proprietor both of heaven and earth, and of all things in them:* Ps. 24 : 1, "The earth is the Lord's and the fulness thereof;" and 50 : 10, "Every beast of the forest is mine, and the cattle upon a thousand hills." By him and of him are all things; and for his will and pleasure they are, and were created.

2. *This great and absolute Lord hath granted to man a large charter of the world.* When he had taken an exact inventory of those goods with which he had furnished this great house, the universe, (he " saw every thing that he had made, and behold, it was very good," Gen. 1 : 31;) then he set man to live in it as his tenant, and freely gave him the use of and dominion over all the works of his hands, Gen. 1 : 28, " Replenish the earth and subdue it, and have dominion over all the fish of the sea, and over the fowl of the air, and over every living thing that moveth upon the earth." So the Psalmist, Ps. 115 : 16, " The heaven, even the heavens are the Lord's; but the earth hath he given to the children of men." A large and regal gift, whereby he hath made over all sublunary things to man; reserving to himself the sovereignty and supreme lordship of all, and requiring only from man the homage and payment of obedience. Yet,

3. *This large charter and donation gave no particular propriety to any:* neither, if man had continued in his happy and innocent estate, would there have been any need of *mine* or *thine*, or any partition of these earthly possessions; but common blessings had been enjoyed in common, and all things which covetousness and corruption now ravine after, would have been as promiscuously enjoyed and used as the common light and air, and each particular man's share in those blessings would have been sufficient and satisfactory. But,

4. Sin entering into the world, *men's desires grew immoderate after these earthly enjoyments, and their attempts to attain them injurious to others;* so that it became necessary to prescribe bounds and limits to them, and to

divide among them what before lay in common among all; that each man knowing his assigned portion, might rest satisfied with it, and be restrained from the unjust invasion and usurpation of another's right. And,

5. This could no otherwise be effected but by *human laws, by mutual compact and agreement, declaring what should be accounted as every man's right and property.* So that it is law which is the great determiner of property; and there is nothing *mine* or *thine*, farther than this assigns it to us. Indeed equity must sometimes interpose to moderate the letter of the law; for, in some cases, should we rigorously prosecute our right, and insist upon every punctilio that we may call our due, this, although it would not be unjust, yet it would be justice turned into gall and wormwood; it would be a breach and violation of the law of Christ and of charity, which requires us rather to part with our own in small matters, than to be vexatious or contentious in recovering or defending it.

Thus you see how all right and property first came into the world: a general right, by the donation of God; a particular right by the sanction of laws, alloting to each man his portion, which to invade or usurp from him, is injustice or theft.

Whence it follows that where there is no society in occupation of any part of the earth, the right accrues to the first possessor; and where things are found which appertain to none, they fall to the first seizer; for there can be no theft committed where there is no precedent title. If any therefore should providentially be cast into some desert and uninhabited part of the world, the general charter that God hath given to mankind of possessing the earth, empowers them to seize on it as theirs; and they may lawfully make use of the blessings of it in common, till, by mutual consent, they shall divide to each other their part and portion; but after such a partition is made, to use the same liberty is no longer lawful, but theft and robbery.

Thus you see what *theft* is, and that this law of God prohibiting us to steal what is another's, doth presuppose a law of man, which maketh property and causeth things to become either ours or another's.

But there are MANY KINDS OF THEFT.

1. The first kind of theft is *the taking away of what rightfully belongs to another, whether God or man.*

(1.) Of this sort the highest and chief is that committed *against God by sacrilege,* which is an alienating from God whatever he hath appropriated to himself, or whatever is on good grounds dedicated to the encouragement and maintenance of his honor and service.

Indeed the alienating of what hath been given to superstitious or idolatrous uses cannot be justly included in the sin of sacrilege; for it was not so much given to God as to ignorance and superstition; therefore our ancestors have done well and piously in dissolving those nests and cages of unclean birds that were so numerous and burthensome in these kingdoms; but withal, in my judgment, they would have done much better if they had converted their revenues to some public use, either for the benefit of the church or the commonwealth, rather than to their own private and particular gain.

But where any thing is indeed consecrated to God and set apart for the maintenance and encouragement of his worship and service, it is no less than sacrilege and robbing of God to alienate any part of this to any secular use, or to detain it from that use to which it was separated.

Of this God himself grievously complains, Mal. 3 : 8, 9, " Will a man rob God ?" as if it were a sin so heinous as that it is hardly to be supposed any man would be guilty of it. What! not allow thàt God his share among them who had liberally afforded them all things to enjoy! " Yet ye have robbed me. But ye say, Wherein have we robbed thee? In tithes and offerings. Ye are cursed with a curse; for ye have robbed me, even this whole nation."

Certainly those things which are appointed for the worship and service of God, whether they be so originally by divine right or not, yet cannot be alienated nor detained without involving the persons or the nation that doeth thus in a most direful curse; for this is no other than a robbing God of his right.

(2.) Theft is committed *against men* by *an unjust seizing or detaining what of right belongs to them.* And this may be done either by *fraud* or *force:* therefore our Savior in reciting the commandments mentions them both Mark, 10 : 19, " Do not steal: defraud not."

This is a sin, moreover, that God hath threatened with many severe curses and punishments.

The *temporal* punishment which the Scripture awards to it is a fourfold and sometimes a fivefold restitution, as you may see, Exod. 22 : 1; therefore Zaccheus, when he was converted, offers a fourfold restitution to those whom he had wronged, " Luke, 19 : 8, " If I have taken any thing from any man by false accusation, I restore him fourfold."

And yet, besides this restitution, it seems that sometimes the offenders were to be put to death, especially if the circumstances of their theft added cruelty and oppression to it. This appears in the parable of Nathan. 2 Sam. 12. When he had most artificially aggravated the crime of the rich man in taking away the poor man's lamb, he so raised David's compassion and indignation that he pronounced this sentence, verse 5, 6, " The man that hath done this thing shall surely die; and he shall restore the lamb fourfold, because he did this thing, and because he had no pity." So you see that, even under the law of Moses, it was not unlawful in some cases to punish a thief with death, though the usual and prescribed punishment was restitution.

God also leaves a curse upon what is gotten by theft and deceit. A curse that will blast and consume all such wicked increase. They put it into a bag with holes, and, by some unperceivable providence, it strangely wastes and slips away between their fingers. But, usually, luxury and intemperance devour what is got by theft and rapine—God, by his righteous judgment, making one sin the vengeance of another. Some secret withering curse seizeth upon it, and what is thus wickedly added to our former possessions, will rub its rust and canker upon them all; and, if restitution be not duly made, will insensibly prey upon them and consume them; therefore, saith the wise man, Proverbs, 21 : 7, " The robbery of the wicked shall destroy them;" and Jer. 17 : 11, " As the partridge sitteth on eggs, and hatcheth them not, so he that getteth riches, and not by right, shall leave them in the midst of his days, and at his end shall be a fool." Many times God raiseth up those against them who deal with them as they have dealt with others; and when these spunges are full of what they have unjustly sucked up, they shall be squeezed, and made to refund their ill-gotten treasure. Thus God threatens the Chaldeans, Hab. 2 : 8, "Because thou hast spoiled many nations, all the remnant of the people shall spoil thee." Such unjust gettings tend only to poverty; and in this sense it is no solecism to say they have but gained a loss, and treasured for themselves and their posterity want and beggary. Therefore, as you desire to thrive in the world, and to have your earthly comforts multiplied, so be sure that no gain of robbery, or oppression, or fraud and deceit, be found in your hands; for this will devour even what you have gotten lawfully.

Again, not only is theft against men threatened with severe curses and punishments, but *anxieties and perplexities of mind always accompany ill-gotten wealth*. This is a sin so much against the very light of nature, that conscience, if it be not utterly stupified and senseless, will be still molesting and haunting men with troublesome thoughts and reflections; besides, the fear of detection, and the shame and punishment which will follow upon it, must needs be a continual disturbance to them. Whereas, what is gotten with a good conscience, and in an honest and lawful calling, whether it be more or less, brings this contentment with it, that a man may quietly sit down and rejoice in that portion which the providence and bounty of his gracious God and heavenly Father have here afforded him. He drinks no widow's tears nor orphan's blood. He eats not the flesh of the poor, nor breaks the bones of the needy. His conscience gnaws not upon him whilst he is feeding on what his honest labor and industry have prepared for him; and although it be but a bit of bread and a cup of water that he can procure, yet is he entertained at a continual feast. His fare may be but mean, yet his cheer, his joy and comfort is great, and the coarsest morsel he eats is far more savory to him than all the heightened delicacies of rich oppressors, whose consciences mingle gall and wormwood with their most pleasant bits, and gnaw and grind them as they grind the faces of the poor and needy. Therefore, saith the wise man, Prov. 16 : 8, " Better is a little with righteousness, than great revenues without right." And the Psalmist, Ps. 37 : 16, " A little that a righteous man hath is better than the riches of many wicked."

Further, this sin of robbery and deceit *provokes God to cut men off by some untimely stroke and immature judgment*—and that, either by the hand of human justice with shame and reproach, or of divine justice with wrath and vengeance. For so we find it threatened, Ps. 55 : 23, " Thou, O God, shalt bring them down into the pit of destruction : bloody and deceitful men shall not live out half their days :" that is, they shall not lengthen out their days to that period which the course and strength of nature might seem to promise them; but the hand of God shall cut them off in the vigor and midst of their flourishing years. But, however it may fare with them in this life, however they may escape the reproach of men and the sword of justice, yet,

They who commit this sin *shall certainly be eternally cursed and eternally miserable.* Their ill-gotten goods shall not be able to redeem their souls, nor bribe the justice of God, nor give them the least solace and comfort. And what wretched fools are they who must eternally perish for gaining things that perish here, and bring everlasting torments upon themselves for that which before brought them vexations and disquietude! 1 Cor. 6 : 10, "Nor thieves, nor covetous, nor drunkards, nor revilers, nor extortioners shall inherit the kingdom of God." Where then shall their portion be but in that lake which burneth with fire and brimstone unquenchable? Where the Lord will spoil their very souls, as the wise man's expression is, Prov. 22 : 23, "Rob not the poor; for the Lord will plead their cause, and will spoil the soul of those that spoiled them." Thus you see in what various ways God hath threatened that he will punish this sin.

But before I can proceed farther, here are *two questions* to be answered.

Question 1. *Whether in no case it be lawful to steal.* What if the necessity be so urgent that I must certainly perish or else relieve myself by this means?

I say we ought not to do it in any case, for theft is in itself a sin, and there can be no necessity to sin; for every man is bound rather to choose the greatest evil of sufferings than to commit the least evil of sin.

Indeed such necessity doth somewhat mitigate the heinousness of the offence; but that is not at all considerable in the direction of our practice, since it continues a sin still, and deserves eternal damnation. The wise man tells us, Prov. 6 : 30, 31, "Men do not despise a thief if he steal to satisfy his soul when he is hungry;" but this must be understood only comparatively, viz. that the reproach and infamy which attend such a one are not so great as that of an adulterer, as it appears verse 32, as if he should say, "To be an adulterer is a far fouler reproach than to be a needy thief." Yet he adds, " If he be found he shall restore sevenfold; he shall give all the substance of his house:" that is, though his necessity and hunger may take off somewhat from the shame, yet it shall not from the punishment of his offence, but he shall restore that which he hath stolen sevenfold. Not that the restitution should be seven times as much as the theft, for the utmost that the law requires was but a fivefold restitution, Exod. 22 : 1; but as the word sevenfold is most frequently used in Scripture to signify that which is complete and perfect, so is it here, " he shall restore sevenfold," that is, he shall make a full and satisfactory restitution.

Since therefore the punishment of theft shall not be relaxed upon the plea of indigence and necessity, it is apparent that necessity cannot justify any from the guilt of theft.

Hence, let your wants be what they will or can be, you ought not to supply them by any such wicked and unlawful courses, whatever Aquinas says to the contrary, 22 de q. 66, art. 7. If God hath given thee strength and ability, thou oughtest to labor and to use thine honest industry to procure necessaries; if not, thou oughtest to implore the charity and benevolence of others whose hearts God may open to thy relief. Or if thou shouldst meet with such cruel *Diveses* who will contribute nothing to thy support, thou oughtest rather, with godly *Lazarus*, to die in thine integrity than to steal any thing from them, which, although it be their superfluity, yet it is not thy right without their donation.

Question 2. What shall we judge of the Israelites spoiling the Egyptians of their jewels, of which we read, Exod. 12 : 35, 36 ?

I answer: In *this action there was no theft committed.* For,

(1.) The supreme dominion of all things is the Lord's, and he may justly transfer the right and property where he pleaseth. Therefore the Israelites being commanded by the Lord to take these things of the Egyptians, took only what was rightfully their own, being made so by him who hath the sovereign power of all things both in heaven and earth.

(2.) These things which they thus took might be well considered in lieu of their wages, which were not given them for their long service in Egypt. Therefore it was but righteous in God to consign over these riches of the Egyptians to the Israelites as a reward for their tedious servitude. Those who, by the command of the supreme Lord of all, take that which is but a due reward for their labor, cannot certainly be condemned as guilty of theft. And this, it seems, was their plea, when in the time of Alexander the Great, so many ages after the thing was done, the Egyptians sued the Jews by a juridical process, to recover what was taken from them. But,

(3.) This example is extraordinary and special, and not to be pleaded nor introduced into practice. For certain it is that they had a most express command from God to spoil the Egyptians. But whosoever shall pretend any such warrant now, by revelation or the impulse of his private spirit, may well be censured for enthusiasm and condemned for robbery. Thus I have done with the first and greatest kind of theft: taking away what rightfully belongs to another, whether God or man.

2. Another kind of theft is, *oppression and unreasonable exaction.*

And this especially is the sin of superiors towards

their inferiors: taking advantage, either upon their weakness or their necessity, to impose most unequal conditions upon them, and such as they cannot bear without their detriment or ruin; contrary to that law which God gave unto his people, Lev. 25 : 14, "If thou sell ought unto thy neighbor, or buyest ought at thy neighbor's hand, ye shall not oppress one another." Thus, those who set their lands to the sweat and toil of others at too hard a rate, so that the laborious tenant cannot subsist by his industry; those that let out money at a biting interest, or rigidly exact it from insufficient persons; great ones who fright the meaner into disadvantageous bargains, and force them through fear to part with what they enjoy at an under price; these, and others like them, though they may not be condemned by human laws, which give too much permission to men to make the utmost advantage of their own, yet they are guilty by the law of God, and their sin is no less than oppression, which is a sin hateful both to God and man. The prophet Micah, chap. 3 : 2, 3, calls it a "flaying off their skin from off them, and their flesh from off their bones;" and "chopping them in pieces as for the pot, and as flesh for the caldron." All unmercifulness and hard dealings with others are a kind of theft; for the law of nature, and much more the law of charity, binds thee so to deal with others that they may have no cause to complain of thee to God, and in the bitterness of their spirits to imprecate his wrath and vengeance upon thee.

3. Another kind of theft is, *detaining from another what is his due either by equity or compact.*

And how many are there whose profuse riot and luxury are maintained upon the intrusted goods of others, whilst the poor creditor in the meantime hath no other satisfaction but good words, and scarce any thing to live upon but his own tears and sighs! And how many withhold the hire of the laborer, who, when he hath wearied himself in their service, is denied that small reward which he requires for his necessary refreshment! Yea, not only denying it, but even deferring it beyond the time that they can conveniently be without it, is a kind of theft and oppression. Deut. 24 : 14, 15, " Thou shalt not oppress a hired servant that is poor and needy. At his day thou shalt give him his hire, neither shall the sun go down upon it; for he is poor, and setteth his heart upon it: lest he cry against thee unto the Lord, and it be sin unto thee." Yea, in all thy bargains and agreements, though they be never so much to thine own prejudice, thou art bound to stand to them, unless the other will voluntarily release thee from the obligation; for this is one of the characters given of a godly person, Ps. 15 : 4, " He that sweareth," and covenanteth "to his own hurt, and changeth not," but upon demand is ready and willing to fulfil his agreement. How much more heinous and abominable is it, when men have already received the full value of their compact, unjustly to withhold what they have agreed to give! which is no better than to take their labor or their goods from them by violence and robbery; yea, and in one respect worse, inasmuch as it adds falsehood to stealth.

4. Another kind of theft is *in buying and selling*.

And this is a very large and voluminous deceit; for the subtlety of men hath found out so many artifices to defraud and overreach one another, that to recount them is almost as hard as to escape them. Here come in the false weights and the false measures which are an "abomination to the Lord," Prov. 11 : 1 ; false and counterfeited wares; overcommending or undervaluing of goods for advantage, and many other unjust contrivances which men's consciences can better suggest to them than any discourse. The apostle hath sufficiently cautioned and threatened such men, 1 Thess. 4 : 6, " Let no man go beyond or defraud his brother in any matter; because that the Lord is the avenger of all such." Believe it, there is a day coming when the false weights shall be themselves weighed, and the scanty measures measured by a standard that is infallibly true. Possibly thou mayest deal so cunningly, that those whom thou overreachest can have no advantage against thee nor right themselves by law; but remember that the great Judge will avenge them upon thee at the last day. Then all accounts shall be balanced, and so much found resting due which thou shalt certainly pay, though not to those whom thou hast wronged, yet to the justice of God who is the great and universal creditor.

Besides these several kinds of theft, there are likewise *many other kinds*, as prodigality in wasting what should satisfy the just demands of others, taking wages and reward for what we do not endeavor conscientiously to perform; selling that which we have no right to dispose of, or things which ought not to be sold; taking bribes for justice, or rewards for injustice. But I shall not particularly insist upon these and many others that might be mentioned.—Thus we have seen what the *negative* part of this precept is, or what is *forbidden* in this commandment.

II. As every *negative* implies in it a *positive*, let us now see what is the duty here REQUIRED.

This is twofold: that every one of us should have some calling, and that all of us should be contented in the state and condition of life in which Divine providence hath placed us.

1. The command is, *thou shalt not steal;* therefore *every man ought to have a calling* by which he may comfortably subsist, and by his labor and industry may provide at least necessaries for himself and family. For he that provideth not for his family "hath denied the faith," saith the Apostle, "and is worse than an infidel."

(1.) Some there are *who live without any calling at all.* Such are like idle drones that consume the labor of others, lazy vagabonds to whom the greatest charity would be correction, who only serve to devour misplaced alms and defraud the truly poor of their relief. Yea, if I should rank with these a company of superfluous debauched gentlemen, I think I should do them no great injury; such I mean who are neither serviceable to God nor their country, who have nothing of true worth and gentility in them, but are a company of lewd and desperate characters, the most unprofitable members in the commonwealth, and good for nothing but to kill and destroy one another in their drunken quarrels. I know there is no necessity for manual employment and labor to those whom God hath liberally endowed with his earthly blessings; but yet they may have a calling, and within their own sphere may find employment enough to take up their time and thoughts, and such as may make them the most beneficial men on earth, and truly honored and loved by others; for by their authority, their example, the ampleness of their patrimony and revenues, and the dependence that others have upon them, they may be as influential to pro mote goodness and virtue as too commonly they are to promote vice and villany; and to such truly generous spirits who intend to be so employed, let me commend the careful perusal of an excellent treatise directed to them, entitled, "The Gentleman's Calling." But yet withal, if they should condescend to some stated vocation and course of life, it would be no disparagement to their gentility; for certainly Adam was as much a gentleman, and had as large demesnes as any of them, and yet God thought fit to place him in Eden that he might *dress* and *keep* the garden. But as some have no employment,

(2.) Others *have an unlawful employment*, whose only work is to instruct in vice, and excite men to it. And how many such are there who live by provoking and encouraging the wickedness of others, and continually make use of all the allurements that might entice to evil; and recommend debauchery, first to the fancy and then to the will and affections!

(3.) Others have indeed an honest and a lawful calling, but they are *negligent and slothful* in it. Sloth tendeth to poverty, Prov. 6 : 10, 11, "Yet a little sleep, a little slumber, a little folding of the hands to sleep : so shall thy poverty come as one that travelleth," drawing nearer and nearer to thee by soft and silent degrees; "and thy want as an armed man," who, though his pace be slow by reason of the weight of his armor, yet his assaults are more irresistible and destructive. And poverty tempts to theft, Prov. 30 : 9, " Lest I be poor, and steal." And therefore this command, which forbids theft, must, by consequence, enjoin labor and industry in those lawful callings wherein the Divine providence hath set us, according to that of the apostle, Eph. 4 : 28, " Let him that stole, steal no more; but rather let him labor, working with his hands the thing which is good, that he may have to give to him that needeth," and so, by his industry, of a thief become a benefactor and alms-giver.

2. It requires us to be *contented with that portion of earthly comforts which our heavenly Father allots to us.*

" Be content with those things ye have." Heb. 13 : 5. And certainly he that is not content with what God allows him, lies under a grievous temptation, by fraudulent and unjust courses, to carve out his own condition to himself, and to invade the rights and property of others. Discontent and covetousness are the root of all injustice. He that thinks himself wronged in that he hath not as much as some others, will be apt, either through fraud or violence, to increase his own by wronging of others.

Let us therefore check this ripening temper betimes, and not think that we have too little and others too much; but whatsoever God affordeth us, let us account it sufficient provision and a child's portion; and although it be but food and raiment, neither the most delicate nor the most sumptuous, yet, " having food and raiment, let us be therewith content," as the apostle exhorts us, 1 Tim. 6 : 8. Let us look upon all other things as superfluous or indifferent, and not murmur though we should never obtain them; for whatever is needful to thy subsistence God's providence and blessing upon thy industry will furnish thee with; and what is not needful to this, is not worth thy envy and repining.

3. I shall only subjoin a word or two to those who are *conscious to themselves that they have wronged others* of what was their due, and either withheld or taken from them what by law and equity belonged to them.

Let such know that they are bound to make them a perfect and plenary satisfaction, by making an entire and plenary restitution, if the thing they have stolen or purloined be still extant and in their hand; or if not, then by making a full and satisfactory compensation. Yea, be the thing great or small, more or less, though it should seemingly tend to the loss of thy credit by acknowledging such a wrong, or visibly tend to thy impoverishing or undoing to restore it, yet notwithstanding, thou art bound to restore every farthing of that of which thou hast wronged and defrauded thy brother. Nor is it enough to confess the sin before God and to beg pardon at his hands, but thou must likewise render unto man what is his due, and what thou unjustly keepest from him, whether it be his by thy promise or by his own former possession, as ever thou hopest to obtain pardon for thy sin from the mercy of God; yea, and thou art bound likewise, to the very utmost of thy power, to make him recompense for all the damage which he hath in the meantime sustained by thy unjust withholding of his right and due from him; or else thou shalt never obtain pardon and remission for thy guilt. And the reason is, because, as long as you detain what is another's, so long you continue in the commission of the same sin; for unjust possession is a continued and prolonged theft, and certainly repentance can never be true nor sincere while we continue in the sin of which we seem to repent; and thy repentance not being true, pardon shall never be granted thee.

But you will say, "What if those whom we have wronged be since dead? How can restitution be made to them?"

I answer: In this case thou art bound to make it to

their children, or their nearest relations, to whom it is to be supposed that what thou hast wrongfully detained would have descended and been left by them. Or, if none of these can be found, nor any to whom of right it may belong, then God's right takes place, as he is the great Lord and proprietor of all things; and thou oughtest, besides what thou art obliged to give of thine own, to bestow it on the works of charity and piety, for it is then escheated to him. Yet, withal, thou hast great reason to bewail that thou hast so long deferred the restitution of it to the right owner till now thou hast made thyself incapable of doing it.

This possibly may seem a hard lesson, and doubtless it is so in a world so full of rapine and injustice; but yet, as hard as it is, this is the rule of christianity, this is the inflexible law of justice, and without this you live and die without all hopes of obtaining pardon, **by continuing in your sins impenitently.**

THE NINTH COMMANDMENT.

Thou shalt not bear false witness against thy neighbor.

The former commandment provides for the security of every man's *property*, that he may suffer no wrong nor detriment in his goods; this provides for the preservation of his *good name*, which is a much dearer possession. For "A good name," saith the wise man, Prov. 22 : 1, "is rather to be chosen than great riches," and therefore it ought to be preserved and guarded by us, although not delicately and nicely, yet tenderly and with respect. Whoso contemns fame will soon prostitute virtue, and those who care not what others say, will shortly arrive to such impudence of sinning as not to care what they themselves do.

Indeed a good name is so excellent a blessing, that there is but one thing to be preferred before it, and that is a good conscience. When these two stand in competition, credit must give place to duty; and in this case it is far better to lose our repute with men, than our acceptance and reward with God. It oftentimes so happens, through the ignorance and general corruption of mankind, that what is honest, and pure, and just, is yet not of good report amongst them: piety is but affectation, strictness of life a peevish hypocrisy, the cross a scandal, Christ himself a wine-bibber, a friend of publicans and sinners, his doctrine heresy, and his miracles impostures. And if thou lightest upon any such froward and perverse censurers, as too many such there are in all ages, "who think it strange," as the apostle speaks, "that ye run not with them to the same excess of riot, speaking evil of you," seek not by any base and sinful compliance to redeem their good opinion, but rather glory in the testimony of their railing, and account all their reviling speeches to be but so many votes for your blessedness. "Blessed are ye when men shall revile you, and persecute you, and shall speak all manner of evil against you falsely for my sake." Mat. 5 : 11.

Never covet a good name by bad actions. For what will all the concurring applause of the whole world signify to thee, if yet thy conscience condemn thee louder than they can extol thee? This is but to have music at the door, when all the while there is chiding and brawling within. It is far better that others should wound thy credit than thou thy conscience. That is a wound which their tongues can never lick whole again. All the reputation thy popular sinning can bring thee will be but like hanging bells at a horse's ears, when all the while his back is galled with his burthen. Whoever will be a christian must resolve to go through bad report as well as good: he should desire the one, but not anxiously refuse the other. And if any will bespatter him, let him be careful that it be only with their own dirt, and not with his—with their own malice, and not his miscarriages. And whilst he thus keeps his conscience clear, he may be assured that his credit shall be cleared up at that day when all their unjust reproaches shall but add a crown and diadem of glory to his head.

But where a good name is consistent with a good conscience, we ought to prize and value it as one of the choicest of God's blessings in this world, and to use all lawful means to preserve it. For,

1. *A good name will render a man more serviceable to God*, and *the fitter instrument to promote his honor and glory in the world.*

And therefore the wise man, Eccl. 7 : 1, compares a good name to "precious ointment," and in the comparison gives it the preference. For as precious ointment diffuses its fragrancy through the room where it is poured forth, and affects all that are in it with its delightful odor; so do men's gifts, when they are perfumed with a good name, delight and attract others, and by a sweet and powerful charm allure them to imitate and practise those virtues which they see to be so commendable. And therefore we find it the apostle's care, 2 Cor. 6 : 3, to give "no offence in any thing, that the ministry might not be blamed." Though it be our great folly to estimate men's counsels by their own practice, since a diseased physician may prescribe a wholesome medicine, yet so it comes to pass, whether through the curse of God or the prejudice of men, that those who have lost their credit, have, together with it, lost all opportunities and advantages of doing good in the world: let their talents be never so great and their gifts never so eminent, yet if once this dead fly be gotten into this box of ointment, it will corrupt it and render it unsavory to all. And the devil hath no policy so successful to make the gifts of those whom he fears might shake his kingdom unuseful, as either to tempt them to the commission of some infamous and scandalous sin, or to tempt others falsely to calumniate and report such profligate crimes concerning them; then he knows such a one is disarmed and made unserviceable, and if he can but once blast the leaves, the fruit will seldom come to any maturity and perfection. Therefore as you desire to be serviceable to God in promoting his glory, and to the world in promoting their good and benefit, which is the great end of our being and the only thing worth living for, so endeavor, by all wise and honest means, to keep up your good name. Be good, and appear to be so. "Let your light so shine before men, that they seeing your good works, may glorify your Father which is in heaven." Mat. 5 : 16.

2. *A good name, as it gives us advantage of doing good to others, lays an obligation upon us of being good ourselves.*

For if the world be so kindly mistaken as to report well of us without any desert, yet this cannot but stimulate us, if we have any ingenuousness, and engage us to deserve it, and thus happily turn that which was praise into motive. Or if they give us but our due commendation, and our virtue justly challengeth this fame, yet still it will engage us to do things worthy of ourselves, and worthy of the common estimate that men put upon us, that we may not fall short of what we have been, or what they still repute us to be. This is a laudable ambition, which seeks by virtue to maintain that credit which by virtue we have acquired. And doubtless when other arguments have been baffled by a temptation, this hath been a sheet anchor to the soul, and hath often held it in the greatest storms when the wind and waves have beat most furiously against it. "Should I consent to this sin, what a blot and dishonor should I get to myself! How should I be able to look good men in the face again? Would not this sin brand me for a hypocrite in their esteem? Would they ever look upon me or receive me with affection after this fall? Should I not carry the disgrace and scar of this wound visibly upon me to my grave? No, one sin shall never ruin all the comfort and all the repute gained through so many years, and I, who have been so long exemplary as a christian, will not by this one act make myself a scorn to the wicked and a shame to the godly." And by these considerations he rejects a temptation that perhaps ran down all other considerations before it. But a man of a lost and desperate credit sins impudently without any such restraint upon him; he thinks it is but in vain for him to abstain from any wickedness, for, whether he doth or not, people will still believe him guilty; his credit is so disfigured and his name so infamous that he thinks he cannot be worse than he is already reported, and so rubs his forehead and outfaces censure, and with a brazen impudence cares not how wicked he is nor how many know him to be so. Thus you see how cautious we ought to be in maintaining our own good name.

But this command requires us to preserve the repute and good name of OTHERS as well as our own. It forbids

The sin of *lying*, of *detraction and slander*, and of *base soothing and unworthy flattery*.

In the first place, the command prohibits LYING; and this is a sin which comprehends under it all other violations of this precept, for slander and flattery are both of them lies, different only in manner and circumstances; and as lying is a sin large and comprehensive in its nature, so it is general and universal in its practice. We may well complain, with the holy prophet, that "Truth is perished from the earth."

And here I shall show *what a lie is*, with the different sorts of lies, and then the *heinousness and aggravation* of this common sin.

I. A lie, according to Augustin's definition of it, is A VOLUNTARY SPEAKING OF AN UNTRUTH WITH AN INTENT TO DECEIVE.

In a lie therefore there must be these three ingredients. There must be *the speaking of an untruth; it must be known to us to be an untruth; and it must be with a will and intent to deceive him to whom we speak it, and to lead him into error.* Hence,

1. *Parables and figurative speeches are no lies.* For neither as to the drift and scope of them are they falsehoods, nor yet are they spoken with an intent to deceive, but rather to instruct the hearers, and so they have neither the matter nor the form of a lie.

The Scripture abounds with these tropical expressions, which although, in the proper signification of the words, they cannot be verified of the thing to which they are applied, yet do they very fully agree to them in their figurative and transferred sense. Thus Jotham's parable of trees choosing them a king was aptly accommodated to the sense which he meant, and which those that heard him well enough understood. And thus our Savior Christ calls himself a *door*, signifying by that metaphor that by him alone we must enter into heaven and eternal life; a *vine*, signifying that without our incision into him and spiritual union to him, whereby we derive grace from his plenitude and fulness of grace as the branches do sap and juice from the stock, we shall be cast out as withered and fruitless branches, fit for nothing but to be burned. Innumerable other metaphors are every where dispersed throughout the Scriptures.

And besides metaphors, the Scripture useth *hyperboles*. I shall only instance in that famous one, John, 21 : 25, " Many other things Jesus did, the which, if they should be written every one, I suppose that even the world itself could not contain the books that should be written." This high expression the evangelist uses to indicate the great number of the miracles and remarkable passages of our Savior's life, and to signify that he did very many other things which are not on record.

And sometimes the Scripture useth *ironical taunts*. Thus in that bitter sarcasm of Elijah to the priests of Baal, 1 Kings, 18 : 27, "He mocked them, and said, cry aloud; for he is a god." Ironical speeches of this kind are so far from being intended to create error in the minds of men, or to confirm them in it, that they are spoken on purpose to convince them of their errors and make them appear to be shameful and ridiculous, and therefore are no lies.

But here we must take this caution, that in using such figurative speeches we ought so to *circumstantiate* them that the hearers may easily perceive the drift and scope of our discourse, or at least that they may be assured that we intend some other meaning by them than what the words do *properly* and *in themselves* bear. Otherwise, though it may not be a lie in us, yet it may be an occasion of error and mistake in them.

2. *Every falsehood is not a lie.* For though it hath the matter, yet it may want the form and complement to make it such. For many times men speak and report that which

is not true, which yet they themselves do believe to be true; and so they are rather deceived than deceivers, and perhaps are far from any intention of imposing on the credulity of others. Such a one is not so much to be accused of lying, as of folly and rashness in reporting that for truth the certainty of which is not clear and evident to himself.

3. *A man may speak that which is true, and yet be a liar in so doing.* As in these two cases:

When we report that to be a truth, which, although it be so, yet we believe it to be a falsehood, and report it with an intent to deceive those that hear us. Or,

When we report the figurative words of another, leaving out those circumstances which might make them appear to be figurative. Therefore they are called *false witnesses* which came in against Christ and testified that he said he was " able to destroy the temple of God and to build it in three days," Mat. 26 : 60, in which, though there were many falsifications of the words of our Savior, yet had they reported the very words that he spake, they had nevertheless been false witnesses, because by their testimony they wrested them to another sense than what Christ intended by them; for certainly he is a liar who reports my words with a purpose to beget a wrong construction of them, as much as he who reports me to have spoken what I never said.

4. *It is no lie to conceal part of the truth when it is not expedient nor necessary to be known.* Thus, 1 Sam. 16 : 2, God himself instructs Samuel, when he sent him to anoint David king over Israel, that he should answer, he came *to sacrifice to the Lord;* which was truth, and one end of his going into Bethlehem, though he had also another, which he prudently concealed.

5. *A man may act contrary to what he before said, if the circumstances of the thing be altered, without being guilty of lying.* Of this we have frequent examples in the Scripture. Thus, Gen. 19 : 2, the angels tell Lot that they would not come into his house, but would " abide in the street all night;" yet, upon his importunity and earnest entreaties, they went in with him. And thus Peter, with some heat and vehemency of his humility, refused that Christ should wash his feet, John, 13 : 8, " Thou shalt never wash my feet;" but when he was instructed in the significancy of this condescension of our Savior, he not only permits, but entreats him to do it. So likewise in all things of such a nature we may lawfully change our words upon the change of our minds, and upon the inducement of some circumstances that were not known or considered by us, we may, without the imputation of lying, do otherwise than we before resolved and declared. But here must be heedful caution :

That the actions be not such as we are bound to perform by divine precept;

Nor such as we have bound ourselves to by the voluntary obligation of a vow made unto God;

Nor such that our not doing them, or doing otherwise than we have promised, shall be hurtful or prejudicial to others. For if I have promised another that which is beneficial to him, however I may change my opinion, yet I must not change my purpose; but, unless he will release me, or hath forfeited the benefit of my promise by failing in the conditions of it, I stand engaged to perform what I have plighted to him.

Thus you see what a lie is, and what is not a lie.

The sum of all I shall contract in this description of

it: A lie is a falsehood, either real or supposed so by us spoken purposely and with an intention to deceive another. And therefore, neither falsehoods not thought to be so, nor figurative speeches, nor truth partly concealed, nor the change of our mind and purposes upon the changing and alteration of circumstances, can be chargeable with the foul and scandalous sin of lying.

As to the *different sorts of lies*, they are usually distinguished into three kinds: the jocular, the officious, and the pernicious lie.

1. The *jocular lie* is a lie framed to excite mirth and laughter, and to deceive the hearer only to please and divert him. Though it may seem very harmless to deceive men into mirth and recreation, yet truth is such an awful and severe thing that it ought not to be contradicted; no, not in jest. And God reckons it as a sin against the Israelites, Hos. 7 : 3, that they made "the king and princes glad," or merry, "with their lies."

2. The *officious lie* is a lie which is told for another's benefit and advantage, and seems to make an abundant compensation for its falsehood by its use and profit. But yet neither can this excuse it from being a sin; for since a lie is intrinsically evil in itself, let the advantage that accrues by it be never so great, we ought not to shelter either ourselves or others under that rotten refuge. That stated maxim holds universally true in all cases; *we ought not to do evil that good may come thereof.* Therefore, although thine own life or thy neighbor's depends upon it, yea, put the case, it were not only to save his life but to save his soul, couldst thou by this means most eminently advance the glory of God or the general good and welfare of the church, yet thou oughtest not to tell the least

he to promote these great and blessed ends. This the apostle takes for granted, Rom. 3 : 7.

And here, as this passage may seem at first glance somewhat obscure, I shall briefly expound it. *If the truth of God hath more abounded through my lie unto his glory, why yet am I also judged as a sinner?* The words as they stand seem to be favorable to such a beneficial lie; but if we consider the scope and drift of them, we shall see that they clearly condemn it. For the apostle had, in the foregoing verses, taught that the unrighteousness and sins of men did occasionally conduce to the manifestation of the justice and veracity of God, in fulfilling his threatenings upon them. Against this position he raiseth an objection, verse 5, If the unrighteousness of men commend and illustrate the righteousness of God, how then can God be just in taking vengeance on those sins by which he is glorified? To this the apostle answers two ways:

He *abhors the consequence*, verse 6. *God forbid* that we should think him unjust because he punisheth those sins which accidentally serve for the manifestation of his glory. For if God were unjust, how then should he judge the world?

He *answers, by putting a like case and giving a like instance*, verse 7, " If the truth of God hath more abounded through my lie—why yet am I judged as a sinner?" As if he had said, " By the like reason as you infer that it would be unrighteous in God to punish those who are the occasion of so much glory to him through their sins, by the like, I might infer, that if by my lie I might glorify God, I were not to be accounted a sinner for lying." But this, saith he, verse 8, is a most wicked consequence, and such as would justify the slanders of those who report that we affirm it lawful *to do evil that good may come, whose damnation is just:* that is, it is just with God to damn those who slander us with such a gross untruth; and it is just with God to damn those who hold so wicked and destructive a doctrine.

So you see that nothing could be more expressly spoken against these officious lies than what the apostle here produceth in this place. He asserts, in general, *that we must not do evil that good may come thereof;* and he instanceth in particular, *that we must not lie, although the glory of God may be promoted by it.*

3. The *malicious and pernicious lie is a lie devised on purpose for the hurt and damage of my neighbor.* And this is the worst and the most heinous sort of all, and hath nothing that might excuse or extenuate it. It shows a heart brimful of the bitterness of malice, when this passion works out at the mouth in slanderous reports and false accusations. All lies are in themselves sinful; but this is the vilest and most abominable of all.

II. The AGGRAVATIONS OF THIS SIN. Consider,

1. It is *a sin that makes you most like unto the devil.*

The devil is a spirit, and therefore, gross carnal sins cannot correspond to his nature. His sins are more refined and intellectual; such as are pride and malice, deceit and falsehood, John, 8 : 44, "He is a liar, and the father of it." And the more malice goes into the composition of any lie, the more nearly it resembles him. This is the first-born of the devil; the beginning of his strength; for by lies he prevailed over wretched man; hence it is his darling and beloved sin, and the greatest instrument of promoting his kingdom. It is that which, in his own mouth, ruined all mankind in the gross, when he falsely suggested to our first parents that they should be as gods; and that which he still puts into the hearts and mouths of men to ruin and destroy their souls and the souls of others, Acts, 5 : 3, " Why hath Satan filled thine heart to lie to the Holy Ghost?" "When he speaketh a lie, he speaketh of his own," saith our Savior. And certainly, when we speak a lie we repeat only what he prompts and dictates to us. Thou never liest but thou speakest aloud what the devil whispered softly to thee; the old serpent lies folded round in thy heart, and we may hear him hissing in thy voice. And therefore when God summoned all his heavenly attendance about him, and demanded who would persuade Ahab to go up and fall at Ramoth-Gilead, an evil spirit that had crowded in amongst them steps forth and undertakes the office, as his most natural employment, and that wherein he most of all delighted, 1 Kings, 22 : 22, " I will go forth and be a lying spirit in the mouth of all his prophets." Every lie thou tellest, consider that the devil sits upon thy tongue, breathes falsehood into thy heart, and forms thy words and accents into deceit.

2. Consider that it is *a sin most contrary to the nature of God, who is truth itself.* It is sin that he hates and abominates, Prov. 6 : 16, 17, " These six things doth the Lord hate; yea, seven are an abomination unto him: a proud look, a lying tongue," &c.; and Prov. 12 : 22, " Lying lips are an abomination to the Lord." Hence we have so many express commands given us against this sin, Lev. 19 : 11, " Ye shall not deal falsely, nor lie one to another." Col. 3 : 9, " Lie not one to another." " Wherefore, putting away lying, speak every man truth to his neighbor." Eph. 4 : 25.

3. Consider that it is *a sin that gives in a fearful evidence*

against us that we belong to the devil and are his children; for he is the father of lies and of liars. God's children will imitate their heavenly Father in his truth and veracity. And it is a very observable place, Isa. 63:8, "Surely," saith God, "they are my people; children that will not lie; so he was their Savior."

4. Consider *how dreadfully God hath threatened this sin with eternal death.* Scarce any one sin more expressly and particularly. Rev. 22:15, "Without," even in outer darkness, "are dogs—and murderers, and idolaters, and whosoever loveth or maketh a lie."

5. A lie *showeth a most degenerate and cowardly fear of men, and a most daring contempt of the great God.* Whoever lies, does it out of a base and sordid fear lest some evil and inconvenience should come to him by declaring the truth. And this Montaigne, in his Essays, gives as the reason why the imputation of lying is the most reproachful ignominy that one man can lay upon another, and that which most passionately moves them to revenge; because, saith he, "To say a man lieth, is to say that he is audacious towards God and a coward towards men." Lib. 2, c. 18.

6. *Mankind generally account lying a most infamous and reproachful sin.* A liar loseth all credit and reputation amongst men; and he who hath made himself scandalous by lying, is not believed when he speaks truth. Yea, it is so odious and foul a sin that we find it generally esteemed worse than other sins; and the avoiding of this is thought a good excuse for the commission of others; for when men are moved with some violent passion they often resolve to do those things which, when their passion is allayed, they must look upon as grievous sins; yet, rather than be false to their word, and so censured for

lying, they will venture to perpetrate them. Thus Herod, for his oath's sake, beheaded John the Baptist. And the common excuse for rash and unwarrantable actions is, " I said I would do thus or thus, and therefore I thought myself bound in honor to do it."

7. It is *a sin that God will detect, and which exposeth those who are guilty of it to shame and contempt.* Lying lips are " but for a moment." Prov. 12 : 19. And when they are found out, as usually they are, by their own forgetfulness and the interfering of their own speeches, how shameful will their sin be to them! And the reward they shall have for it is, that those who have accustomed themselves to lying shall not be believed when they speak truth.

Thus much concerning the *heinousness* and *aggravation* of the sin of lying.

There remain two other violations of this commandment; the one is by *slander and detraction*, the other by *base flattery and soothing ;* and both may respect either ourselves or others.

I shall now speak of the common sin of SLANDER and DETRACTION : a sin that is reigning and triumphant in this our age, and if I should likewise say in this place, I think I should not myself be guilty of it by that censure.

Slander and *detraction* seem somewhat to differ. *Slander*, properly, is *a false imputation of vice*, but *detraction* is *a causeless diminishing report of virtue.* The one traduceth us to be what indeed we are not, the other lessens what we really are, and both are highly injurious to our good name and reputation, the best and dearest of all our earthly possessions.

When a man's life and actions are so blameless and exemplary that even malice itself is ashamed to vent its venom by base slanders lest it should appear to be malice, and the reproach should light rather upon the reporters than him whom they seek to defame, then it betakes itself to those little sly arts of nibbling at the edges of a man's credit and clipping away the borders of his good name, that it may not pass so current in the world as before. Thus when any are so just as to give others their due commendation either for learning, or wisdom, or piety, or any other perfection, either of grace or of nature, you shall have those who lie in wait to cut off other men's esteem. If they see it so strongly fortified by the conspicuousness of it and the general vote of the world that they dare not attack the whole, they lurkingly assault part of it, and what they cannot altogether deny they will endeavor to diminish: "It is true, such a man is, as you say, learned and knowing, but withal so knowing as to know that too. He is wise, but his wisdom is rather politic than generous, and all his designs are biassed with self-ends. He is charitable, but his charity seems too indiscreet; or if you did not proclaim his good works he himself would. He is pious and devout indeed, poor man, after his way, and according to his knowledge." Thus by these blind hints they endeavor either to find or to make a flaw in another man's reputation, well knowing that a cracked name, like a cracked bell, will not sound half so clear and loud in the ears of the world as else it might. Thus you see what slanders and detractions are. I remark,

1. *A man may be a self-slanderer and a self-detracter.* Such are those who traduce and defame themselves, and either assume to themselves those wickednesses which

they have not committed, or blameably conceal those gifts and excellencies they are endowed with, when they are called to discover them for the glory of God and the public good.

Some slander themselves *out of hope of reward*, when they suppose that the crimes they boast of may be accepted as services by others. Thus, when Saul had slain himself, an Amalekite falsely reports to David that he had slain him—hoping to obtain a reward from him for despatching his enemy.

Sometimes men impiously boast of those sins which they never did and never durst commit, merely *out of a braving humor of vain-glory*, and that among their debauched companions they may gain the reputation of valiant and daring sinners.

Others falsely accuse themselves of those sins of which they were never guilty, *out of a despairing and dejected spirit*. Thus many a poor soul that hath labored under severe convictions, begins first to doubt, and then to conclude that he hath certainly committed the unpardonable sin against the Holy Ghost, and, in extreme anguish and horror, crieth guilty, and confesseth the indictment that is falsely drawn up against him by the calumny of the devil and his own dark fears and melancholy.

Sometimes men detract from themselves *out of a lying and dissembled humility*, making this kind of detraction only a bait for commendation; as knowing the ball will rebound back the farther to them the harder they strike it from them. This is usually an artifice of proud and arrogant persons; and those who cannot endure to be contradicted in any thing else, would be very loth you should yield to them in this.

And, lastly, others detract from themselves *out of a too bashful modesty*, or to avoid some troublesome and unpleasing employments which they are called unto. Thus we find Moses, Exod. 4 : 10, making many excuses that he was "not eloquent," but "slow of speech and slow of tongue;" and all because he was loth to undertake that difficult and dangerous charge of bringing out the children of Israel from the bondage of Egypt.

All these kinds of self-slander and detraction are evil, and some of them most vile and abominable.

2. There is *a slandering of and detracting from another*, wronging him unjustly in his fame and reputation, which we ought tenderly to preserve and cherish. God and nature have intrusted us mutually with each other's good name. Thy brother's credit is put as a precious *deposit* into thy hands, and if thou wickedly lavishest it out by spreading false rumors of him, or carelessly keepest it, by suffering others to do so when it is in thy power to justify him, know assuredly that it will be strictly required of thee, for in this respect every man is his brother's keeper.

This slandering of others may be either in *judicial process* or in *common and ordinary converse*.

(1.) In *judicial process*. And then it is truly and properly false-witnessing—when thou risest up against thy brother in judgment, and attestest that which thou knowest to be false and forged, or which thou art not most infallibly assured to be true. And this sin is the more heinous and dreadful on account of two aggravating circumstances that attend it.

Since usually all actions in law and judgment concern either *the person or the estate* of thy brother, by a false witness thou not only wrongest him in his name and reputation, but also either his person or his estate, and so thou art not only a slanderer but a thief or murderer. " A hypocrite with his mouth destroyeth his neighbor." Prov. 11 : 9. And by so much the more odious is thy crime, in that thou pervertest the law, which was intended to be a fence and safeguard to every man's property, and turnest it against itself, making it the instrument of thy injustice and cruelty. The Psalmist, Psal. 52 : 2, compares Doeg's malicious tongue to a sharp razor; and certainly when thou givest a false testimony against thy brother, thy tongue is a sharp razor, it not only wounds his credit but cuts his throat.

Again, since usually all judicial proceedings exact from the witnesses a tremendous oath solemnly taken by the name of the great God of heaven, to give in a false testimony is not only to be guilty of slander but of *perjury* too.

Yea, and let me add one thing more to make it a most accumulate wickedness; such a false testimony is not only slander and perjury, but it is *blasphemy* too. For what else is it but to bring the most holy God, who is eternal truth, to confirm a falsehood and a lie ? What can be a higher affront to his most sacred Majesty than this ? For a sworn witness is therefore accepted because he brings God in to be a witness too. And wilt not thou tremble, O wretch, to cite God to appear a witness to that which a thousand witnesses within thee (I mean thy own conscience) do all depose to be false and forged; and so to transfer thy injustice, and rapine, and bloody murder upon him, and shelter them all under the shadow of his veracity and faithfulness !

You see then how horrid an impiety this is; and yet

how common it is, not only those who by this wicked means suffer wrong, but others who are conversant in such judiciary trials do too truly report.

May it please God to put it into the hearts of our rulers to enact more severe and rigorous laws against those who are found guilty of it! It is sad to think that whereas a thief shall be adjudged to death (in England) for stealing some petty inconsiderable matter, and perhaps too for the relief of his pressing necessities; yet two villains that have conspired together by false accusations and perjured testimonies to take away a man's whole estate, or possibly his life, should for these far greater crimes be sentenced to so easy a punishment that only shame and reproach make up the severest part of it. Certainly methinks it were but just that the least they should suffer should be a retaliation of their intended mischiefs, and that the same they designed against their brother should be inflicted on themselves; whether it be loss of life or loss of goods and estate. It is but equity that the plotters and artificers of mischief should perish by their own craft. And if this rigor and wholesome severity were used, we should not have so many oaths set out to hire, nor would any make it a trade to be a witness; but innocency would be secured under the protection of the laws, and the laws themselves be innocent of the ruin of many hundreds, who by this means fall into the snares of ungodly men. Of this one thing I am sure, that God himself thought it a most equitable law when he thus provided for the safety of his people Israel: Deut. 19: 18–20, " If the witness be a false witness, and testify falsely against his brother, then shall ye do unto him as he had thought to do unto his brother: so shalt thou put the evil away from among you;

and those which remain shall hear and fear, and shall henceforth commit no more any such evil among you."

(2.) There is a slandering of others *in our common and ordinary converse*. And this is either *open and avowed*, in their presence and to their faces; or *secret and sly*, behind their backs.

The *open and avowed* is also twofold. One way is by *reviling and railing speeches*, as Shimei barked at David, 2 Sam. 16 : 7, " Come out, thou bloody man, and thou man of Belial." And I wish that our streets and houses did not, to their great disgrace and reproach, echo with such clamor; and that too many did not rake together all the dirty expressions which their wit and malice will serve them to invent only to throw into one another's faces. A sin which, as it is sordid and base in itself, so it chiefly reigns among those who are of a mean condition; but wherever found, is a disparagement to human nature, a sin against civil society, and argues men guilty of much folly and brutishness; and I am sure it is a transgression of that express command of the apostle, Eph. 4 : 31, 32, " Let all bitterness, and wrath, and anger, and clamor, and evil-speaking be put away from you, with all malice; and be ye kind one to another, tender-hearted, forgiving one another, even as God for Christ's sake hath forgiven you."

The other way of open, avowed slander is by *bitter taunts and sarcastical scoffs*. And this is usually an applauded sin among the more refined sort of men, who take a pride and glory in exposing others and making them ridiculous, thinking their own wit never looks so beautiful as when it is dyed in other's blushes. But this is a most scurrilous and offensive way, wherein certainly he hath the most advantage, not who hath most wit, but that hath least modesty. These kinds of tauntings are sometimes such as the apostle calls *cruel mockings*, and reckons up as one part of those persecutions which the primitive christians endured. Heb. 11 : 36. As Nero for his barbarous sport wrapped up the christians in beasts'. skins and then set dogs to worry them; so these disguise their brethren in false and antic shapes, and then fall upon them and beat them.

Again, there is a more *secret and sly* conveyance of slander, by *backbiting, whispering, and the carrying up and down of tales.* Like those busy tongues, Jer. 20 : 10, that would fain find or make themselves some employment, saying, *Report, and we will report.* And so a false and slanderous rumor shall, like the river Nile, spread over the whole land, and yet the head of it be never known: it shall pass on to the indelible blot and infamy of thy neighbor, and the first author of it lie hid and concealed in the crowd, as some fishes will in the mud which they themselves have stirred. Against this sort of men Solomon, in his book of Proverbs, is very severe; and there is no one wickedness which that excellent compendium of wisdom and morality doth more inveigh against than this of whispering about another man's disgrace, Prov. 18 : 8, "The words of a tale-bearer are as wounds, and they go down into the innermost parts of the belly." And this he repeats again, chap. 26 : 22, intimating that the wound which such a tongue makes is deep, but yet hid and secret, and therefore the more incurable. And Prov. 16 : 28, "A whisperer separateth chief friends." He is, as it were, the devil's truchman and interpreter between them both, and goeth to one and buzzeth in his ear what such a one said of him, although perhaps it be altogether false; and when he hath by this means got some angry and choleric speeches from him, goes and reports them back to the other; and so by his wicked breath blows up the coals of strife and dissension between them. Therefore the wise man tells us, "Where no wood is, the fire goeth out; so, where there is no tale-bearer the strife ceaseth." Prov. 26 : 20. The apostle cautions the Corinthians against this sin, 2 Cor. 12 : 20, "I fear lest, when I come, I shall not find you such as I would—lest there be among you debates, envyings, wraths, strifes, backbitings, whisperings, swellings, tumults;" and he reckons it up among the black catalogue of those crimes, for the which "God gave up" the heathen "to a reprobate mind, to do those things which are not convenient; being filled with all unrighteousness—full of envy, murder, debate, deceit, malignity, whisperers, backbiters, haters of God, despiteful, proud, boasters, inventors of evil things." Rom. 1 : 28–30. Now one of the chief artifices of this sort of men is to calumniate strenuously, according to that old maxim of the devil, *Calumniare fortiter, et aliquid adhærebit*, "Slander stoutly, and somewhat will stick behind;" for though the wound may possibly be healed, yet the scar will still remain, and be a blemish to a man's reputation as long as he lives.

But then again there is another kind of slander and detraction, *when a man divulgeth those imperfections and faults which are truly in his neighbor, without being called or necessitated to do it.* For sometimes truth itself may be a slander, when it is spoken with an evil design to the hurt and prejudice of another.

Indeed, if thou be duly called to witness in judgment; or if it be in thy own defence and vindication, when, if thou dost not discover him that is guilty, thou thyself mayst be supposed to be the person; or if the crime be such as ought not to escape unpunished; or if he remain contumacious after more private admonition, in which case our Savior commands us to tell it to the church: or lastly, when it is for the safety and security of another, who might else be wronged should we conceal from him the mischiefs which others intend him: in these cases it is both lawful and expedient to make known the faults of thy brother.

But then be sure that thou do it not with any secret delight and exultation that thou hast his credit to trample upon, to raise thine own the higher; but with that true grief and sorrow of heart which may evince to all the world that nothing but conscience and a sense of thy duty enforced thee to publish his shame, which thou wouldst be willing to hide at the price of any thing but sin and thine own shame.

But, alas! it is strange to consider the depravity of our nature, how we delight in other men's sins, and are secretly glad when their miscarriages give us an occasion to reproach and disgrace them. How many are big with such stuff, and go in pain till they have disburthened themselves into the ears of others! And some are such ill dissemblers of their joy, that they do it with open scorn and irrision. Others are more artificially malicious, and with a deep sigh and a downcast look, and a whining voice and an affected slowness, whisper to one, "Alas! did you not hear of such a gross miscarriage by such a one?" and then whisper the same thing to another, and a third; and when they have made it as public as they can, hypocritically desire every one to keep it secret, for that they would be loth their neighbor should come to any disgrace and trouble about it. Believe it, sirs, this, though the matter you report be never so true, is nothing else but slander; because it is done to no good end, but only to feed your own malice, and, like flies, to lie sucking the galled backs and sores of others. And therefore we find that Doeg, though he told nothing but the truth, 1 Sam. 22 : 9, 10, yet is by David challenged as a liar and slanderer. Ps. 52.

Having thus shown what this sin of slander is, I shall give some brief RULES AND DIRECTIONS, which, through the grace of God, may be serviceable to keep you from this common sin; and then such as may show how you ought to demean yourselves under the lash of other men's slanderous tongues.

1. *How to keep yourselves from slandering others.*

(1.) If thou wouldst keep thyself from being a slanderer of others, *addict not thyself violently to any one party or persuasion of men.* For party spirit will beget prejudice, and prejudice is the jaundice of the soul, which represents other men and their actions in the color which our own disease puts upon them. And indeed we have all generally such a good conceit of ourselves, that it is a very hard and difficult matter to have a good esteem for others who are not of our judgment and of our way. And this makes us, first, very willing to hear some evil of them; for because we think that what we do is good, we cannot cordially think them good who do not judge and act as we ourselves do, and so our minds are prepared to entertain reports against them from others, and then to spread them abroad ourselves. And I cannot but impute to this the great uncharitableness of our days, wherein love and brotherly kindness lie murdered under the violence of different persuasions, and different modes, and divers ways of worshipping one and the same God and our Lord Jesus Christ. Hence all those lying rumors and lying wonders that one party invents to beat down the other. Both suffer from each other's envenomed tongues, and between both, truth suffers, and charity perishes, and is utterly lost. For shame, O christians! Is this the way to promote God's cause or Christ's kingdom? Doth he or it stand in need of your lies? Will you speak wickedly for God, and talk deceitfully for him? Shall his honor be maintained by the devil's inventions? I shall not speak partially; but wheresoever the fault lies, there let the censure fall—that it is certainly a very strong presumption of a weak and bad cause, when the refuge and support of it are lies.

(2.) If thou wouldst not be guilty of slander, *be not busy in other men's affairs*. Keep thine eyes within doors and thy thoughts at home. Inquire not what others say nor what others do, but look to thine own affairs, and guide them with discretion. Thou hast work enough at home, within thine own heart, and in thine own house; and if thou art careful to manage that well, thou wilt scarcely have either time or inclination to receive or divulge bad reports of others. And therefore the apostle joins idleness and tattling together, "They learn to be idle, wandering about from house to house; and not only idle, but tattlers also, and busy-bodies, speaking things which they ought not." 1 Tim. 5 : 13. They are *idle*, and yet *busy-bodies*, very idly busy, who, because they care not to employ their hands, set their tongues on work, and suffer them to walk through the world abusing and lashing every one they meet. A true description of a company of giddy flies in our times, that are always roving from house to house, and skipping about, now to this man's ear, and by and by to that, and buzzing reports of what ill they have heard or observed of others.

(3.) Take another rule. If thou wouldst not be guilty of slander, *be frequent in reflecting on thine own miscarriages, or thy proneness to fall into the same or greater faults.* When thou hearest or knowest of any foul and scandalous sin committed by another, look backwards upon thine own life and actions. Canst thou find no blots in thy copy? Is the whole course of thy life fair written upon thy conscience? If not, how canst thou without shame to thyself upbraid thy brother with his miscarriages, when thou thyself hast been guilty of the like or greater? Or why, O hypocrite, "beholdest thou the mote that is in thy brother's eye, and seest not the beam that is in thine own?" Methinks our shame for our own sins should be a covering to our brother's, and when we ourselves are guilty, we should not be so malicious nor foolish as to reproach ourselves by reproaching him; for thus to eclipse and darken his good name is but as when the moon eclipseth the sun, her own darkness and obscurity is made the more evident by it.

Or if God by his restraining grace hath kept thee from those wickednesses into which he hath suffered others to fall, yet then look inward, view and search thine own heart, ransack over thy corrupted nature, and there thou shalt find those, yea, and far greater abominations than those, like beds of twisted serpents knotting and crawling within thee. Say with thyself, "How can I reproach him who hath but copied forth mine own nature? How can I expose his infamy who hath but done what I have much ado to keep myself from doing? Possibly the same temptation might have prevailed over me too, had God let it loose upon me. I owe my preservation, not to any difference that was between us, but only to the free and abounding grace of God: by this it is that I stand; and shall I reproach him for falling, who should also myself have fallen were I not strongly upheld by another?" Thus I say, by reflecting on ourselves we shall be withheld from being injurious in our censures and in our reports of others, we shall hardly divulge their real miscarriages, much less accuse and slander them with false and forged ones. This is the apostle's rule, Gal. 6 : 1, " Brethren, if a man be overtaken in a fault, ye, which are spiritual, restore such a one in the spirit of meekness; considering thyself lest thou also be tempted."

(4.) If you would not be guilty of slander, *listen not to those who are slanderers and detracters.* Lend not your ears to those who go about with tales and whispers, whose idle business it is to tell news of this man and the other; for if these kinds of flies can but blow in your ears, the worms will certainly creep out at your mouths. For all discourse is kept up by exchange, and if he bring thee one story, thou wilt think it incivility not to repay him with another for it; and so they chat over the whole neighborhood, accuse this man, and condemn another, and suspect a third, and speak evil of all. I wish that the most of our converse were not taken up this way, in recounting stories of what passed between such and such, when all is to no other end but to bring an evil report upon them. Now, if any such backbiters haunt thee, who make it their trade to run up and down with tales and news, give them no countenance, listen not to their detractions, but rather sharply rebuke them and silence their slanderous tongues; and this will either drive the slander from them or the slanderer from thee. "The north wind driveth away rain, so doth an angry countenance a backbiting tongue." Prov. 25 : 23.

(5.) If you would not be slanderers of others, *be not self-lovers.* For self-love always causeth envy, and envy detraction. An envious man cannot endure another's praise, and therefore seeketh all he can to blast it by false reports and lying slanders, as if all that were detracted from another were added to his own reputation. When his neighbor's fame begins to grow tall and to spread about him, he then seeks what he can to cut it down, because he thinks it hinders his prospect, and the world cannot take so fair a view of him as he desires, therefore he is still hewing at it, sometimes with oblique and sometimes with direct blows, sometimes striking at his talents and sometimes at his piety; and if he can but make these fall in the esteem of the world, then he thinks none shall be so much respected and honored as himself. A man that is a self-lover thinks all due to himself: all praise and commendation must run in his channel, or else it takes a wrong course, and he accounts just so much taken from him as is ascribed to another, and this puts him upon this base art of detraction, that by depressing others he may advance himself, and raise the structure of his own fame upon the ruins of his neighbor's. Therefore if thou wouldst not slander others, be sure do not too much admire thyself. For self-applause and self-esteem is like a pike in a pond, that will eat up and devour all about it, that itself may thrive and grow upon them.

(6.) *Be not too ready to entertain suspicious and evil surmises against others.* For if thou begin to suspect evil of another, the next thing is to conclude it, and the next to report it. This suspicion is a strange shadow that every action of another will cast upon our minds, especially if we be beforehand a little disaffected towards them. Thus very dreams increased suspicion against Joseph in his brethren. And if once a man be out of esteem with us, let him then do what he will, be it never so virtuous and commendable, suspicion will still be the interpreter; and where suspicion is the interpreter of men's actions, slander and detraction will be the gloss and comment upon them. Indeed suspicion is always too hasty in concluding, and many times our jealousies and distrusts upon very small occasions prompt us to conclude that what we have thus surmised is certainly come to pass, and so we take shadows for enemies, and report that confidently for truth which yet we never saw acted but only in our own fancies.

Now, notwithstanding that this sin of slander and detraction is so great and heinous, yet may it not be justly feared that many place their whole religion in it, and think themselves so much the better by how much the worse they think and report of other men? Do they not think it a piece of zeal and warmth for the worship and service of God, to cry down all as superstitious that do not worship him in their way? Do they not make it, if not a part, yet a sign of holiness, to be still finding fault and crying out against others; to be censorious and clamorous? Such a class of men they represent as all lewd and profane, and such a class as all rebellious and hypocrites; and then, to justify their censures, they instance possibly in two or three, of whom perhaps they know no more than the bare names.

And what tends all this to but mutual exasperation? Those that do not believe them are exasperated against the reporters, and those who do believe them are exasperated against the slandered.

And as it tends to exasperation, so likewise it encou rageth and hardeneth many in their sins. For when they hear so much evil blazed abroad in the world, and few or none escape without having some foul blot rubbed upon them, or infamous crime reported of them whether truly or falsely, how natural that many should think that sin and wickedness is no such strange thing, and so embolden themselves to commit that which they hear is so common.

I beseech you therefore, christians, for the peace of the church, which else will continue sadly rent and divided; for the sake of christianity, which else will be discredited and reviled; for your brethren's sake, who else will be discouraged or exasperated, be very cautious what reports you either receive or make of others. Their good name is very precious, precious to God when their blameless conversation warrants it, and precious to themselves. However, unless there be absolute necessity, and you are constrained to do it for the glory of God and the good of others, divulge not their imperfections though they be real, and in no case whatever feign or devise false rumors concerning them. "Take heed lest, if ye bite and devour one another, ye be not consumed one of another," and one with another. These are rules to keep you from being guilty of slander against others.

2. But if any are guilty of raising an ill report against you, observe these following *rules and directions how you ought to demean yourselves in this case.*

(1.) *If the reproach they cast on thee be true and deserved,* though they perhaps have sinned in disclosing it to the world, yet *make this use of it: go thou and disclose it in thy most humble and penitent confessions unto God;* yea, and if thou art called thereunto by due form of law, give glory unto God by confessing it before men. Men possibly may upbraid thee with it, but by this course God will forgive thee, without upbraiding thee.

(2.) If thou art *falsely charged* with that which never was in thy heart to do, *yet improve this providence to stir thee up to pray the more fervently that God would for ever keep thee from falling into that sin with which others slander thee:* so shall all their reproaches be thrown merely into the air, and fall at last heavy on their own heads, whilst thou rejoicest in the innocency of thine own soul.

(3.) *If any unjustly slander thee, revenge not thyself upon them by slandering them again.* I must confess that this is a very hard lesson, and requires almost an angelical perfection to perform it well. We read in the Epistle of St. Jude, that when Michael and the devil contended "about the body of Moses," the holy angel "durst not bring a railing accusation" against that wicked spirit, but only said, "The Lord rebuke thee." And so, when men of devilish spirits spew out their slanders and broach all the malicious accusations that their father the great accuser hath ever suggested to them, return not slander for slander; for so the devil would teach thee to be a devil; but with all quietness and meekness desire of God to rebuke their lies and calumnies, and by all wise and prudent means vindicate thyself, clear up thine integrity, and make it appear that though "the archers have shot at thee and sorely grieved thee with their arrows, even bitter words;" yet still "thy bow remaineth in its strength." What saith the apostle? 1 Pet. 3 : 9, Render not "evil for evil, or railing for railing." And indeed whoever doth so seeks only to heal a wound in his name by making a much deeper one in his conscience.

(4.) *When thou art falsely aspersed and slandered, refer thyself and appeal to the all-knowing God:* retire into the peace and refuge of thine own conscience, and there shalt thou find enough for their confutation and thy comfort.

Know that a good name may be in the power of every slanderous tongue to blast; but they cannot corrupt thy conscience to vote with them. Possibly, it is only the excellence and eminence of thy grace that offends them: if so, glory in it; for the reproaches of wicked men are the best testimonials that can be given of an excellent and singular christian. In a strict and holy conversation there is such contradiction to the loose and profane of the world, as at once both convinces and vexes them, reproves and provokes them. And if thou dost thus reproach them by thy life, wonder not at it if they again reproach thee by their lying slanders. Be not too solicitous how they esteem thee. It is miserable to live upon the reports and opinions of others; let us not much reckon what they say, but what reports our own consciences make; and if a storm of obloquy and reproaches, railings and slanders, do at any time patter upon us, how sweet is it to retire inwards to the calm innocency of our own hearts! there are a thousand witnesses which will tell us we have not deserved them. How comfortable is it to remit our cause to God, and to leave our vindication to him for whose cause we suffer reproach! Thus Jeremiah appeals to God: "I heard the defaming of many—Report, say they, and we will report it. But, O Lord of hosts, thou that triest the righteous, and seest the reins and the heart, unto thee have I opened my csaue." Ch. 20 : 10, 12. Thus, if whilst wicked men are maliciously conspiring how to blot and sully our names, we can but keep our consciences clear, what need we much trouble ourselves how the wind blows abroad, since we are harbored under the retreat of a peaceable heart? They may possibly persuade others to believe their calumnies; but God, who searcheth the heart and conscience, knows that we are injured; and he is hastening on a day wherein he will clear up our righteousness; and then the testimony of a good conscience shall put ten thousand slanderers to silence.—Thus I have spoken of this sin, slander and detraction.

The *third* sin against this commandment is BASE FLATTERY, which is a quite opposite extreme to the other, as both are opposite to truth. There is either *self-flattery*, or the *flattering of others*.

1. There is a *self-flattery*. And indeed every man is, as Plutarch well observed, his own greatest flatterer. However empty and defective we may be, yet we are all apt to love ourselves, perhaps without a rival, and to be puffed up with a vain conceit of our own imaginary perfections, to applaud and commend ourselves in our own thoughts and fancies, and to think that we excel all others in what we have, and what we have not we despise as nothing worth. From this abundance of a vain heart

break out arrogant boastings of ourselves, contemning of others, and a presumptuous intruding ourselves into those employments and functions which we are no way able to manage. Learn, therefore, O christian, to take the just measure of thyself. Let it not be too scanty, for that will make thee pusillanimous and cowardly, and through an extreme of modesty render thee unserviceable to God and the world. But rather let it be too scanty than too large, for this will make thee proud, arrogant and assuming; and by exercising thyself in things too high for thee, thou wilt but spoil whatsoever thou dost rashly and overweeningly venture upon. If thou art at any time called or necessitated to speak of thyself, let it rather be less than the truth than more; for the tongue is of itself very apt to be lavish when it hath so sweet and pleasing a theme as a man's own praise. Take the advice of Solomon: "Let another man praise thee, and not thine own mouth; a stranger, and not thine own lips." Prov. 27:2.

2. There is a *sinful flattering of others*, and that either by an immoderate extolling of their virtues, or what is worse, by a wicked commendation even of their very vices. This is a sin most odious to God, who hath threatened to "cut off all flattering lips." Psalm 12:3. But especially it is most detestable in ministers, whose very office and function it is to reprove men for their sins, if they shall "daub with untempered mortar," and "sew pillows under men's elbows," crying "Peace, peace, when there is no peace to the wicked," only that they may lull them asleep in their security; they do but betray their souls, and the blood of them God will certainly require at their hands.

THE TENTH COMMANDMENT.

Thou shalt not covet thy neighbor's house: thou shalt not covet thy neighbor's wife; nor his man-servant, nor his maid-servant, nor his ox, nor his ass, nor any thing that is thy neighbor's.

Thus are we at last, through the Divine assistance, arrived to the tenth and last precept of the moral law.

Indeed the papists, and after them some protestants, divide it into two, making these words, *thou shalt not covet thy neighbor's wife,* to be one entire command; and then putting together the other branches of it, *thou shalt not covet thy neighbor's house, nor his servant,* &c. to piece up the last. And then, withal, to keep the number of the commandments from swelling beyond a decalogue, or *ten* words, some join the first and second together into one; and the papists, in propounding the commandments to the people, wholly leave out the *second,* fearing they may be corrupted by hearing it, because it speaks too boldly against their idolatry and image-worship.

But how infinitely rash is it for vile wretches either to invert or defalcate, and as it were to decimate the laws of the great God, by the which they and all their actions must be judged at the last day!

And certainly were it not that they might the better conceal from the ignorant common people the dangerous and heretical words of the second commandment, they could have lain under no temptation at all to do a thing altogether so unreasonable as the dividing of this tenth commandment into two; for on the same ground might they as well have divided it into seven, since there are many more concupiscences mentioned in it than that of our neighbor's wife and of his house. And if each of these must constitute a distinct precept, why not also, *thou shalt not covet his man-servant: thou shalt not covet his ox,* &c.

Besides, the order of the words makes clearly against them. For whereas they make, *thou shalt not covet thy neighbor's wife* to be the ninth, in the text those words, *thou shalt not covet thy neighbor's house* go before them, so that either they must needs confess it to belong to the tenth, or else must grant a most unintelligible hyperbaton both of sense and words, such as would bring in utter confusion and disorder amongst those laws which God certainly prescribed us in a most admirable method and disposition.

But to speak no more of this, I shall first consider *the sin here prohibited,* and then close up with *some practical use and improvement.*

I. The sin here prohibited is CONCUPISCENCE, or an unlawful lusting after what is another man's.

For since God had in the other commandments forbidden the *acts* of sin against our neighbor, he well knew that the best means to keep men from committing sin in act would be to keep them from desiring it in heart; and therefore he who is a Spirit imposeth a law on our spirits, and forbids us to *covet* what before he had forbidden us to perpetrate. It is true that other precepts are spiritual likewise, and their authority reacheth to the mind and the most secret thoughts and imaginations of the heart; for our Savior, Mat. 5, accuseth him of adultery that doth but lust after a woman, and him of murder that is but angry with his brother without a cause; and it is a most certain rule, that whatever precept prohibits the outward act of any sin, prohibits likewise the inward propension and desires of the soul towards it. But because these are not plainly and literally expressed in the former commands, therefore the infinite wisdom of God thought it fit to add this last command, wherein he doth expressly arraign and condemn the very first motions of our hearts towards any sinful object; and whereas, before he had commanded us not to kill, not to steal, not to commit adultery, not to slander and bear false witness; now in the last place, for the greater security that these his laws should not be violated, he commands us not so much as to *harbor in our hearts* any desire towards these. So that this tenth commandment may well be called *Vinculum Legis, the bond of the whole law;* and it is especially the bond that strengthens and confirms the second table; for because all our outward actions take their first rise from our inward motions and concupiscence, there is no such way to provide for our innocency as to lay a check and restraint upon these.

Concupiscence is sometimes taken in Scripture in a good sense, but more often in an evil. There is an honest and lawful concupiscence, when we desire those things which are lawful, to which we have right, and of which we have need. There is likewise a holy and pious, and a wicked and sinful concupiscence. We have both together, Gal. 5 : 17,

"The flesh lusteth against the spirit, and the spirit against the flesh."

It is only concerning this *sinful* concupiscence that we are at present to speak. This evil concupiscence is the first-born of original sin; the first essay and expression of that corruption which hath seized on us and on all the wretched posterity of Adam. For in original sin, besides the guilt which results from the imputation of the primitive transgression to us, and makes us liable to eternal death, there is likewise an universal depravation of our natures, consisting, *first*, in *a loss of those spiritual perfections wherewith man was endowed in his creation,* which is the defacing of the image of God stamped on our nature in knowledge, righteousness and true holiness; and *secondly*, and consequent upon this, in *a violent propension and inclination to whatsoever is really evil and contrary to the holy will and commands of God,* and this is the image of the devil, into which man, by his voluntary apostasy and defection, hath transformed himself.

This inordinate inclination of the soul to what is evil and sinful is properly the *concupiscence* forbidden in this commandment. For the soul of man being an active and busy creature, must still be putting forth itself in actions suitable to its nature. Before the fall man enjoyed supernatural grace, though in a natural way; which enabled him to point every motion of his soul towards God, and to fix him as the object and end of all his actions; but, forfeiting this grace by the fall, and being left in the hands of mere nature, all his actions now, instead of aspiring to God, pitch only on the creature. And this becomes sin to us, not merely because we affect and desire created good, for that is lawful, but because we affect and desire it in an inordinate manner, that is, without affecting and desiring God. And thus the soul not being able, without grace and the image of God, to raise its operations to God, pitched upon low, sinful objects, to the neglect and slighting of God and the great concerns of heaven. This is, in the general, that inordinate disposition of the soul which is here called coveting or concupiscence.

There are *four degrees* of this sinful concupiscence.

1. There is the *motus primo primi,* or *the first film and shadow of an evil thought,* the imperfect embryo of a sin before it is well shaped in us or hath received any lineaments and features. And these the Scripture calls the imaginations of the thoughts of men's hearts, Gen. 6 : 5, " God saw that every imagination of the thoughts of man's heart was only evil continually :" that is, the very first figment and flushing of our thoughts is evil and corrupt. Indeed, some of these are injected by the devil. Many times he assaults the dearest of God's children with horrid temptations, and importunately casts into their minds strange thoughts of questioning the very being of God, the truth of the Scriptures, the immortality of the soul, future rewards and punishments, and such other blasphemous, hideous and unshapen monsters, against the very fundamentals of religion, for the truth of which they would willingly sacrifice their very lives as a testimony to them. These indeed are not their sins, although they are their great troubles and afflictions; for they come only from a principle without them, and they are merely passive and sufferers by them, so long as they are watchful to abhor and resist them, and to cast these fiery darts of the devil back again into his face. But then there are other first motions arising in our hearts towards those

sins which are more delightful and pleasant to our sensual inclinations: these, whatsoever the papists say to the contrary, as soon as ever they do but begin to heave and stir in our breasts, are truly sins, and do in their measure pollute and defile the soul; for the soul of man is like a clear mirror, upon which if you only breathe you sully it and leave a dimness upon it. So truly, the very first breathings of an evil thought and desire in our souls do sully their beauty and dim their lustre, and render the image of God less conspicuous in them than it was before.

2. A farther degree of this concupiscence is, *when these evil motions are entertained in the sensual mind with some measure of complacency and delight.*

When a sinful object offers itself to a carnal heart, there is a kind of inward pleasing titillation that affects it with delight, and begets a kind of sympathy between them. As in natural sympathies a man is taken and delighted with an object before he knows the reason why he is so; so likewise in this sinful sympathy between a carnal heart and a sensual object, the heart is taken and delighted with it before it hath had time to consider what there is in it that should so move and affect it. At the very first sight and glimpse of a person we many times find that we conceive some more particular respect for him than possibly for a whole crowd of others, though all may be equally unknown to us; so on the very first glimpse and apparition of a sinful thought in our minds, we find that there is something in it that commands a particular regard from us, that unbosoms and unlocks our very souls to it, even before we have the leisure to examine why.

3. Hereupon follows *assent and approbation of the sin in the practical judgment*, which, being blinded and forcibly carried away by the violence of corrupt and carnal affections, commends the sin to the executive faculties.

The understanding is the great trier of every deliberate action, so that nothing passeth into act which hath not first passed examination and censure there; whether this or that action is to be done is the great question canvassed in this court, and all the powers and faculties of the soul wait what definitive sentence will be here pronounced, and so accordingly proceed. Now here two things do usually appear and put in their plea to the judgment against sin; God's law, and God's advocate, conscience; the law condemns, and conscience cites that law. But then the affections step in and bribe the judge with profit, or pleasure, or honor, and thereby corrupt the judgment to give its vote and assent unto sin.

4. When any sinful motion hath thus gotten an allowance and pass from the judgment, then it *betakes itself to the will for a decree*. The judgment approves it, and therefore the will must now resolve to commit it, and then the sin is fully perfected and formed within, and there wants nothing but opportunity to bring it forth into act.

Thus you see what this concupiscence is, and the degrees of it, viz. the first bubblings up of evil thoughts in our hearts, our complacency and delight in them, (as indeed it is very hard and much against corrupt nature not to love these first-born of our souls,) the assent and allowance of our judgment, and the decree and resolution of our wills. Each of these is forbidden in this commandment.

But if the sin proceeds any further, it then exceeds the

bounds and limits of this commandment, and falls under the prohibition of some of the former, which forbid the outward acts of sin.

Thus much concerning evil concupiscence in the general.

But here is mention likewise made of several particular objects of it: *thy neighbor's house*, his *wife*, his *servants*, his *cattle*, (under which are comprehended all sorts of his possessions,) and all is included under the last clause, *nor any thing that is thy neighbor's*. So that, to desire to take from him either his life, or his good name, or his virtue, is this condemned covetousness; as well as a desire to take from him his temporal possessions and enjoyments.

II. I shall close all with some PRACTICAL USE AND IMPROVEMENT.

1. *Learn here to adore the unlimited and boundless sovereignty of the great God.*

His authority immediately reacheth to the very soul and conscience, and lays an obligation on our very thoughts and desires, which no human laws can do. It is but a folly for men to intermeddle with or impose laws upon that of which they can take no cognizance, and therefore our thoughts and desires are free from their censure any farther than they discover themselves by overt acts. But though they escape the commands and notice of men, yet they cannot escape God. *He seeth not as men see, neither judgeth he as men judge: the secrets of all hearts are open and bare before his eyes:* he looks through our very souls, and there is not the least hint of a thought, not the least breath of a desire stirring in us but it is more distinctly visible to him than the most opake bodies are unto us. "The Lord knoweth the thoughts of man, that they are vanity." Ps. 94 : 11. And therefore his law, like his knowledge, reaches unto the most secret recesses of the soul, searches every corner of the heart, judges and condemns those callow lusts which men never espy; and if these find harbor and shelter there, condemns thee as a transgressor, and guilty of eternal death, how plausible soever thy external demeanor may be. Wherefore,

2. *Content not thyself with an outward conformity to the law, but labor to approve thy heart in sincerity and purity unto God:* otherwise thou art but a pharisaical hypocrite, and washest only the outside of the cup, when within thou art still full of unclean lusts.

This was the corrupt doctrine of the scribes and pharisees, that the law reached only to the outward man; and although we entertained and cherished wicked desires and evil purposes in our hearts, yet so long as they did not break forth into outward crimes, they were not to be imputed unto us, nor did God account them as sins. And this St. Paul confesseth of himself, that whilst he was trained up in pharisaical principles, he did not understand the inward motions of lusts to be sins.

But, alas, this is but gilding over a dry and rotten post, which, though it may look beautiful to men, yet, when God comes to examine it, will not abide the fiery trial. Thou art as truly a murderer, a thief, an adulterer in God's sight, if thou dost but harbor bloody, unclean, unjust thoughts in thy heart, as thou wouldst be in men's if thou shouldst actually kill, or steal, or wallow in the open and professed acts of uncleanness.

Indeed, most men do herein grossly delude themselves, and if they can but refrain from the outward commission of gross and scandalous sins, they very seldom reflect on their heart-lusts, which, like deep ulcers, rankle inwardly, and perhaps grow incurable, when all the while they may be skimmed over with a fair and inoffensive life. Although the heart estuate and boil over with malicious, revengeful, lascivious thoughts, yet they usually dispense with these, and their natural conscience indulgeth them without disturbance.

But deceive not yourselves—*God is not mocked*, nor can he be imposed upon by external shows, neither will he judge of thee as others do, or as thou thyself dost.

I know it is a very difficult thing to convince men of the great evil that there is in sinful thoughts and desires, and therefore very difficult to persuade them to labor against them; for because they do not openly obtrude themselves, therefore men think they carry in them but small guilt and little danger. Every man that hath but a remnant of conscience left him will beware of gross and notorious crimes, that carry the mark of hell and damnation visibly stamped upon their foreheads, such as he that can without reluctance commit them, must needs own himself for the apparent offspring of the devil. But for "an invisible thought, a notion, a desire, a thing next to nothing—this certainly I may please myself withal, for this can hurt no one. By a malicious purpose I wrong no man, by a covetous desire I extort from no man, and what so great evil then can there be in this ?"

It is true, indeed, wert thou only to deal with men, whom immaterial things touch not, there were no such great evil in them; but when thou hast likewise to do with an immaterial and spiritual God, before whom thy very thoughts and desires appear as substantial and considerable as thy outward actions, then know that these fall under his censure here, and will fall under his revenge hereafter.

Now were this persuasion effectually wrought into the minds of men, is it possible they could indulge themselves as they do in vain, frothy, unclean, malicious thoughts and desires? Is it possible they could so closely brood on these cockatrice eggs which will bring forth nothing but serpents to sting them to eternal death? Is it possible they could delight in rolling and tossing a sin to and fro in their fancy, and by imagining it, make the devil some recompense for not daring to commit it? Certainly such men are altogether unacquainted with the life and power of true grace, when those sins which they dare not act, yet they dare with pleasure contemplate and dally with in their fancies and imaginations.

Turn therefore your eyes inwards. Bewail and strive against that natural concupiscence which lodgeth there, and never content thyself that thou hast dammed up the streams of thy corruption from overflowing thy life and actions, till thou hast in some good measure dried up the fountain of it.

3. See here the best and the surest method to keep us from the outward violation of God's laws, which is to *mortify our corrupt concupiscence and desires.*

And therefore, as I told you, the wisdom of God hath set this commandment in the last place, as a fence and guard to all the rest. *Thou shalt not covet*, and then certainly *thou shalt not kill*, nor *steal*, nor *commit adultery*, nor *bear false witness*, but be kept pure from all outward defilements of the flesh when thou art thus cleansed from the inward defilements of the spirit.

For from these it is that all the more visible sins of our lives and actions have their supply. Therefore saith our Savior, "Out of the heart proceed evil thoughts murders, adulteries, fornications, thefts, false witness, blasphemies." Mat. 15 : 19. Observe that he puts evil thoughts in the front, as the leader of all this black regiment; for out of this evil treasure of the heart men bring forth evil things; and all the fruits of the flesh, the grapes of Sodom and the clusters of Gomorrah, receive their sap and nourishment from this root of bitterness.

It ought therefore most deservedly to be the great and chief care of every christian to lay the axe to this root, to purge and heal this fountain that sends forth such corrupt and poisonous streams, to keep his heart clean from sinful thoughts and affections, and then his life will be clean by consequence. And therefore God very pressingly requires this, Jer. 4 : 14, "O Jerusalem, wash thy heart from wickedness—how long shall vain thoughts lodge within thee ?"

And let me add, that unless we make this our chief care, unless we do most solicitously observe this last commandment, all our care in observing the former commands will be utterly in vain, not only in respect to our acceptance and reward with God, but as to any good issue and effect. All other endeavors will be as hopeless as to attempt the cure of an ulcerous body without purging it, where the corruption will quickly break forth again; or to attempt the emptying of a pond that hath many springs still rising up in the bottom of it, which will soon grow as full as ever it was.

THE END.

www.ingramcontent.com/pod-product-compliance
Lightning Source LLC
Chambersburg PA
CBHW021826220426
43663CB00005B/148